15-MINUTE
ITALIAN
LEARN IN JUST 12 WEEKS

T0104151

Francesca Logi

Penguin
Random
House

REVISED EDITION
DK LONDON
Senior Editor Ankita Awasthi Tröger
Senior Art Editor Clare Shedden
Illustrators Peter Bull Art Studio and Dan Crisp
Managing Editor Carine Tracanelli
Managing Art Editor Anna Hall
US Editor Heather Wilcox
US Executive Editor Lori Hand
Production Editor Gillian Reid
Senior Production Controller Poppy David
Jacket Design Development Manager Sophia MTT
Associate Publishing Director Liz Wheeler
Art Director Karen Self
Publishing Director Jonathan Metcalf

DK DELHI
Project Editor Nandini D. Tripathy
Senior Art Editor Ira Sharma
Project Art Editor Anukriti Arora
Assistant Art Editor Sulagna Das
Managing Editor Soma B. Chowdhury
Senior Managing Art Editor Arunesh Talapatra
Jacket Designer Juhi Sheth
Senior Jacket Designer Suhita Dharamjit
Senior Jackets Coordinator Priyanka Sharma-Saddi
DTP Coordinator Pushpak Tyagi
DTP Designers Rakesh Kumar, Mrinmoy Mazumdar,
Nityanand Kumar
Hi-res Coordinator Neeraj Bhatia
Production Editor Vishal Bhatia
Production Manager Pankaj Sharma
Pre-production Manager Balwant Singh
Senior Picture Researcher Sumedha Chopra
Picture Research Manager Taiyaba Khatoon
Creative Head Malavika Talukder

**Language content for Dorling Kindersley by
g-and-w publishing.
Additional translations for 2023 edition by
Andiamo! Language Services Ltd.**

This American Edition, 2023
First American Edition, 2005
Published in the United States by DK Publishing
1745 Broadway, 20th Floor, New York, NY 10019

Copyright © 2005, 2012, 2018, 2023
Dorling Kindersley Limited
DK, a Division of Penguin Random House LLC
24 25 26 27   10 9 8 7 6 5 4 3 2
003–334019–Jul/2023

A catalog record for this book
is available from the Library of Congress.
ISBN 978-0-7440-8081-0

DK books are available at special discounts when
purchased in bulk for sales promotions, premiums,
fundraising, or educational use. For details, contact:
DK Publishing Special Markets, 1745 Broadway,
20th Floor, New York, NY 10019
SpecialSales@dk.com

Printed in China
www.dk.com

Contents

How to use this book

Twelve themed chapters are broken down into five daily 15-minute lessons, allowing you to work through four teaching units and one practice unit each week. The lessons cover a range of practical themes, including leisure, business, food and drink, and travel. A reference section at the end contains a menu guide and English-to-Italian and Italian-to-English dictionaries.

Warm up
Each day starts with a warm-up that encourages you to recall vocabulary or phrases you have learned previously.

Instructions
Each exercise is numbered and introduced by instructions that explain what to do. In some cases, additional information is given about the language point being covered.

Text styles
Distinctive text styles differentiate Italian, English, and the pronunciation guide.

Audio
This icon indicates that you should listen to audio recordings in order to do the exercise. See page 7 for details of how to access and use the audio app.

12 · WEEK 1

1 WARM UP
1 minute

Say the Italian for as many members of the family as you can (pp10–11).

Say "**I have two sons**" (pp10–11).

La mia famiglia
MY FAMILY

The Italians have two ways of saying you: **Lei** is the formal version, and **tu** is the informal version for family, friends, and young people. This means that there are also different words for *your* (below). It's a good idea to use the formal version until you are addressed by the other person as **tu**.

2 WORDS TO REMEMBER
5 minutes

The Italian words for *my* and *your* vary depending on the gender and number of the following noun. They are usually preceded by *il, la, i,* or *le,* except when referring to a singular family member. Familiarize yourself with these words, then test yourself using the cover flap.

mio/mia
mee-oh/me-eah
my (masculine/feminine singular)

miei/mie
mee-ayee/mee-ay
my (masculine/feminine plural)

tuo/tua
too-oh/too-ah
your (informal masculine/feminine singular)

tuoi/tue
too-oh-ee/too-ay
your (informal masculine/feminine plural)

suo/sua
soo-oh/soo-ah
your (formal masculine/feminine singular)

suoi/sue
soo-oh-ee/soo-ay
your (formal masculine/feminine plural)

Questi sono i miei genitori.
kwaystee sonoh ee mee-ayee jeneetoree
These are my parents.

3 IN CONVERSATION

Lei ha figli?
lay ah fillyee
Do you have any children?

Sì, ho due figlie.
see, oh dooay feellyay
Yes, I have two daughters.

Queste sono le mie figlie. E Lei?
kwestay sonoh lay mee-ay feellyay. ay lay
These are my daughters. And you?

In conversation
Illustrated dialogues reflecting how vocabulary and phrases are used in everyday situations appear throughout the book.

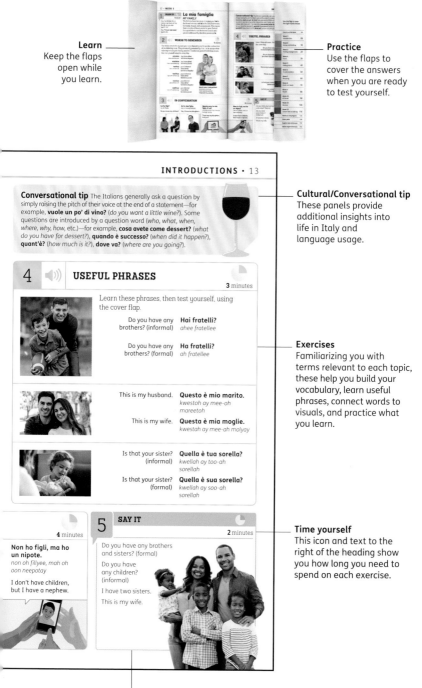

Learn
Keep the flaps open while you learn.

Practice
Use the flaps to cover the answers when you are ready to test yourself.

INTRODUCTIONS · 13

Conversational tip The Italians generally ask a question by simply raising the pitch of their voice at the end of a statement—for example, **vuole un po' di vino?** (do you want a little wine?). Some questions are introduced by a question word (who, what, when, where, why, how, etc.)—for example, **cosa avete come dessert?** (what do you have for dessert?), **quando è successo?** (when did it happen?), **quant'è?** (how much is it?), **dove va?** (where are you going?).

Cultural/Conversational tip
These panels provide additional insights into life in Italy and language usage.

4))) USEFUL PHRASES

3 minutes

Learn these phrases, then test yourself, using the cover flap.

Do you have any brothers? (informal)	**Hai fratelli?**	*ahee fratellee*
Do you have any brothers? (formal)	**Ha fratelli?**	*ah fratellee*
This is my husband.	**Questo è mio marito.**	*kwestoh ay mee-oh mareetoh*
This is my wife.	**Questa è mia moglie.**	*kwestah ay mee-ah molyay*
Is that your sister? (informal)	**Quella è tua sorella?**	*kwellah ay too-ah sorellah*
Is that your sister? (formal)	**Quella è sua sorella?**	*kwellah ay soo-ah sorellah*

Exercises
Familiarizing you with terms relevant to each topic, these help you build your vocabulary, learn useful phrases, connect words to visuals, and practice what you learn.

4 minutes

Non ho figli, ma ho un nipote.
non oh fillyee, mah oh oon neepotay

I don't have children, but I have a nephew.

5 SAY IT

2 minutes

Do you have any brothers and sisters? (formal)

Do you have any children? (informal)

I have two sisters.

This is my wife.

Time yourself
This icon and text to the right of the heading show you how long you need to spend on each exercise.

Say it
In these exercises, you are asked to apply what you have learned using different vocabulary.

»

Practice

At the end of every week's lessons, a practice unit lets you test yourself on what you have learned so far. A recap of selected elements from previous lessons helps reinforce your knowledge.

Test yourself
Use the cover flap to conceal the answers while you practice.

Reference

This section appears at the end of the book and brings together all the words and phrases you have learned over the weeks. While the menu guide focuses on food and drink, the dictionary lists Italian translations of common words and phrases.

Dictionaries
Mini-dictionaries provide ready reference from English to Italian and Italian to English for 2,500 words.

Menu guide
Use this guide as a reference for food terminology and popular Italian dishes.

PRONUNCIATION GUIDE

Many Italian sounds will already be familiar to you, but a few require special attention. Take note of how these letters are pronounced:

c   an Italian **c** is pronounced *ch* before *i* or *e* but *k* before other vowels: **cappuccino** *kappoocheenoh*

ch pronounced *k* as in *keep*

g   pronounced *j* as in *jam* before *i* or *e* but *g* as in *get* before other vowels

gh pronounced *g* as in *go*

gn pronounced *ny* like the sound in the middle of onion

gli pronounced *ly* like the sound in the middle of million

h   **h** is always silent: **ho** *oh* (*I have*)

r   an Italian **r** is trilled like a Scottish *r*

s   an Italian **s** can be pronounced either *s* as in *see* or *z* as in *zoo*

sc pronounced *sh* as in *ship* before *i* or *e* but *sk* as in *skip* before other vowels

z   an Italian **z** is pronounced *ts* as in *pets*

Italian vowels tend to be pronounced longer than their English equivalents, especially:

e   as the English *lay*

i   as the English *keep*

u   as the English *boot*

After each word or phrase, you will find a pronunciation transcription. Read this, bearing in mind the tips above, and you will achieve a comprehensible result. But remember that the transcription can only ever be an approximation and that there is no real substitute for listening to native speakers.

HOW TO USE THE AUDIO APP

The free audio app accompanying this book contains audio recordings for all numbered exercises on the teaching pages, except for the Warm Up and Say It exercises (look out for the audio icon). There is no audio for the practice pages.

To start using the audio with this book, download the **DK 15 Minute Language Course** app on your tablet or smartphone from the App Store or Google Play and select your book from the list of available titles. Please note that this app is not a stand-alone course but designed to be used together with the book to familiarize you with the language and provide examples for you to repeat aloud.

There are two ways in which you can use the audio. The first is to read through the 15-minute lessons using just the book, then go back and work with the audio and the book together. Or you can combine the book and the audio from the start, pausing the app to read the instructions on the page.

You are encouraged to listen to the audio and repeat the words and sentences out loud until you are confident you understand and can pronounce what has been said. Remember that repetition is vital for language learning. The more often you listen to a conversation or repeat an oral exercise, the more the new language will sink in.

SUPPORTING AUDIO
This icon indicates that audio recordings are available for you to listen to.

FREE AUDIO APP

1 WARM UP
1 minute

The Warm Up panel appears at the beginning of each topic. Use it to reinforce what you have already learned and to prepare yourself for moving ahead with the new subject.

Buongiorno
HELLO

In Italy, a firm handshake usually accompanies an introduction or meeting in a formal situation. In a casual setting, many people greet relatives and friends with a kiss on each cheek, but usually only when they haven't met, or are not going to see each other, for a while. Men often greet each other with a hug.

2 WORDS TO REMEMBER
2 minutes

Familiarize yourself with these words by reading them aloud several times, then test yourself by concealing the Italian on the left with the cover flap.

Buongiorno *bwonjornoh*	Hello/Good day (formal)
Piacere *peeahcheray*	Pleased to meet you
Grazie *gratseeay*	Thank you
Buonasera/ Buonanotte *bwonasayrah/ bwonanottay*	Good evening/ Good night
Arrivederci *arreevederchee*	Goodbye (formal)

Ciao! *chow* Hi!/Bye! (informal)

3 IN CONVERSATION: FORMAL
3 minutes

Buongiorno. Mi chiamo Suzi Lee.
bwonjornoh. mee keeamoh soozee lee

Hello. My name's Suzi Lee.

Buongiorno. Marco Paoletti, piacere.
bwonjornoh. markoh pa-olettee, peeahcheray

Hello. Marco Paoletti, pleased to meet you.

Piacere.
peeahcheray

Pleased to meet you.

4 🔊 PUT INTO PRACTICE

3 minutes

Read the Italian on the left and follow the instructions to complete this dialogue. Then, test yourself by concealing the Italian on the right with the cover flap.

Buonasera. | **Buonasera signora.**
bwonasayrah | *bwonasayrah seennyorah*

Good evening.
Say: Good evening madam.

Mi chiamo Marta. | **Piacere.**
mee keeamoh martah | *peeahcheray*

My name is Marta.
Say: Pleased to meet you.

Cultural tip
The Italians greet each other with **signore** (*sir*) and **signora** (*madam*) much more than English-speakers do. These titles are also used with surnames: **signor Paoletti, signora Bernardini**. The use of **signorina** (*miss*) is not recommended.

5 🔊 USEFUL PHRASES

3 minutes

Learn these phrases by reading them aloud several times, then test yourself by concealing the Italian on the right with the cover flap.

What's your name? | **Come si chiama?**
 | *komay see keeamah*

See you soon. | **A presto.**
 | *ah prestoh*

See you tomorrow. | **A domani.**
 | *ah domanee*

6 🔊 IN CONVERSATION: INFORMAL

3 minutes

Allora, a domani?
allorah, ah domanee

So, see you tomorrow?

Sì, ciao, a domani.
see, chow, ah domanee

Yes, goodbye, see you tomorrow.

Ciao. A presto.
chow. ah prestoh

Goodbye. See you soon.

1 WARM UP

1 minute

Say "**hello**" and "**goodbye**" in Italian (pp8–9).

Now, say "**My name is…**" (pp8–9).

Say "**sir**" and "**madam**" (pp8–9).

I parenti
RELATIVES

In Italian, some words for family relationships can have several meanings. For example, **fratelli** can mean both brothers and siblings. **Nipote** can mean four different things: nephew, niece, grandson, and granddaughter. For nephew and grandson you use the masculine **il nipote**, while for niece and granddaughter you use the feminine **la nipote**.

2 🔊 MATCH AND REPEAT

5 minutes

Look at the people in this scene and match their numbers to the vocabulary list on the left. Then, test yourself by concealing the Italian on the left, using the cover flap.

① **il padre**
eel padray

② **la madre**
lah madray

③ **la sorella**
lah sorellah

④ **il fratello**
eel fratelloh

⑤ **la figlia**
lah feelyah

⑥ **il figlio**
eel feelyoh

⑦ **la nonna**
lah nonnah

⑧ **il nonno**
eel nonnoh

father **①** mother **②**

sister **③** brother **④**

daughter **⑤** son **⑥**

grandmother **⑦** grandfather **⑧**

Conversational tip The word for *the* varies depending on whether the noun it refers to is masculine or feminine. For example, **il fratello** (*brother*) is masculine, but **la sorella** (*sister*) is feminine. **Il** and **la** change to **l'** before a vowel. Feminine plurals use **le**, masculine plurals **i**. However, masculine singular words starting with a *z* or *s + consonant* use **lo**; masculine plurals starting with a vowel, *z*, or *s + consonant* use **gli**.

3 🔊 **WORDS TO REMEMBER:** RELATIVES

4 minutes

la moglie
lah molyay
wife

il marito
eel mareetoh
husband

Familiarize yourself with these words, then test yourself, using the cover flap.

uncle	**lo zio** *loh tzeeoh*
aunt	**la zia** *lah tzeeah*
cousin	**il cugino/la cugina** *eel koojeenoh/lah koojeenah*
in-laws	**i suoceri** *ee swocheree*
I have four children.	**Ho quattro figli.** *oh kwattroh feelyee*
We have two daughters.	**Abbiamo due figlie.** *abbeeahmoh dooay feelyeeay*
I have a sister.	**Ho una sorella.** *oh oonah sorellah*
I have two brothers.	**Ho due fratelli.** *oh dooay fratellee*

Sono sposato/sposata.
sono spozatoh/spozatah
I'm married (male/female).

4 🔊 **WORDS TO REMEMBER:** NUMBERS

5 minutes

Familiarize yourself with these words, then test yourself, using the cover flap.

Note that the word for *a/an* or *one* changes to match gender: **un figlio** (*a son*, masculine) and **una figlia** (*a daughter*, feminine). **Un** changes to **uno** in front of **z** or **s + consonant**: **uno zio** (*an uncle*), **uno sport** (*a sport*). **Una** changes to **un'** before a vowel: **un'amica** (*a female friend*).

To make plurals, a final **-a** in a noun usually changes to **-e**: **una figlia/due figlie** (*one daughter/two daughters*), while a final **-o** or **-e** usually changes to **-i**: **un fratello/tre fratelli** (*one brother/three brothers*) and **una madre/quattro madri** (*one mother/four mothers*).

one	**uno** *oonoh*
two	**due** *dooay*
three	**tre** *tray*
four	**quattro** *kwattroh*
five	**cinque** *cheenkway*
six	**sei** *say*
seven	**sette** *settay*
eight	**otto** *ottoh*
nine	**nove** *novay*
ten	**dieci** *deeaychee*

1 | WARM UP
1 minute

Say the Italian for as many members of the family as you can (pp10–11).

Say "**I have two sons**" (pp10–11).

La mia famiglia
MY FAMILY

The Italians have two ways of saying *you*: **Lei** is the formal version, and **tu** is the informal version for family, friends, and young people. This means that there are also different words for *your* (below). It's a good idea to use the formal version until you are addressed by the other person as **tu**.

2 WORDS TO REMEMBER
5 minutes

The Italian words for *my* and *your* vary depending on the gender and number of the following noun. They are usually preceded by *il*, *la*, *i*, or *le*, except when referring to a singular family member. Familiarize yourself with these words, then test yourself using the cover flap.

mio/mia *mee-oh/me-eah*	my (masculine/ feminine singular)
miei/mie *mee-ayee/mee-ay*	my (masculine/ feminine plural)
tuo/tua *too-oh/too-ah*	your (informal masculine/ feminine singular)
tuoi/tue *too-oh-ee/too-ay*	your (informal masculine/ feminine plural)
suo/sua *soo-oh/soo-ah*	your (formal masculine/ feminine singular)
suoi/sue *soo-oh-ee/soo-ay*	your (formal masculine/ feminine plural)

Questi sono i miei genitori.
*kwaystee sonoh ee
mee-ayee jeneetoree*
These are my parents.

3 IN CONVERSATION

Lei ha figli?
lay ah fillyee

Do you have any children?

Sì, ho due figlie.
see, oh dooay feellyay

Yes, I have two daughters.

Queste sono le mie figlie. E Lei?
kwestay sonoh lay mee-ay feellyay. ay lay

These are my daughters. And you?

Conversational tip The Italians generally ask a question by simply raising the pitch of their voice at the end of a statement—for example, **vuole un po' di vino?** (*do you want a little wine?*). Some questions are introduced by a question word (*who, what, when, where, why, how,* etc.)—for example, **cosa avete come dessert?** (*what do you have for dessert?*), **quando è successo?** (*when did it happen?*), **quant'è?** (*how much is it?*), **dove va?** (*where are you going?*).

4 ◀)) USEFUL PHRASES

3 minutes

Learn these phrases, then test yourself, using the cover flap.

Do you have any brothers? (informal)	**Hai fratelli?** *ahee fratellee*
Do you have any brothers? (formal)	**Ha fratelli?** *ah fratellee*

This is my husband. **Questo è mio marito.**
kwestoh ay mee-oh mareetoh

This is my wife. **Questa è mia moglie.**
kwestah ay mee-ah molyay

Is that your sister? (informal) **Quella è tua sorella?**
kwellah ay too-ah sorellah

Is that your sister? (formal) **Quella è sua sorella?**
kwellah ay soo-ah sorellah

4 minutes

Non ho figli, ma ho un nipote.
non oh fillyee, mah oh oon neepotay

I don't have children, but I have a nephew.

5 SAY IT

2 minutes

Do you have any brothers and sisters? (formal)

Do you have any children? (informal)

I have two sisters.

This is my wife.

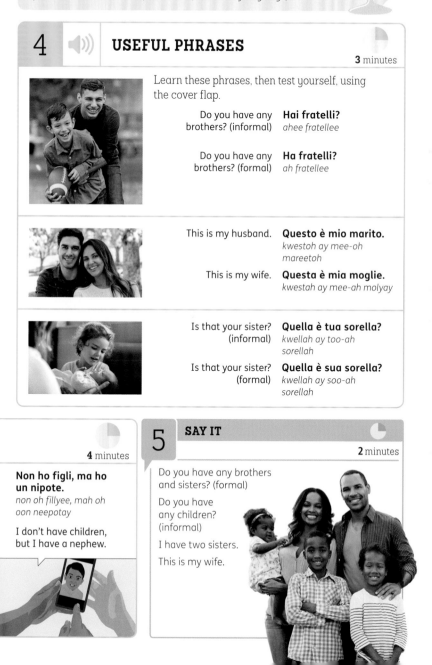

1 WARM UP
1 minute

Say "**See you soon**" (pp8–9).

Say "**I am married**" (pp10–11) and "**This is my wife**" (pp12–13).

Essere e avere
TO BE AND TO HAVE

There are some essential verbs that you can use to make a range of useful expressions. The first of these are **essere** (*to be*) and **avere** (*to have*). In Italian, the verb form varies according to the pronoun (*I, you, he, she*, and so on). The pronoun itself is often omitted, as it is implied by the verb.

2 ◁)) **ESSERE**: TO BE

5 minutes

Practice **essere** (*to be*) and the sample sentences, then test yourself, using the cover flap. Note that descriptive words can have different endings, depending on what is being described.

(io) sono *(ee-oh) sonoh*	I am
(tu) sei *(too) say*	you are (informal singular)
(Lei) è *(lay) ay*	you are (formal singular)
(lui/lei) è *(loo-ee/lay) ay*	he/she/it is
(noi) siamo *(noy) see-ahmoh*	we are
(voi) siete *(voy) see-aytay*	you are (plural)
(loro) sono *(loroh) sonoh*	they are

Sono inglese.
sonoh eenglesay
I'm English.

Sono stanco. *sonoh stankoh*	I'm tired.
È contenta? *ay kontayntah*	Is she happy?
Siamo italiani. *see-ahmoh eetahleeahnee*	We're Italian.

3 🔊 AVERE: TO HAVE

5 minutes

Practice **avere** (*to have*) and the sample sentences, then test yourself, using the cover flap.

Ha dei broccoli?
ah day brokkolee
Do you have any broccoli?

I have	**(io) ho**	*(eeoh) oh*
you have (informal singular)	**(tu) hai**	*(too) ahee*
you have (formal singular)	**(Lei) ha**	*(lay) ah*
he/she/it has	**(lui/lei) ha**	*(loo-ee/lay) ah*
we have	**(noi) abbiamo**	*(noy) abbeeahmoh*
you have (plural)	**(voi) avete**	*(voy) avetay*
they have	**(loro) hanno**	*(loroh) annoh*

Marco has a meeting.	**Marco ha una riunione.** *markoh ah oonah reeooneeonay*
Do you have a cell phone?	**Ha un cellulare?** *ah oon chaylloolaray*
How many brothers and sisters do you have?	**Quanti fratelli ha?** *kwantee fratellee ah*

4 🔊 NEGATIVES

4 minutes

It is easy to make sentences negative in Italian. Just put **non** in front of the verb: **non siamo inglesi** (*we're not English*), **non ho fratelli** (*I don't have any brothers*). Read these sentences aloud, then test yourself, using the cover flap.

la bicicletta
lah beechee-klettah
bicycle

He's not married.	**Non è sposato.** *non ay spozatoh*
I'm not sure.	**Non sono sicuro/a.** *non sonoh seekooroh/ah*
We don't have any children.	**Non abbiamo figli.** *non abbeeamoh feelyee*

Non ho l'auto.
non oh la-ootoh
I don't have a car.

Ripassa e ripeti
REVIEW AND REPEAT

How many?

❶ tre
tray

❷ nove
novay

❸ quattro
kwattroh

❹ due
dooay

❺ otto
ottoh

❻ dieci
deeaychee

❼ cinque
cheenkway

❽ sette
settay

❾ sei
say

Hello

**❶ Buongiorno,
mi chiamo...**
*bwonjornoh,
mee keeamoh...*

❷ Piacere.
peeahcheray

**❸ Sì, e ho due figli.
E Lei?**
*see, ay oh dooay
feelyee. ay lay*

**❹ Arrivederci.
A domani.**
*arreevederchee.
ah domanee*

---

1 HOW MANY?

2 minutes

Say these numbers in Italian, then test yourself, using the cover flap.

❶ ❷ ❸ ❹ ❺ ❻ ❼ ❽ ❾

---

2 HELLO

4 minutes

You meet someone in a formal situation. Join in the conversation, replying in Italian, following the numbered English prompts.

Buongiorno, mi chiamo Susanna.
❶ Hello. My name is... [your name].

Questo è mio marito, Piero.
❷ Pleased to meet you.

Lei è sposato/a?
❸ Yes, and I have two sons. And you?

Noi abbiamo tre figlie.
❹ Goodbye. See you tomorrow.

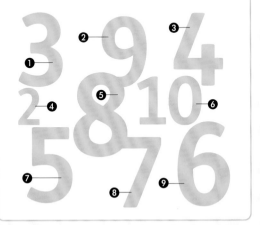

3 BE OR HAVE

5 minutes

Fill in the blanks with the correct form of **avere** (*to have*) or **essere** (*to be*).

❶ (noi) ____ italiani.
❷ (noi) ____ quattro figli.
❸ (lei) ____ inglese.
❹ (Lei) ____ un fratello?
❺ (io) ____ sposato/a.
❻ (voi) ____ figli?
❼ (io) non ____ il cellulare.
❽ (tu) ____ sicuro.

Be or have

❶ **siamo**
see-ahmoh

❷ **abbiamo**
abbeeahmoh

❸ **è**
ay

❹ **ha**
ah

❺ **sono**
sonoh

❻ **avete**
avetay

❼ **ho**
ho

❽ **sei**
say

4 RELATIVES

4 minutes

Name these family members in Italian.

grandmother ❶ grandfather ❷
❸ father ❹ mother
sister ❺ brother ❻
❽ son
daughter ❼

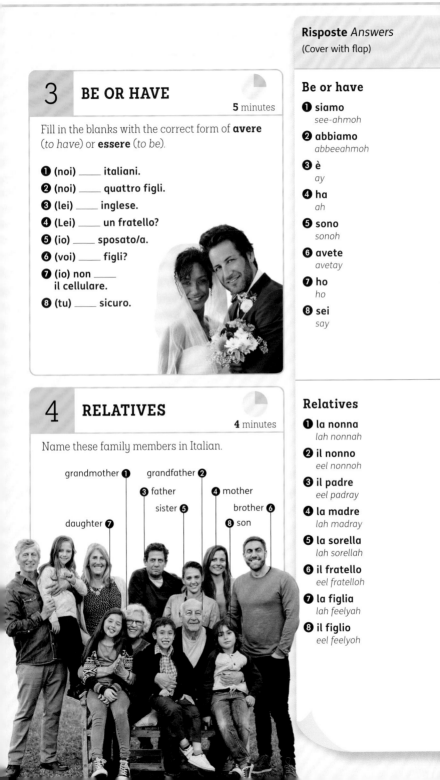

Relatives

❶ **la nonna**
lah nonnah

❷ **il nonno**
eel nonnoh

❸ **il padre**
eel padray

❹ **la madre**
lah madray

❺ **la sorella**
lah sorellah

❻ **il fratello**
eel fratelloh

❼ **la figlia**
lah feelyah

❽ **il figlio**
eel feelyoh

Al bar
IN THE CAFÉ

1 WARM UP
1 minute

Count to ten (pp10–11).

Remind yourself how to say "**hello**" and "**goodbye**" (pp8–9).

Ask "**Do you have a cell phone?**" (pp14–15).

In an Italian **café-bar**, you can get coffee in the morning accompanied by plain or filled croissants. Pastries, sandwiches, snacks, and soft or alcoholic drinks are also available. You can either stand at the counter or sit at a table (some with waiter service), which can be more expensive. It is usual to tip the server, but a good rounding up will be enough.

2 WORDS TO REMEMBER

Familiarize yourself with these words, then test yourself, using the cover flap.

la tisana *lah teezanah*	herbal or fruit tea
il tè con latte *eel tay kon lattay*	tea with milk
il panino *eel paneenoh*	sandwich
lo zucchero *loh tsookkeroh*	sugar
il caffè macchiato *eel kaffay makeeatoh*	espresso with a little milk

il cappuccino
eel kappoocheenoh
coffee with frothy milk

il caffè espresso
eel kaffay espressoh
espresso

3 IN CONVERSATION

Vorrei un cappuccino, per favore.
vorray oon kappoocheenoh, per favoray

I'd like a cappuccino, please.

Altro, signora?
altroh, seennyorah

Anything else, madam?

Ha delle brioche?
ah dellay breeosh

Do you have any croissants?

Cultural tip A standard coffee is a small, black **espresso**. Italians are not big tea drinkers, and when they do have tea, they add some lemon rather than milk. If you want milk, ask for **un po' di latte freddo** (*a little cold milk*).

la brioche
lah breeosh
croissant

4 🔊 USEFUL PHRASES 5 minutes

Learn these phrases, then test yourself, using the cover flap.

Un caffè americano, per favore.
oon kaffay amereekanoh, per favoray

A black coffee, please.

Altro?
altroh

Anything else?

Anche una brioche, per favore.
ankay oonah breeosh, per favoray

A croissant, too, please.

Quant'è?
kwantay

How much is that?

4 minutes

Sì, certo.
see, chertoh

Yes, certainly.

Allora, prendo due brioche. Quant'è?
allorah, prendoh dooay breeosh. kwantay

I'll have two croissants, then. How much is that?

Otto euro, per favore.
ottoh ayooroh, per favoray

Eight euros, please.

<table>
<tr><td>

1 **WARM UP**

1 minute

Say "**I'd like**" (pp18–19).

Say "**I don't have a brother**" (pp14–15).

Ask "**Do you have any croissants?**" (pp18–19).

</td><td>

Al ristorante
IN THE RESTAURANT

There are a variety of eating places in Italy. You can find snacks at a **bar** (pp18–19), but for a more hearty meal, head to a **trattoria**, which is an informal, traditional restaurant serving typical local dishes. In a more formal **ristorante**, it is often necessary to book a table. A **pizzeria** is a relaxed and cheap way of dining out and is ideal for big groups.

</td></tr>
</table>

2 ◀)) MATCH AND REPEAT

5 minutes

Match the numbered items to the list, then test yourself, using the cover flap.

❶ **il piattino**
eel peeahteenoh

❷ **la tazza**
lah tattsah

❸ **il bicchiere**
eel beekkyayray

❹ **la forchetta**
lah forkettah

❺ **il coltello**
eel koltelloh

❻ **il cucchiaio**
eel kookee-ayoh

❼ **il piatto**
eel peeattoh

❽ **il tovagliolo**
eel tovallyohloh

cup ❷   glass ❸

saucer ❶

❹ fork   ❻ spoon

knife ❺   plate ❼   napkin ❽

3 ◀)) IN CONVERSATION

Buongiorno, ha un tavolo per quattro? *bwonjornoh, ah oon tavoloh per kwattroh*	**Ha la prenotazione?** *ah lah prenotatseeonay*	**Sì, a nome Gatti.** *see, anomay gattee*
Hello, do you have a table for four?	Do you have a reservation?	Yes, in the name of Gatti.

4 🔊 WORDS TO REMEMBER

3 minutes

Familiarize yourself with these words, then test yourself, using the cover flap.

Sto pranzando con la mia famiglia.
stoh prantsandoh kon lah meeah fameelyah
I'm having lunch with my family.

menu	**il menù**	*eel menoo*
wine list	**la lista dei vini**	*lah leesta day veenee*
starters	**gli antipasti**	*lly anteepastee*
first main course	**i primi piatti**	*ee preemee peeattee*
second main course	**i secondi piatti**	*ee seekondee peeattee*
desserts	**i dessert**	*ee dessert*
breakfast	**la colazione**	*lah kolatseeonay*
lunch	**il pranzo**	*eel pranzoh*
dinner	**la cena**	*lah chenah*

5 🔊 USEFUL PHRASES

2 minutes

Learn these phrases, then test yourself, using the cover flap.

What do you have for dessert? **Cosa avete come dessert?**
kozah avaytay komay dessert

The bill, please. **Il conto, per favore.**
eel kontoh, per favoray

4 minutes

Benissimo. Che tavolo vuole?
beneesseemoh. kay tavoloh vwolay

Very good. Which table do you want?

Vicino alla finestra, per favore.
veecheenoh allah feenestrah, per favoray

Near the window, please.

Certo. Ecco.
chertoh. ekkoh

Of course. Here you are.

1 **WARM UP**
1 minute

Say "**I am married**" (pp12–13) and "**I'm not sure**" (pp14–15).

Ask "**Do you have a fork?**" (pp20–21).

Say "**I'd like a sandwich**" (pp18–19).

Le pietanze
DISHES

Italy is famous for its cuisine and the quality of its restaurants. The traditional Mediterranean cuisine is vegetable- and legume-based, with fish also featured prominently. Each region has its own specialities. Pasta is a typically Italian dish, prepared in a variety of ways. Most restaurants will have a good range of dishes for vegetarians and vegans.

2 🔊 **MATCH AND REPEAT**
4 minutes

Match the numbered items to the list, then test yourself, using the cover flap.

❶ **la verdura**
lah vairdoorah

❷ **la frutta**
lah froottah

❸ **il formaggio**
eel formajjoh

❹ **la frutta secca**
la froottah sekkah

❺ **la minestra**
lah meenestrah

❻ **il pollo**
eel polloh

❼ **la pasta**
lah pastah

❽ **il pesce**
eel peshay

❾ **i frutti di mare**
ee froottee dee maray

❿ **la carne**
lah karnay

❶ vegetables ❷ fruit ❸ cheese ❹ nuts ❺ soup ❻ poultry ❼ pasta ❽ fish ❾ seafood ❿ meat

Cultural tip In many restaurants, you will be able to choose from cheaper set menus, **il menù fisso** or **il menù turistico**. **L'insalata** (*salad*) is generally served as **il contorno** (*side dish*) and will need to be ordered separately, like all other sides.

3 🔊 WORDS TO REMEMBER: COOKING METHODS

3 minutes

Familiarize yourself with these words, then test yourself, using the cover flap. Note that the ending of these words may vary, depending on the gender of item described.

fried (m/f)	**fritto/a**	*freettoh/ah*
grilled	**alla griglia**	*allah greellyah*
roasted (m/f)	**arrosto**	*arrostoh*
boiled (m/f)	**lesso/a**	*layssoh/ah*
steamed	**al vapore**	*al vaporay*
rare (meat)	**al sangue**	*al sangway*

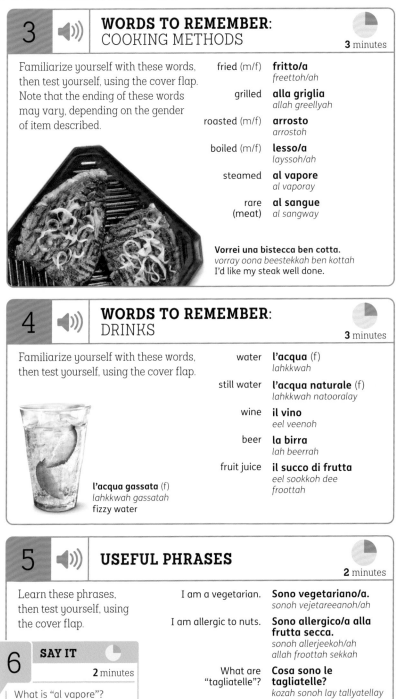

Vorrei una bistecca ben cotta.
vorray oona beestekkah ben kottah
I'd like my steak well done.

4 🔊 WORDS TO REMEMBER: DRINKS

3 minutes

Familiarize yourself with these words, then test yourself, using the cover flap.

water	**l'acqua** (f)	*lahkkwah*
still water	**l'acqua naturale** (f)	*lahkkwah natooralay*
wine	**il vino**	*eel veenoh*
beer	**la birra**	*lah beerrah*
fruit juice	**il succo di frutta**	*eel sookkoh dee froottah*

l'acqua gassata (f)
lahkkwah gassatah
fizzy water

5 🔊 USEFUL PHRASES

2 minutes

Learn these phrases, then test yourself, using the cover flap.

I am a vegetarian.	**Sono vegetariano/a.** *sonoh vejetareeanoh/ah*
I am allergic to nuts.	**Sono allergico/a alla frutta secca.** *sonoh allerjeekoh/ah allah froottah sekkah*
What are "tagliatelle"?	**Cosa sono le tagliatelle?** *kozah sonoh lay tallyatellay*

6 SAY IT

2 minutes

What is "al vapore"?

I'm allergic to seafood.

I'd like a beer.

1 **WARM UP** **1** minute

What are "**breakfast**," "**lunch**," and "**dinner**" in Italian (pp20–21)?

Say "**I**," "**you**" (informal), "**he**," "**she**," "**we**," "**you**" (plural), "**they**" (pp14–15).

Volere
TO WANT

In this section, you will learn the present tense of a verb that is essential to everyday conversation—**volere** (*to want*)—as well as a useful polite form, **vorrei** (*I would like*). Remember to use this form when requesting something, because **voglio** (*I want*) may sound too strong.

---

2 🔊 **VOLERE**: TO WANT

6 minutes

Practice **volere** (*to want*) and the sample sentences, then test yourself, using the cover flap.

(io) voglio *vollyoh*	I want
(tu) vuoi *vwoee*	you want (informal singular)
(Lei) vuole *vwolay*	you want (formal singular)
(lui/lei) vuole *vwolay*	he/she/it wants
(noi) vogliamo *vollyamoh*	we want
(voi) volete *voletay*	you want (plural)
(loro) vogliono *vollyonoh*	they want

Lei vuole un'auto nuova. *lay vwolay oon a-ootoh nwovah* — She wants a new car.

Vogliamo andare in vacanza. *vollyamoh andaray een vakantsah* — We want to go on vacation.

Voglio delle caramelle. *vollyoh dellay karamayllay* I want some candy.

Conversational tip In Italian, **del**, the word for *some*, changes depending on what follows. For example, **voglio del caffè** (*I want some coffee*, masculine singular), **voglio della birra** (*I want some beer*, feminine singular), **voglio dei limoni** (*I want some lemons*, masculine plural), and **voglio delle caramelle** (*I want some candy*, feminine plural). **Della** may be shortened to **dell'** before a vowel.

3 ◀)) POLITE REQUESTS

4 minutes

There is a form of **volere** used for polite requests: **(io) vorrei** (*I would like*), as in **vorrei un caffè** (*I'd like a coffee*). Practice the sample sentences, then test yourself, using the cover flap.

I'd like a beer.	**Vorrei una birra.** *vorray oonah beerah*
I'd like a table for tonight.	**Vorrei un tavolo per stasera.** *vorray oon tavoloh per staserah*
I'd like the menu, please.	**Vorrei il menù, per favore.** *vorray eel menoo, per favoray*

4 ◀)) PUT INTO PRACTICE

4 minutes

Complete this dialogue, then test yourself, using the cover flap.

Buonasera. Ha la prenotazione?
bwonasayrah. ah lah prenotatseeonay

Good evening. Do you have a reservation?

No, ma vorrei un tavolo per tre.
noh, mah vorray oon tavoloh per tray

Say: No, but I would like a table for three.

Benissimo. Che tavolo vuole?
beneesseemoh. kay tavoloh vwolay

Very good. Which table do you want?

Vicino alla finestra, per favore.
veecheenoh allah feenestrah, per favoray

Say: Near the window please.

Ripassa e ripeti
REVIEW AND REPEAT

Risposte *Answers*
(Cover with flap)

At the table

❶ la frutta secca
la froottah sekkah

❷ lo zucchero
loh tsookkeroh

❸ i frutti di mare
ee froottee dee maray

❹ la carne
lah karnay

❺ il bicchiere
eel beekkyayray

1   AT THE TABLE

Name these items in Italian.

❶ nuts

sugar ❷

❸ seafood

meat ❹

glass ❺

This is my…

❶ Questo è mio marito.
kwestoh ay meeoh mareetoh

❷ Questa è mia figlia.
kwestah ay meeah feellyah

❸ Queste sono le mie sorelle.
kwestay sonoh lay meeay sorellay

2   THIS IS MY…

4 minutes

Say these sentences in Italian.
Use **mio**, **mia**, **miei**, or **mie**.

❶ This is my husband.

❷ This is my daughter.

❸ These are my sisters.

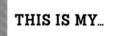

I'd like…

❶ Vorrei una brioche.
vorray oonah breeosh

❷ Vorrei un cappuccino.
vorray oon kappoocheenoh

❸ Vorrei lo zucchero.
vorray loh tsookkeroh

❹ Vorrei un caffè espresso.
vorray oon caffay espressoh

3   I'D LIKE…

3 minutes

Say you'd like these items in Italian.

croissant ❶   ❷ cappuccino   ❸ sugar

❹ espresso

At the table

6 **la pasta**
lah pastah

7 **il formaggio**
eel formajjoh

8 **il coltello**
eel koltelloh

9 **il tovagliolo**
eel tovallyohloh

10 **la birra**
lah beerrah

6 pasta

7 cheese

knife **8**

9 napkin

10 beer

4 minutes

4 RESTAURANT

4 minutes

You arrive at a restaurant. Join in the conversation, replying in Italian, following the numbered English prompts.

Buonasera.
1 Good evening, I would like a table for six.

Ha la prenotazione?
2 Yes, in the name of Gatti.

Benissimo.
3 I'd like the menu, please.

Vuole anche la lista dei vini?
4 No. Fizzy water, please.

Ecco.
5 I don't have a glass.

Restaurant

1 **Buonasera, vorrei un tavolo per sei.**
bwonasayrah, vorray oon tavoloh per say

2 **Sì, a nome Gatti.**
see, anomay gattee

3 **Vorrei il menù, per favore.**
vorray eel menoo, per favoray

4 **No, acqua gassata, per favore.**
noh, ahkkwah gassatah, per favoray

5 **Non ho il bicchiere.**
non oh eel beekkyeray

I giorni e i mesi
DAYS AND MONTHS

1 **WARM UP**
1 minute

Say "**He is**" and "**They are**" (pp14–15).

Say "**He is not**" and "**They are not**" (pp14–15).

What is Italian for "**my mother**" (pp10–11)?

In Italian, the days of the week (**i giorni della settimana**) and months of the year (**i mesi dell'anno**) do not have capital letters. You generally use **in** with months: **in ottobre** (*in October*), but you use nothing with days: **lunedì** (*on Monday*). However, when you mean every Monday, you use the article (**il/la**): **il lunedì** (*on Mondays*).

---

2 **WORDS TO REMEMBER**: DAYS
5 minutes

Familiarize yourself with these words, then test yourself, using the cover flap.

lunedì *loonedee*	Monday
martedì *martedee*	Tuesday
mercoledì *merkoledee*	Wednesday
giovedì *jovedee*	Thursday
venerdì *venerdee*	Friday
sabato *sabatoh*	Saturday
domenica *domeneekah*	Sunday
oggi *ojjee*	today
domani *domanee*	tomorrow
ieri *yayree*	yesterday

Ci vediamo domani.
chee vedeeamoh domanee
See you tomorrow.

Ho una prenotazione per oggi.
oh oonah prenotatseeonay per ojjee
I have a reservation for today.

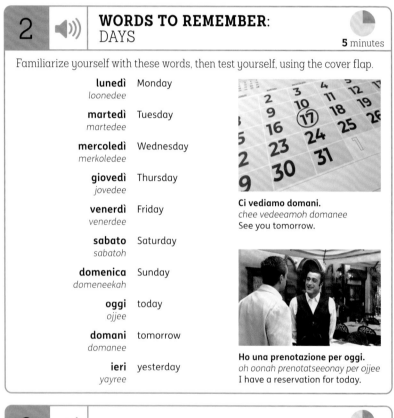

---

3 **USEFUL PHRASES**: DAYS
2 minutes

Learn these phrases, then test yourself, using the cover flap.

La riunione non è martedì.
lah reeooneeonay non ay martedee
The meeting isn't on Tuesday.

La domenica lavoro.
lah domeneekah lavoroh
I work on Sundays.

4 WORDS TO REMEMBER: MONTHS

5 minutes

Familiarize yourself with these words, then test yourself, using the cover flap.

Il nostro anniversario di matrimonio è in luglio.
eel nostroh anneeversareeoh dee matreemoneeoh ay een loollyoh
Our wedding anniversary is in July.

January	**gennaio**	*jennaheeoh*
February	**febbraio**	*febbraheeoh*
March	**marzo**	*martsoh*
April	**aprile**	*apreelay*
May	**maggio**	*majjeeoh*
June	**giugno**	*jooneeoh*
July	**luglio**	*loollyoh*
August	**agosto**	*agostoh*
September	**settembre**	*settembray*
October	**ottobre**	*ottobray*
November	**novembre**	*novembray*
December	**dicembre**	*deechembray*
month	**mese**	*mezay*
year	**anno**	*annoh*

Natale è in dicembre.
natalay ay een deechembray
Christmas is in December.

5 USEFUL PHRASES: MONTHS

2 minutes

Learn these phrases, then test yourself, using the cover flap.

My children are on vacation in August. **I miei bambini sono in vacanza in agosto.**
ee mee-ayee bambeenee sonoh een vakantsah een agostoh

My birthday is in June. **Il mio compleanno è in giugno.**
eel mee-oh kompleahnnoh ay een jooneeoh

<table>
<tr><td>

1

WARM UP

1 minute

Count in Italian from
1 to 10 (pp10–11).

Say "**I have a reservation**"
(pp20–21).

Say "**The meeting is on
Wednesday**" (pp28–29).

</td><td>

L'ora e i numeri
TIME AND NUMBERS

Italians use the 12-hour clock on a day-to-day basis
and the 24-hour clock in official contexts, such as
timetables, sometimes adding **di mattina** (*in the
morning*), **di pomeriggio** (*in the afternoon*), **di sera**
(*in the evening*), or **di notte** (*at night*). To say the
time, you say **sono le...**, as in **sono le dieci** (*it's ten
o'clock*), except for *it's one o'clock*, which is **è l'una**.

</td></tr>
</table>

2 🔊 WORDS TO REMEMBER: TIME

4 minutes

Familiarize yourself with these words, then
test yourself, using the cover flap.

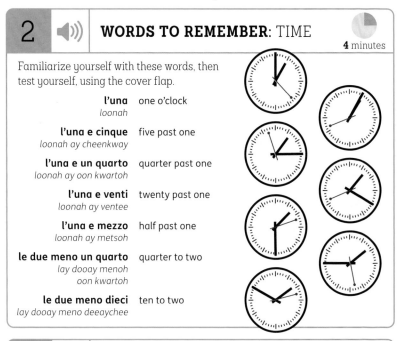

l'una *loonah*	one o'clock
l'una e cinque *loonah ay cheenkway*	five past one
l'una e un quarto *loonah ay oon kwartoh*	quarter past one
l'una e venti *loonah ay ventee*	twenty past one
l'una e mezzo *loonah ay metsoh*	half past one
le due meno un quarto *lay dooay menoh oon kwartoh*	quarter to two
le due meno dieci *lay dooay meno deeaychee*	ten to two

3 🔊 USEFUL PHRASES

2 minutes

Learn these phrases, then test yourself,
using the cover flap.

Che ore sono? *kay oray sonoh*	What time is it?
A che ora vuole la colazione? *ah kay orah voo-olay lah kolatseeonay*	What time do you want breakfast?
Ho una prenotazione per le dodici. *oh oonah prenotatseeonay per lay dodeechee*	I have a reservation for twelve o'clock.

4 🔊 WORDS TO REMEMBER: HIGHER NUMBERS

6 minutes

In Italian, when you say 21, 31, etc., you say **ventuno**, **trentuno**, and so on. After that just put the two numbers together: **ventidue** (22), **ventitré** (23), **trentadue** (32), **trentatré** (33), etc.

To say the date, you generally use the cardinal number in Italian: **oggi è il 26 aprile** (*today is 26th April*). The exception is the first day of the month, when you say *the first*, as in **domani è il primo febbraio** (*tomorrow is the first of February*).

Familiarize yourself with these words, then test yourself, using the cover flap.

eleven	**undici**	*oondeechee*
twelve	**dodici**	*dodeechee*
thirteen	**tredici**	*traydeechee*
fourteen	**quattordici**	*kwattordeechee*
fifteen	**quindici**	*kweendeechee*
sixteen	**sedici**	*sedeechee*
seventeen	**diciassette**	*deechassettay*
eighteen	**diciotto**	*deechottoh*
nineteen	**diciannove**	*deechannovay*
twenty	**venti**	*ventee*
thirty	**trenta**	*trentah*
forty	**quaranta**	*kwarantah*
fifty	**cinquanta**	*cheenkwantah*
sixty	**sessanta**	*sessantah*
seventy	**settanta**	*settantah*
eighty	**ottanta**	*ottantah*
ninety	**novanta**	*novantah*
hundred	**cento**	*chentoh*
three hundred	**trecento**	*traychentoh*
thousand	**mille**	*meellay*
ten thousand	**diecimila**	*deeaycheemeelah*
two hundred thousand	**duecentomila**	*dooaychentomeelah*
one million	**un milione**	*oon meeleeonay*

Ho pagato ottantacinque euro con pagamento contactless.
Oh pagatoh ottantacheenkway ayooroh kon pagamayntoh contactless
I've paid eighty-five euros by contactless payment.

5 SAY IT

2 minutes

twenty-five

sixty-eight

eighty-four

ninety-one

five to ten

half past eleven

What time is lunch?

1 WARM UP
1 minute

Say the days of the week in Italian (pp28–29).

Say "**It's three o'clock**" (pp30–31).

What's the Italian for "**today**," "**tomorrow**," and "**yesterday**" (pp28–29)?

Gli appuntamenti
APPOINTMENTS

Business in Italy is generally conducted more formally than in Britain or the United States; always address business contacts as **Lei** (formal *you*). Italians, especially those working in offices, banks, and public services, tend to take a short lunch break and often eat at their workplace or at street food kiosks.

2 USEFUL PHRASES
5 minutes

Learn these phrases, then test yourself, using the cover flap.

Fissiamo un appuntamento per domani?
feesseeamoh oon appoontamentoh per domanee
Shall we meet tomorrow?

Con chi?
kon kee
With whom?

Quando è libero/a?
kwandoh ay leeberoh/ah
When are you free?

Mi dispiace, sono impegnato/a.
mee deespeeachay, sonoh eempennyatoh/ah
I'm sorry, I'm busy.

Va bene giovedì?
vah benay jovedee
How about Thursday?

Per me va bene.
per may vah benay
That's good for me.

Benvenuto.
benvenootoh
Welcome.

la stretta di mano
lah strettah dee manoh
handshake

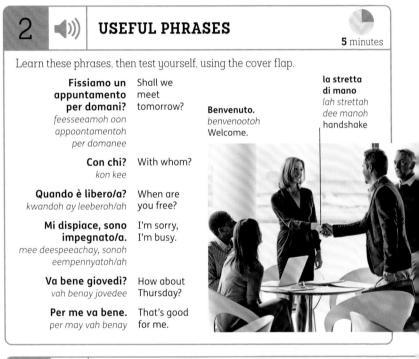

3 IN CONVERSATION

Buongiorno. Ho un appuntamento.
bwonjornoh. oh oon appoontamentoh

Hello. I have an appointment.

Con chi?
kon kee

With whom?

Con il signor Baroni.
kon eel seennyor baronee

With Mr. Baroni.

4 PUT INTO PRACTICE

5 minutes

Complete this dialogue, then test yourself, using the cover flap.

Fissiamo un appuntamento per giovedì?
feesseeamoh oon appoontamentoh per jovedee

Shall we meet on Thursday?

Say: Sorry, I'm busy on Thursday.

Mi dispiace, giovedì sono impegnato.
mee deespeeachay, jovedee sonoh eempennyatoh

Quando è libero?
kwandoh ay liberoh

When are you free?

Say: Tuesday afternoon.

Martedì pomeriggio.
martedee pomereejjoh

Per me va bene.
per may vah benay

That's good for me.

Ask: At what time?

A che ora?
ah kay orah

Alle quattro, se per Lei va bene.
allay kwattroh, say per lay vah benay

At four o'clock, if that's good for you.

Say: It's good for me.

Per me va bene.
per may vah benay

---

4 minutes

Benissimo, a che ora?
beneesseemoh, ah kay orah

Very good, at what time?

Alle tre, ma sono un po' in ritardo.
allay tray, mah sonoh oon poh een reetardoh

At three o'clock, but I'm a little late.

Non si preoccupi. Prego, si accomodi.
non see prayokkoopee. pregoh, see akkomodee

Don't worry. Take a seat, please.

1 WARM UP
1 minute

Say "**I'm sorry**" (pp32–33).

What is the Italian for "**I'd like an appointment**" (pp32–33)?

How do you say "**With whom?**" in Italian (pp32–33)?

Al telefono
ON THE TELEPHONE

The emergency number for **i carabinieri** (*military police*) is 112, and for **la polizia** (*police*), it is 113. Dial 115 for **i vigili del fuoco** (*fire services*) and 118 for **l'ambulanza** (*ambulance*). All are free from cell phones or landlines in the country. To make international calls from Italy, dial the access code 00, then the country code, area code (omit the initial 0), and phone number. The country code for Italy is 39.

2 MATCH AND REPEAT

Match the numbered items to the list, then test yourself, using the cover flap.

❶ **gli auricolari**
lly awreekolaree

❷ **le cuffie**
lay kooffeeay

❸ **il telefono**
eel telayfonoh

❹ **il cellulare**
eel chelloolaray

❺ **il caricabatterie**
eel karikabatereeay

❻ **la carta SIM**
la karta seem

❼ **la segreteria telefonica**
la segretereeah telayfoneekah

❶ earphones ❷ headphones

❹ cell phone

112

❺ charger ❻ SIM card

Vorrei comprare una carta SIM.
vorray kompraray oonah karta sim
I'd like to buy a SIM card.

3 IN CONVERSATION

Pronto? Bonanni.
prontoh? bonannee

Hello? Bonanni's.

Buongiorno. Vorrei parlare con il dottor Pieri.
bwonjornoh. vorray parlaray kon eel dottor pyayree

Hello. I'd like to speak to Dr. Pieri.

Chi parla?
kee parlah

May I know who's calling?

5 SAY IT
2 minutes

I'd like to speak to
Mr. Pacitti.

Can I leave a message
for Giulia?

Can she call me back
on Wednesday, please?

4 minutes

❸ telephone

answering machine ❼

4 🔊 USEFUL PHRASES
3 minutes

Learn these phrases. Then, test yourself,
using the cover flap.

I'd like the number
for Mario.

**Posso avere il numero
di Mario?**
*possoh averay eel
noomayroh dee mareeoh*

I'd like to speak to
Federico Martini.

**Vorrei parlare con
Federico Martini.**
*vorray parlaray kon
fedayreekoh marteenee*

Can I leave a
message?

**Posso lasciare
un messaggio?**
*possoh lasharay
oon messajjoh*

Sorry, I have the
wrong number.

**Scusi, ho sbagliato
numero.**
*skoozee, oh sballyatoh
noomayroh*

5 minutes

**Luciano Salvetti, della
tipografia Bartoli.**
*loochanoh salvettee, della
teepografeeah bartolee*

Luciano Salvetti of
Bartoli Printers.

**Mi dispiace, la linea è
occupata.**
*mee deespeeachay, lah
leeneah ay okkoopatah*

I'm sorry. The line is busy.

**Può farmi richiamare,
per favore?**
*puoh farmee reekeeamaray,
per favoray*

Can he call me
back, please?

Ripassa et ripeti
REVIEW AND REPEAT

Telephones

❶ il cellulare
eel chelloolaray

❷ il telefono
eel telayfonoh

**❸ la segreteria
telefonica**
*la segretereeah
telayfoneekah*

❹ le cuffie
lay kooffeeay

❺ la carta SIM
la karta seem

1 · TELEPHONES

Name these items in Italian.

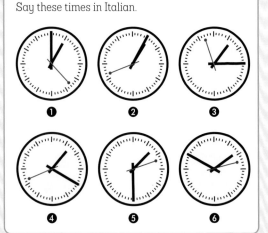

❶ cell phone

❷ telephone

❸ answering machine

headphones ❹

When?

❶ The meeting is
on Thursday.

❷ I want to go on
vacation tomorrow.

❸ My birthday is
in August.

❹ Our anniversary
is in December.

2 · WHEN?

2 minutes

What do these sentences mean?

❶ La riunione è giovedì.

❷ Voglio andare in vacanza domani.

❸ Il mio compleanno è in agosto.

❹ Il nostro anniversario è in dicembre.

Time

❶ l'una
loonah

❷ l'una e cinque
loonah ay cheenkway

**❸ l'una e
un quarto**
*loonah ay
oon kwartoh*

❹ l'una e venti
loonah ay ventee

❺ l'una e mezzo
loonah ay metsoh

**❻ le due
meno dieci**
*lay dooay
menoh deeaychee*

3 · TIME

3 minutes

Say these times in Italian.

❶ ❷ ❸

❹ ❺ ❻

3 minutes

❺ SIM card

4 MATH

4 minutes

Say the answers to these problems in Italian.

❶ 10 + 6 = ?
❷ 14 + 25 = ?
❸ 66 − 13 = ?
❹ 40 + 34 = ?
❺ 90 + 9 = ?
❻ 46 − 5 = ?

Sums

❶ **sedici**
sedeechee

❷ **trentanove**
trentanovay

❸ **cinquantatré**
cheenkwantatray

❹ **settantaquattro**
settantakwattroh

❺ **novantanove**
novantanovay

❻ **quarantuno**
kwarantoonoh

5 I WANT…

3 minutes

Fill in the blanks with the correct form of **volere** (*to want*).

❶ Signora, _____ un caffè?
❷ Io e Matteo _____ un tavolo per due.
❸ (loro) _____ delle caramelle.
❹ (tu) _____ una birra?
❺ (io) _____ una macchina nuova.
❻ (voi) _____ dei bicchieri?

I want…

❶ **vuole**
vwolay

❷ **vogliamo**
vollyamoh

❸ **vogliono**
vollyonoh

❹ **vuoi**
vwoee

❺ **voglio**
vollyoh

❻ **volete**
voletay

1 WARM UP

1 minute

Count to 100 by tens (pp10–11, pp30–31).

Ask "**At what time?**" (pp30–31).

Say "**It's half-past one**" (pp30–31).

Alla biglietteria
AT THE TICKET OFFICE

In Italy, before getting on the train, you must be sure to validate (**convalidare**) your ticket by stamping it in one of the special small machines installed in every train station for this purpose. Fines are imposed on travelers who have forgotten to validate their tickets. You can also buy tickets online—these don't need to be validated.

2 ◀))) WORDS TO REMEMBER

3 minutes

Familiarize yourself with these words, then test yourself, using the cover flap.

la stazione *lah statseeonay*	station
la prenotazione *la prenotatseeonay*	reservation
il biglietto *eel beellyettoh*	ticket
sola andata *solah andatah*	single
andata e ritorno *andatah ay reetornoh*	return
prima/seconda classe *preemah/sekondah klassay*	first/second class
la coincidenza *la koeencheedentsa*	connection
il cartello *eel kartelloh*	sign

il treno
eel trenoh
train

il passeggero
eel passejjayroh
passenger

La stazione è affollata.
lah statseeonay ay affollahtah
The station is crowded.

il binario
eel beenareeoh
platform

3 ◀))) IN CONVERSATION

Due biglietti per Roma, per favore.
dooay beellyettee per rohmah, per favoray

Two tickets to Rome, please.

Andata e ritorno?
andatah ay reetornoh

Return?

Sì. C'è la prenotazione obbligatoria?
see. chay lah prenotatseeonay obbleegatoryah

Yes. Do I need to reserve seats?

4 USEFUL PHRASES

5 minutes

Learn these phrases, then test yourself, using the cover flap.

Il treno per Firenze è in ritardo.
eel trenoh per firentsay ay een reetardoh
The train to Florence is late.

How much is a ticket to Genoa? | **Quanto costa un biglietto per Genova?**
kwantoh kostah oon beellyettoh per jenovah

Do you accept credit cards? | **Accettate la carta di credito?**
acchettatay lah kartah dee kredeetoh

Do I have to change trains? | **Devo cambiare treno?**
devoh kambeearay trenoh

Which platform does the train leave from? | **Da quale binario parte il treno?**
dah kwalay beenareeoh partay eel trenoh

Are there discounts? | **Ci sono delle riduzioni?**
chee sonoh dellay reedootseeonee

What time does the train to Naples leave? | **A che ora parte il treno per Napoli?**
ah kay orah partay eel trenoh per napolee

Cultural tip Most large railway stations have ticket offices and automatic ticket machines (**la biglietteria automatica**) that accept credit and debit cards, cash, and payments via mobile and digital wallets.

5 SAY IT

2 minutes

Which platform does the train for Genoa leave from?

Three return tickets to Naples, please.

4 minutes

No. Sono trecento euro.
noh. sonoh traychentoh ayooroh

No. It's three hundred euros.

Accettate la carta di credito?
acchettatay lah kartah dee kredeetoh

Do you accept credit cards?

Certo. Il treno parte dal binario uno.
chertoh. eel trenoh partay dal beenareeoh oonoh

Certainly. The train leaves from platform one.

1 WARM UP

1 minute

How do you say "**train**" in Italian (pp38–39)?

What does "**Da quale binario parte il treno?**" mean (pp38–39)?

Ask "**When are you free?**" (pp32–33).

Andare e prendere
TO GO AND TO TAKE

Andare (*to go*) and **prendere** (*to take*) are essential verbs in Italian that you will need to use frequently in everyday conversation as you find your way around. You can also use **prendere** when you talk about food and drink—for example, to say **prendo un caffè** (*I'll have a coffee*).

2 ◀))) **ANDARE**: TO GO

6 minutes

Practice **andare** (*to go*) and the sample sentences, then test yourself, using the cover flap.

(io) vado   I go
(eeoh) vadoh

(tu) vai   you go (informal singular)
(too) vaee

(Lei) va   you go (formal singular)
(lay) vah

(lui/lei) va   he/she/it goes
(looee/lay) vah

(noi) andiamo   we go
(noy) andeeamoh

(voi) andate   you go (plural)
(voy) andatay

(loro) vanno   they go
(loroh) vannoh

Dove va, signora?   Where are you going, madam?
dovay vah, seennyorah

Vorrei andare in treno.   I'd like to go by train.
vorray andaray een trenoh

Vado a Pisa.
vadoh ah peesah
I am going to Pisa.

Conversational tip Italian has no equivalent of the English present continuous tense (which uses the -*ing* ending)—it uses the same verb form for both the present and present continuous. For example, **vado a Roma** means both *I am going to Rome* and *I go to Rome*. The same is true of other verbs—for example, **prendo il treno** means both *I am taking the train* and *I take the train*.

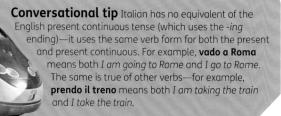

3 ◀)) PRENDERE: TO TAKE

6 minutes

Practice **prendere** (*to take*) and
the sample sentences, then test
yourself, using the cover flap.

I take	**(io) prendo**
	(eeoh) prendoh
you take (informal singular)	**(tu) prendi**
	(too) prendee
you take (formal singular)	**(Lei) prende**
	(lay) prenday
he/she/it takes	**(lui/lei) prende**
	(looee/lay) prenday
we take	**(noi) prendiamo**
	(noy) prendeeamoh
you take (plural)	**(voi) prendete**
	(voy) prendetay
they take	**(loro) prendono**
	(loroh) prendonoh

Prendo la metro tutti i giorni.
prendoh lah metroh toottee ee jornee
I take the metro every day.

I don't want to take a taxi.	**Non voglio prendere un taxi.**
	non vollyoh prenderay oon taxee

Take the first on the left.	**Prenda la prima a sinistra.**
	prenda lah preemah ah seeneestrah

He'll have the veal.	**Lui prende il vitello.**
	looee prenday eel veetelloh

4 ◀)) PUT INTO PRACTICE

2 minutes

Complete this dialogue, then test yourself, using the cover flap.

Dove va?	**Vado alla stazione.**
dovay vah	*vadoh allah statseeonay*

Where are you going?

Say: I'm going to the station.

Vuole prendere la metro?	**No, voglio andare in autobus.**
vwolay prenderay lah metroh	*noh, vollyoh andaray een a-ootoboos*

Do you want to take the metro?

Say: No, I want to go by bus.

1 WARM UP
1 minute

Say "**I'd like to go to the station**" (pp40–41).

Ask "**Where are you going?**" (pp40–41).

Say "**fruit**" and "**cheese**" (pp22–23).

Taxi, autobus e metro
TAXI, BUS, AND METRO

In Italy, you generally don't hail taxis but go to a taxi stand. You can buy bus tickets at a newsagent, which you then validate on the bus. The same tickets can usually also be used on the metro. Some buses and metros also accept contactless and app payments.

2 🔊 WORDS TO REMEMBER
4 minutes

Familiarize yourself with these words, then test yourself, using the cover flap.

l'autobus (m)   bus
la-ootoboos

il pullman   coach
eel poolman

la stazione dei pullman/della metro   coach/ metro station
lah statseeonay day poolman/dellah metroh

la fermata dell'autobus   bus stop
lah fermatah della-ootoboos

il biglietto   fare
eel beellyettoh

il posteggio dei taxi   taxi stand
eel postejjoh day taxee

Passa di qui il 46?
passah dee kwee eel kwarantasay
Does the number 46 stop here?

3 🔊 IN CONVERSATION: TAXI
2 minutes

Al mercato di San Lorenzo, per favore.
al merkatoh dee san lorentsoh, per favoray

To the San Lorenzo market, please.

Benissimo, signore.
beneesseemoh, seennyoray

Very well, sir.

Mi lasci qui, per favore.
mee lashee kwee, per favoray

Can you drop me here, please?

4 🔊 USEFUL PHRASES

4 minutes

Learn these phrases, then test yourself, using the cover flap.

I'd like a taxi to go to the Colosseum.
Vorrei un taxi per andare al Colosseo.
vorray oon taxee per andaray al kolossayoh

Please wait for me.
Mi aspetti, per favore.
mee aspettee, per favoray

How long is the journey?
Quanto dura il viaggio?
Kwantoh doorah eel veeajjoh

Excuse me, how do you get to the Vatican?
Scusi, per andare al Vaticano?
skoozee, per andaray al vateekahnoh

When is the next bus to the Capitol?
Quando passa il prossimo autobus per il Campidoglio?
kwandoh passah eel prosseemoh a-ootoboos per eel kampeedollyoh

Cultural tip Metro lines (**linee della metropolitana**) in Rome are known by their letter. The name of the last station on the line is used to indicate the direction of the train. Naples, Milan, Genoa, Turin, Catania, and Brescia have metro lines, too; these can be navigated in a similar way to Rome's.

6 SAY IT

2 minutes

Do you go to the railway station?

The Vatican, please.

When's the next coach to Rome?

5 🔊 IN CONVERSATION: BUS

2 minutes

Scusi, va al museo?
skoozee, vah al moozayoh

Excuse me, do you go to the museum?

Sì. Non è lontano.
see. non ay lontanoh

Yes. It's not very far.

Può dirmi quando devo scendere?
pwoh deermee kwandoh devoh shenderay

Can you tell me when to get off?

1 WARM UP

1 minute

Say "**I have...**" (pp14–15).

Say "**my father,**" "**my sister,**" and "**my parents**" (pp10–11 and pp12–13).

Say "**I'm going to Rome**" (pp40–41).

In auto
ON THE ROAD

Be sure to familiarize yourself with the Italian rules of the road before driving in Italy. Italian **autostrade** (*highways*) are fast but expensive toll (**il pedaggio**) roads. You usually take a ticket as you join the highway and pay according to the distance traveled as you leave it.

2 🔊 MATCH AND REPEAT

Match the numbered items to the list, then test yourself, using the cover flap.

❶ **il bagagliaio**
eel bagallyaeeoh

❷ **il parabrezza**
eel parabretsah

❸ **il caricabatterie**
eel kareekabattayreeay

❹ **la colonnina di ricarica**
lah kolonneenah dee reekareekah

❺ **lo sportello**
loh sportelloh

❻ **la gomma**
lah gommah

❼ **i fari**
ee faree

❽ **il cavo di ricarica**
eel kavo dee reekareekah

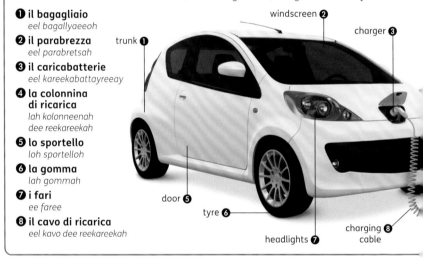

windscreen ❷
charger ❸
trunk ❶
door ❺
tyre ❻
headlights ❼
charging ❽ cable

Cultural tip At self-service stations, the pump shows the fuel being added and the money owed. At unmanned gas stations, you may need to authorize a card payment before the pump starts working. Electric cars can be charged at public charging stations, paid for by card or app, and could take up to half a day to fully charge.

3 🔊 ROAD SIGNS

Senso unico
senso uneekoh
One-way

Rotatoria
rotatoreeah
Roundabout

Dare la precedenza
daray lah prechedentsah
Yield

4 🔊 USEFUL PHRASES

2 minutes

Learn these phrases, then test yourself, using the cover flap.

My indicator doesn't work. **La freccia non funziona.**
lah frechah non foontseeonah

Fill it up, please. **Il pieno, per favore.**
eel pyaynoh, per favoray

4 minutes

charging point/ station ❹

5 🔊 WORDS TO REMEMBER

4 minutes

Familiarize yourself with these words, then test yourself, using the cover flap.

car **l'auto** (f)
la-ootoh

gas **la benzina**
lah bendseenah

diesel **il gasolio**
eel gazolyoh

oil **l'olio** (m)
lohlyoh

engine **il motore**
eel motoray

transmission **il cambio**
eel kambeeoh

flat tire **la gomma a terra**
lah gommah ah terrah

exhaust **la marmitta**
lah marmeettah

driver's license **la patente**
lah patentay

6 SAY IT

2 minutes

My transmission doesn't work.

I have a flat tire.

2 minutes

Diritto di precedenza
deereettoh dee prechedentsah
Priority road

Divieto di accesso
deevyaytoh dee acchessoh
No entry

Sosta vietata
sostah veeaytatah
No parking

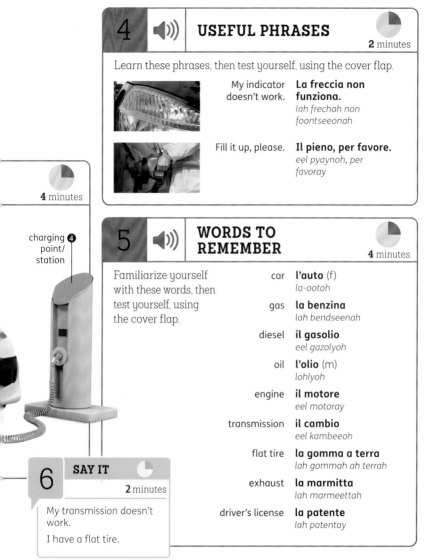

Risposte *Answers*
(Cover with flap)

Ripassa e ripeti
REVIEW AND REPEAT

Transport

❶ l'autobus
la-ootoboos

❷ il taxi
eel taxee

❸ l'auto
la-ootoh

❹ il treno
eel trenoh

❺ la bicicletta
lah beecheeklettah

❻ la metro
lah metroh

1   TRANSPORT

Name these forms of transport in Italian.

❸ car

❷ taxi

❹ train

bicycle ❺

Go and take

❶ va
vah

❷ prendiamo
prendeeamoh

❸ vado
vadoh

❹ prende
prenday

❺ vanno
vannoh

❻ prendi
prendee

2   GO AND TAKE

4 minutes

Fill in the blanks with the correct form of **andare** (*to go*) or **prendere** (*to take*).

❶ Dove _____ **l'autobus?**
(andare)

❷ (noi) _____ **un taxi.**
(prendere)

❸ (io) _____ **a Pisa.** (andare)

❹ _____ **un caffè, signor Gatti?** (prendere)

❺ (loro) _____ **in treno.**
(andare)

❻ (tu) _____ **la seconda a sinistra.** (prendere)

3 minutes

❶ bus

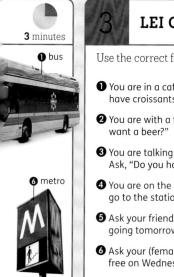

❻ metro

3 LEI OR TU?

4 minutes

Use the correct form of *you*.

❶ You are in a café. Ask, "Do you have croissants?"

❷ You are with a friend. Ask, "Do you want a beer?"

❸ You are talking to a business contact. Ask, "Do you have an appointment?"

❹ You are on the bus. Ask, "Do you go to the station?"

❺ Ask your friend where she's going tomorrow.

❻ Ask your (female) client, "Are you free on Wednesday?"

Lei or tu?

❶ **Ha delle brioche?**
ah dellay breeosh

❷ **Vuoi una birra?**
vwoee oonah beerah

❸ **Ha un appuntamento?**
ah oon appoontamentoh

❹ **Va alla stazione?**
vah allah statseeonay

❺ **Dove vai domani?**
dovay vaee domanee

❻ **È libera mercoledì?**
ay leeberah merkoledee

4 TICKETS

4 minutes

You are buying tickets at a railway station. Join in the conversation, replying in Italian, following the numbered English prompts.

Buongiorno.
❶ I'd like two tickets to Ferrara.

Solo andata o andata e ritorno?
❷ Return, please.

Sono trecento euro.
❸ What time does the train leave?

Alle quindici e dieci.
❹ What platform does the train leave from?

Dal binario sette.
❺ Thank you.

Tickets

❶ **Vorrei due biglietti per Ferrara.**
vorray dooay beellyettee per ferrarah

❷ **Andata e ritorno, per favore.**
andatah ay reetornoh, per favoray

❸ **A che ora parte il treno?**
ah kay orah partay eel trenoh

❹ **Da quale binario parte il treno?**
dah kwalay beenareeoh partay eel trenoh

❺ **Grazie.**
gratseeay

In città
ABOUT TOWN

1 **WARM UP** 🕐
1 minute

Ask "**How do you get to the museum?**" (pp42–43).

Say "**I want to take the metro**" and "**I don't want to take a taxi**" (pp40–41).

Most Italian towns (**le città**) and larger villages (**i paesi**) still have a market day, a thriving community of small shops, and usually a mayor and a town hall. There may be parking restrictions in the town center. In Rome, parking in the central **zona a traffico limitato** is prohibited on weekdays.

2 🔊 **WORDS TO REMEMBER** **4** minutes

Familiarize yourself with these words, then test yourself, using the cover flap.

il benzinaio gas station
eel bentseenaeeoh

l'ufficio turistico (m) tourist office
looffeechoh tooreesteekoh

la piscina swimming pool
lah peesheenah

la biblioteca library
lah beebleeotaykah

3 🔊 **MATCH AND REPEAT** **4** minutes

Match the numbered locations to the list, then test yourself, using the cover flap.

❶ **la chiesa**
lah keeayzah

❷ **il museo**
eel moozayoh

❸ **il ponte**
eel pontay

❹ **la galleria d'arte**
lah gallayreeah darteh

❺ **il centro città**
eel chentroh cheettah

❻ **il municipio**
eel mooneecheepeeoh

❼ **la piazza**
lah peeatsah

❽ **il parcheggio**
eel parkejjoh

town hall ❻

❺ town center

❶ church

❷ museum

❸ bridge

❹ art gallery

4 🔊 USEFUL PHRASES

4 minutes

Learn these phrases, then test yourself, using the cover flap.

Is there an art gallery in town?	**C'è una pinacoteca in città?** *chay oonah peenacotekah een cheettah*
Is it far from here?	**È lontano da qui?** *ay lontanoh da kwee*
There is a swimming pool near the bridge.	**C'è una piscina vicino al ponte.** *chay oonah peesheenah veecheenoh al pontay*
There isn't a library.	**Non c'è una biblioteca.** *non chay oonah beebleeotaykah*

Il duomo è in centro.
eel dwomoh ay een chentroh
The cathedral is in the town center.

5 🔊 PUT INTO PRACTICE

2 minutes

Complete this dialogue, then test yourself, using the cover flap.

Desidera? *dayseedayrah* Can I help you?	**C'è una biblioteca in città?** *chay oonah beebleeotaykah een cheettah*
Ask: Is there a library in town?	
No, ma c'è un museo. *noh, mah chay oon moozayoh* No, but there's a museum.	**E per andare al museo?** *ay per andaray al moozayoh*
Ask: How do I get to the museum?	
È nella piazza. *ay nellah peeatsah* It's in the square.	**Grazie.** *gratseeay*
Say: Thank you.	

❼ square

❽ parking lot

1 WARM UP
1 minute

How do you say "**Near the station**" (pp42–43)?

Say "**Take the first on the left**" (pp40–41).

Ask "**Where are you going?**" (pp40–41).

Le indicazioni
DIRECTIONS

To help you find your way, you'll often find a **pianta della città** (*town map*) situated in the town, usually near the town hall or tourist office. In the older parts of Italian towns, there are often narrow streets in which you will usually find a one-way system in operation. Parking is usually restricted.

2 🔊 WORDS TO REMEMBER

Familiarize yourself with these words, then test yourself, using the cover flap.

il semaforo *eel semaforoh*	traffic lights
la strada *lah stradah*	street/road
l'angolo (m) *langoloh*	corner
l'incrocio (m) *leenkrochoh*	junction
la pianta *lah peeantah*	map
le mappe online *lay mappay onlaeen*	online maps

il monumento
eel monoomentoh
monument

Dove siamo?
dovay seeahmoh
Where are we?

3 🔊 IN CONVERSATION

C'è un ristorante in città?
chay oon reestorantay een cheettah

Is there a restaurant in town?

Sì, vicino alla stazione.
see, veecheenoh allah statseeonay

Yes, near the station.

E per andare alla stazione?
ay per andaray allah statseeonay

How do I get to the station?

5 SAY IT
2 minutes

Turn right at the end of the street.

It's across from the town hall.

It's ten minutes by bus.

4 minutes

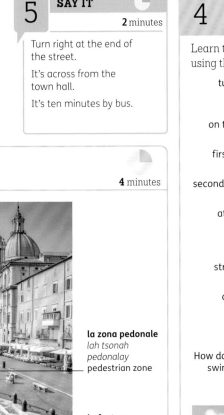

la zona pedonale
*lah tsonah
pedonalay*
pedestrian zone

la fontana
lah fontanah
fountain

4 USEFUL PHRASES
4 minutes

Learn these phrases, then test yourself, using the cover flap.

turn left/right	**giri a sinistra/destra** *jeeree ah seeneestrah/destrah*
on the left/right	**a sinistra/destra** *lah seeneestrah/destrah*
first on the left	**la prima a sinistra** *lah preemah ah seeneestrah*
second on the right	**la seconda a destra** *lah sekondah ah destrah*
at the square, turn left	**alla piazza giri a sinistra** *allah peeatsah jeeree lah seeneestrah*
straight ahead	**sempre dritto** *sempray dreettoh*
at the end of the street	**in fondo alla strada** *een fondoh allah stradah*
across from	**davanti a** *davantee ah*
How do I get to the swimming pool?	**Per andare alla piscina?** *per andaray allah peesheenah*

Mi sono persa.
mee sonoh persah
I'm lost.

4 minutes

Al semaforo giri a sinistra.
al semaforoh jeeree ah seeneestrah

Turn left at the traffic lights.

È lontano?
ay lontanoh

Is it far?

No, cinque minuti a piedi.
noh, cheenkway meenootee ah peeaydee

No, it's five minutes on foot.

1 WARM UP

1 minute

Say "**Is there a museum in town?**" (pp48–49).

How do you say "**At six o'clock**"? (pp30–31).

Ask "**What time is it?**" (pp30–31).

Il turismo
SIGHTSEEING

Most national museums and art galleries close one day a week and on public holidays. It is not unusual, particularly in smaller towns, for shops to close for lunch and on Sundays, and for public buildings and banks to close in the afternoons. City-center shops are usually open all day; some are also open on Sundays, as are shopping centers.

2 WORDS TO REMEMBER

4 minutes

Familiarize yourself with these words, then test yourself, using the cover flap.

la guida *lah gweedah*	guide, guidebook, travel guide
il biglietto *eel beellyettoh*	entrance ticket
l'orario di apertura (m) *lorareeoh dee apertoorah*	opening times
il giorno festivo *eel jornoh festeevoh*	public holiday
la tariffa ridotta *lah tareefah reedotah*	concessionary rate
l'entrata libera (f) *lentratah leebayrah*	free entrance

la visita guidata
lah veeseetah gweedatah
guided tour

Cultural tip Visitors will be asked to pay an entrance fee in most museums, historic buildings, and even in some churches. Reduced rates for **bambini** (*children*), **studenti** (*students*), **pensionati** (*seniors*), and groups are available in most places.

3 IN CONVERSATION

È aperto oggi pomeriggio?
ay apertoh ojjee pomereejjoh

Are you open this afternoon?

Sì, ma chiudiamo alle sei.
see, mah kyoodeeamoh allay say

Yes, but we close at six o'clock.

C'è l'accesso per le sedie a rotelle?
chay lacchayssoh per lay sedeeay ah rotellay

Do you have wheelchair access?

4 USEFUL PHRASES

3 minutes

Learn these phrases, then test yourself, using the cover flap.

What time do you open/close?
A che ora aprite/ chiudete?
ah kay orah apreetay/ keeoodetay

Where are the toilets?
Dove sono i bagni?
dovay sonoh ee banyee

Is there wheelchair access?
C'è l'accesso per le sedie a rotelle?
chay lacchayssoh per lay sedeeay ah rotellay

5  PUT INTO PRACTICE

4 minutes

Complete this dialogue, then test yourself, using the cover flap.

Spiacente. Il museo è chiuso.
speeachentay. eel moozayoh ay keeoozoh

Sorry. The museum is closed.

Ask: Are you open on Mondays?

È aperto il lunedì?
ay apertoh eel loonedee

Sì, ma chiude presto.
see, mah keeooday prestoh

Yes, but we close early.

Ask: At what time?

A che ora?
ah kay orah

3 minutes

Sì, là c'è l'ascensore.
see, lah chay lashaynsoray

Yes, there's an elevator over there.

Grazie. Vorrei quattro biglietti.
gratseeay. vorray kwattroh beellyettee

Thank you. I'd like four entrance tickets.

Ecco a Lei. La guida è gratuita.
ekkoh ah lay. lah gweedah ay gratweetah

Here you are. The guidebook is free.

1 WARM UP

1 minute

Say in Italian "**She is my stepmother**" (pp14–15).

What's the Italian for "**ticket**" (pp38–39)?

Say "**I am going to New York**" (pp40–41).

All'aeroporto
AT THE AIRPORT

Although the airport environment is largely international, it is sometimes useful to be able to ask your way around the terminal in Italian. It's a good idea to make sure you have a few one-euro coins when you arrive at the airport—you may need to pay for a luggage cart.

2 WORDS TO REMEMBER

4 minutes

il check-in *eel chekeen*	check-in
le partenze *lay partentsay*	departures
gli arrivi *lly arreevee*	arrivals
la dogana *lah doganah*	customs
il controllo passaporti *eel kontrolloh passaportee*	passport control
il terminal *eel termeenal*	terminal
l'uscita (f) *loosheetah*	boarding gate
il numero del volo *eel noomeroh del voloh*	flight number

Familiarize yourself with these words, then test yourself, using the cover flap.

Il volo 23 parte dal terminal 2.
eel voloh venteetray partay dal termeenal dooay
Flight 23 leaves from Terminal 2.

3 USEFUL PHRASES

3 minutes

Learn these phrases, then test yourself, using the cover flap.

Il volo da Alghero è in orario?
eel voloh dah algayroh ay een orareeoh
Is the flight from Alghero on time?

Il volo per Londra è in ritardo.
eel voloh per londrah ay een reetardoh
The flight to London is delayed.

Non trovo i miei bagagli.
non trovoh ee mee-ayee bagallyee
I can't find my baggage.

4 PUT INTO PRACTICE

3 minutes

Complete this dialogue, then test yourself, using the cover flap.

Buonasera. Desidera?
bwonasayrah. dayseedayrah

Hello. Can I help you?

Il volo per Milano è in orario?
eel voloh per meelanoh ay een orareeoh

Ask: Is the flight to Milan on time?

Sì, signore.
see, seennyoray

Yes, sir.

Qual è l'uscita del volo?
kwalay loosheetah del voloh

Ask: Which gate does it leave from?

5 MATCH AND REPEAT

4 minutes

Match the numbered items to the list, then test yourself, using the cover flap.

baggage check ❶

boarding pass ❷

ticket ❸

passport ❹

❺ suitcase ❻ carry-on ❼ cart

❶ **lo sportello del check-in**
loh sportelloh del chekeen

❷ **la carta d'imbarco**
lah kartah deembarkoh

❸ **il biglietto**
eel beellyettoh

❹ **il passaporto**
eel passaportoh

❺ **la valigia**
lah valeejah

❻ **il bagaglio a mano**
eel bagallyoh ah manoh

❼ **il carrello**
eel karrelloh

Ripassa e ripeti
REVIEW AND REPEAT

Risposte *Answers*
(Cover with flap)

Places

❶ **il museo**
eel moozayoh

❷ **la chiesa**
lah keeayzah

❸ **il ponte**
eel pontay

❹ **la galleria d'arte**
lah gallayreeah darteh

❺ **il duomo**
eel dwomoh

❻ **il parcheggio**
eel parkejjoh

❼ **la piazza**
lah peeatsah

Car parts

❶ **il parabrezza**
eel parabretsah

❷ **il caricabatterie**
eel kareekabattayreeay

❸ **la colonnina di ricarica**
lah kolonneenah dee reekareekah

❹ **lo sportello**
loh sportelloh

❺ **la gomma**
lah gommah

❻ **il cavo di ricarica**
eel kavo dee reekareekah

1 PLACES

4 minutes

Name these locations in Italian.

❶ museum ❷ church ❸ bridge

❹ art gallery

❺ cathedral

❻ parking lot ❼ square

2 CAR PARTS

Name these car parts in Italian.

windshield ❶

charger ❷

door ❹ tire ❺ charging cable ❻

3 QUESTIONS

4 minutes

Ask the questions in Italian that match these answers:

❶ **Il pullman parte alle otto.**
eel poolman partay allay ottoh

❷ **Il caffè costa due euro e cinquanta.**
eel kaffay kostah dooay ayooroh ay cheenkwantah

❸ **No grazie, non voglio vino.**
noh gratseeay non vollyoh veenoh

❹ **Il treno parte dal binario sette.**
eel trenoh partay dal beenareeoh settay

❺ **Vado a Roma.**
vadoh ah rohmah

❻ **Sì, il diciotto passa di qui.**
see eel deechottoh passah dee kwee

❼ **Il museo è in centro.**
eel moozayoh ay een chentroh

Questions

❶ **A che ora parte il pullman?**
ah kay orah partay eel poolman

❷ **Quant'è il caffè?**
kwantay eel kaffay

❸ **Vuole del vino?**
vwolay del veenoh

❹ **Da quale binario parte il treno?**
dah kwalay beenareeoh partay eel trenoh

❺ **Dove va?**
dovay vah

❻ **Passa di qui il diciotto?**
passah dee kwee eel deechottoh

❼ **Dov'è il museo?**
dovay eel moozayoh

---

3 minutes

❸ charging point/station

4 VERBS

4 minutes

Fill in the blanks with the correct form of the missing verbs.

❶ **(io) _____ inglese.** (essere)

❷ **(noi) _____ l'autobus.** (prendere)

❸ **Il treno _____ a Verona.** (andare)

❹ **(loro) _____ tre bambine.** (avere)

❺ **(tu) _____ un tè?** (volere)

❻ **Quanti figli _____ signora?** (avere)

Verbs

❶ **sono**
sonoh

❷ **prendiamo**
prendeeamoh

❸ **va**
vah

❹ **hanno**
annoh

❺ **vuoi**
vwoee

❻ **ha**
ah

1 **WARM UP**
1 minute

Ask in Italian "**Do you accept credit cards?**" (pp38–39).

Ask "**How much is that?**" (pp18–19)

Ask "**Do you have children?**" (pp12–13).

Prenotare una camera
BOOKING A ROOM

There are different types of accommodations: **l'albergo**, a standard hotel or inn; **la pensione**, a small, usually cheaper family-run hotel; and **gli agriturismi**, farmhouse stays that also offer experiences like wine tasting. Airbnb, offering accommodations in private rooms and homes, is also a popular option.

---

2 ◀))) **USEFUL PHRASES**
3 minutes

Learn these phrases, then test yourself, using the cover flap.

La colazione è compresa?
lah kolatseeonay ay komprezah

Is breakfast included?

Accettate animali domestici?
acchayttatay aneemalee domesteechee

Do you accept pets?

C'è il servizio in camera?
chay eel sayrveetsyoh een kamayrah

Is there room service?

A che ora devo lasciare la camera?
ah kay orah devoh lasharay lah kamayrah

What time do I have to vacate the room?

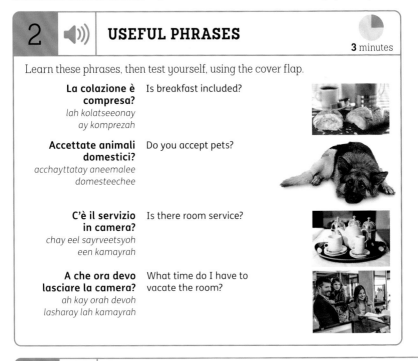

---

3 ◀))) **IN CONVERSATION**

Avete una camera?
avetay oonah kamayrah

Do you have any rooms available?

Sì, abbiamo una matrimoniale.
see, abbeeamoh oonah matreemoneealay

Yes, we have a double room.

È possibile avere anche un lettino?
ay posseebeelay averay ankay oon letteenoh

Is it possible to have a cot as well?

4 🔊 WORDS TO REMEMBER

4 minutes

Familiarize yourself with these words, then test yourself, using the cover flap.

La camera ha la vista sul giardino?
lah kamayrah ah lah veestah sool jardeenoh
Does the room have a view over the garden?

room	**la camera** *lah kamayrah*
single room	**la camera singola** *lah kamayrah seengolah*
double room	**la camera matrimoniale** *lah kamayrah matreemoneealay*
twin room	**la camera a due letti** *lah kamayrah ah dooay layttee*
bathroom	**il bagno** *eel bannyoh*
shower	**la doccia** *lah docchah*
balcony	**il balcone** *eel balkonay*
key	**la chiave** *lah keeavay*
air-conditioning	**l'aria condizionata** (f) *lareeah kondeetseeonatah*
breakfast	**la colazione** *lah kolatseeonay*

5 SAY IT

2 minutes

Do you have a single room, please?

For six nights.

Does the room have a balcony?

Cultural tip Some hotels and **pensioni** will include breakfast in the price of a room; in others, you will be charged extra. Breakfast is often in the style of a buffet and usually includes a choice of coffee or tea, cakes and pastries, bread with jam and butter, cereal, juice, yogurt, and savory items, such as ham and eggs.

5 minutes

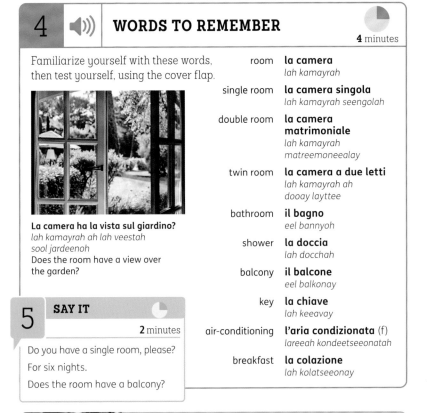

Non c'è problema. Per quante notti?
non chay problemah. per kwantay nottee

No problem. How many nights?

Per tre notti.
per tray nottee

For three nights.

Benissimo. Ecco a Lei la chiave.
beneesseemoh. ekkoh ah lay lah keeavay

Very good. Here's the key.

<table>
<tr><td>

1 **WARM UP**

1 minute

Ask "**Is there...?**" and reply "**There isn't...**" (pp48–49).

What does "**Desidera?**" mean (pp48–49)?

Say "**They don't have any children**" (pp14–15).

</td><td>

In albergo
IN THE HOTEL

Although the larger hotels almost always have bathrooms en suite, there are still some **pensioni** where you may have to share the facilities with other guests. This can also be the case in some **ostelli della gioventù** (*youth hostels*), where families can stay the night in low-cost, reasonably priced rooms.

</td></tr>
</table>

2 ◀))) MATCH AND REPEAT

6 minutes

Match the numbered items to the list, then test yourself, using the cover flap.

1 **le tende**
lay tenday

2 **il cuscino**
eel kusheenoh

3 **il divano**
eel deevanoh

4 **la lampada**
lah lampadah

5 **il guanciale**
eel gwanchalay

6 **il mini bar**
eel meenee bar

7 **il letto**
eel lettoh

8 **la coperta**
lah kopertah

9 **il copriletto**
eel kopreelettoh

10 **il comodino**
eel komodeenoh

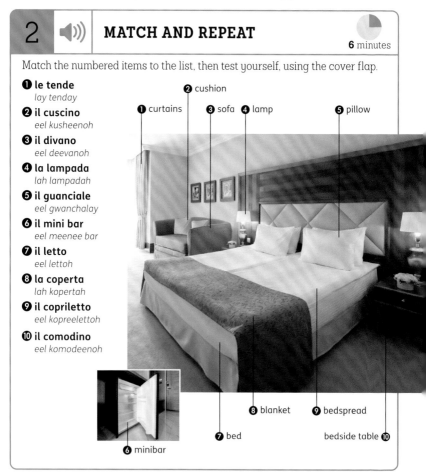

2 cushion
1 curtains **3** sofa **4** lamp **5** pillow
8 blanket **9** bedspread
7 bed bedside table **10**
6 minibar

Cultural tip You'll find that the price of rooms varies according to the season, especially in tourist resorts. The highest prices are charged during the **alta stagione** (*high season*). Accommodations are generally much cheaper in the **bassa stagione** (*low season*). It's a good idea to check before you book.

3 🔊 USEFUL PHRASES

5 minutes

Learn these phrases, then test yourself, using the cover flap.

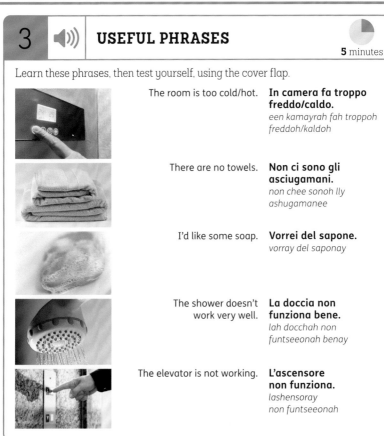

The room is too cold/hot. **In camera fa troppo freddo/caldo.**
een kamayrah fah troppoh freddoh/kaldoh

There are no towels. **Non ci sono gli asciugamani.**
non chee sonoh lly ashugamanee

I'd like some soap. **Vorrei del sapone.**
vorray del saponay

The shower doesn't work very well. **La doccia non funziona bene.**
lah docchah non funtseeonah benay

The elevator is not working. **L'ascensore non funziona.**
lashensoray non funtseeonah

4 🔊 PUT INTO PRACTICE

3 minutes

Complete this dialogue, then test yourself, using the cover flap.

Buonasera. Desidera?
bwonasayrah. dayseedayrah

Hello. Can I help you?

Say: I'd like some pillows.

Vorrei dei guanciali.
vorray day gwanchalee

Il personale ai piani glieli porta subito.
eel personahlay aee peeaneeh llyaylee portah soobeetoh

Housekeeping will bring some right away.

Say: And the television doesn't work.

E la televisione non funziona.
ay lah televeezeeonay non foontseeonah

1 WARM UP
1 minute

Ask "**Can I?**" (pp34–35).

What is Italian for "**the shower**" (pp60–61)?

Say "**I'd like some towels**" (pp60–61).

In campeggio
AT THE CAMPSITE

Camping is popular in Italy, and the country has numerous well-organized campsites, including luxurious glamping sites. The local tourist office can usually provide a list of official campsites in the area where you plan to stay. Respect any signs that say **campeggio vietato** (*camping forbidden*).

2 ◀))) USEFUL PHRASES

Learn these phrases, then test yourself, using the cover flap.

È possibile noleggiare una bicicletta?
ay posseebeelay nolayjjaray oonah beecheeklettah
Can I rent a bicycle?

L'acqua è potabile?
lahkkwah ay potabeelay
Is this drinking water?

È permesso accendere i falò?
ay permessoh acchenderay ee faloh
Are campfires allowed?

È vietata la musica ad alto volume.
ay veeaytatah lah mooseekah ad altoh voloomay
Loud music is forbidden.

Il campeggio è tranquillo.
eel kampayjjoh ay trankweelloh
The campsite is quiet.

la presa di corrente
lah praysah dee korrentay
electrical hook-up

il telo protettivo
eel teloh protetteevoh
fly sheet

la corda
lah kordah
guy rope

il picchetto
eel peekettoh
tent peg

3 ◀))) IN CONVERSATION

Vorremmo una piazzola per tre notti.
vorremmoh oonah peeatsolah per tray nottee

We would like a site for three nights.

Ce n'è una vicino alla piscina.
chay nay oonah veecheenoh allah peesheenah

There's one near the swimming pool.

Qual è il prezzo per una roulotte?
kwalay eel pretsoh per oonah roolott

How much is it for a caravan?

5 SAY IT
2 minutes

I need a site for four nights.

Can I rent a tent?

Where's the electrical hook-up?

---

3 minutes

la direzione del campeggio
lah deeraytseeonay del kampayjjoh
campsite office

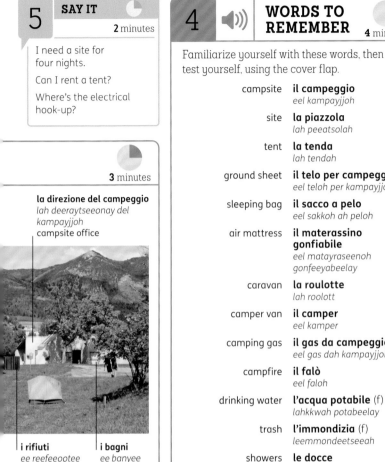

i rifiuti
ee reefeeootee
trash can

i bagni
ee banyee
toilets

---

4 🔊 WORDS TO REMEMBER
4 minutes

Familiarize yourself with these words, then test yourself, using the cover flap.

campsite	**il campeggio**	*eel kampayjjoh*
site	**la piazzola**	*lah peeatsolah*
tent	**la tenda**	*lah tendah*
ground sheet	**il telo per campeggio**	*eel teloh per kampayjjoh*
sleeping bag	**il sacco a pelo**	*eel sakkoh ah peloh*
air mattress	**il materassino gonfiabile**	*eel matayraseenoh gonfeeyabeelay*
caravan	**la roulotte**	*lah roolott*
camper van	**il camper**	*eel kamper*
camping gas	**il gas da campeggio**	*eel gas dah kampayjjoh*
campfire	**il falò**	*eel faloh*
drinking water	**l'acqua potabile** (f)	*lahkkwah potabeelay*
trash	**l'immondizia** (f)	*leemmondeetseeah*
showers	**le docce**	*lay docchay*

---

5 minutes

Quattrocento euro, una notte anticipata.
kwattrohchayntoh ehooroh, oonah nottay anteecheepatah

Four hundred euros, one night in advance.

È possibile affittare un barbecue?
ay posseebeelay affeettaray oon barbeku

Can I rent a grill?

Sì, ma deve versare una cauzione.
see, mah devay versaray oonah kaootseeonay

Yes, but you must pay a deposit.

WARM UP

1 minute

Say "**hot**" and "**cold**" (pp60–61).

What is the Italian for "**room**" (pp58–59), "**bed**," and "**pillow**" (pp60–61)?

Le descrizioni
DESCRIPTIONS

Adjectives are words used to describe people, things, and places. In Italian, you generally put the adjective after the thing it describes—for example, **una camera singola** (*a single room*). However, you will sometimes see them placed before—for example, **una bella donna** (*a beautiful woman*).

2 **WORDS TO REMEMBER**

7 minutes

Adjectives usually change depending on whether the thing described is masculine, feminine, or plural. In most cases, adjectives end in **-o** for masculine singular words and **-a** for the feminine. Plural endings are **-i** for masculine and **-e** for feminine. Some adjectives end in **-e** for the masculine and the feminine, changing to **-i** in the plural. Others never change. Familiarize yourself with these words, then test yourself, using the cover flap.

grande *granday*	big, large
piccolo/piccola *peekkoloh/peekkolah*	small
caldo/calda *kaldoh/kaldah*	hot
freddo/fredda *freddoh/freddah*	cold
buono/buona *bwonoh/bwonah*	good
cattivo/cattiva *katteevoh/katteevah*	bad
lento/lenta *lentoh/lentah*	slow
veloce *velochay*	fast
rumoroso/a *roomorozoh/ah*	noisy
tranquillo/a *trankweelloh/ah*	quiet
duro/dura *dooroh/doorah*	hard
morbido/morbida *morbeedoh/morbeedah*	soft
bello/bella *belloh/bellah*	beautiful
brutto/brutta *broottoh/broottah*	ugly

La montagna è alta.
lah montanyah ay altah
The mountain is high.

La collina è bassa.
lah kolleenah ay bassah
The hill is low.

La casa è piccola.
lah kasah ay peekkolah
The house is small.

La chiesa è vecchia.
lah keeayzah eh vekkeeah
The church is old.

Il paese è molto bello.
Il paese è molto bello.
The village is very beautiful.

3 🔊 USEFUL PHRASES

4 minutes

You can emphasize a description by using **molto** (*very*), **troppo** (*too*), or **più** (*more*) before the adjective. Learn these phrases, then test yourself, using the cover flap.

This coffee is very hot. **Il caffè è molto caldo.**
eel kaffay ay moltoh kaldoh

My room is very noisy. **La mia camera è molto rumorosa.**
lah mee-ah kamayrah ay moltoh roomorosah

The car is too small. **L'auto è troppo piccola.**
la-ootoh ay troppoh peekkolah

I'd like a softer bed. **Vorrei un letto più morbido.**
vorray oon lettoh peeoo morbeedoh

4 🔊 PUT INTO PRACTICE

3 minutes

Complete this dialogue, then test yourself, using the cover flap.

Ecco la camera. **La vista è**
ekkoh lah kamayrah **molto bella.**
lah veestah ay
Here is the bedroom. *moltoh bellah*

Say: The view is
very beautiful.

Il bagno è là. **È troppo piccolo.**
eel bannyoh ay lah *ay troppoh peekkoloh*

The bathroom is over there.

Say: It is too small.

Non abbiamo altre camere. **La prendiamo.**
non abbeeamoh altray *lah prendeeamoh*
kamayray

We don't have any
other rooms.

Say: We'll take it.

Risposte *Answers*
(Cover with flap)

Ripassa e ripeti
REVIEW AND REPEAT

Adjectives

❶ **piccola**
peekkolah

❷ **morbido**
morbeedoh

❸ **buono**
bwonoh

❹ **freddo**
freddoh

❺ **grande**
granday

1 ADJECTIVES

3 minutes

Fill in the blanks with the correct Italian masculine or feminine form of the adjective given in brackets.

❶ **La camera è troppo** _____ . (small)

❷ **Vorrei un guanciale più** _____ . (soft)

❸ **Il caffè è molto** _____ . (good)

❹ **In questo bagno fa** _____ . (cold)

❺ **Vorrei un letto più** _____ . (big)

Campsite

❶ **la roulotte**
lah roolott

❷ **i rifiuti**
ee reefeeootee

❸ **la tenda**
lah tendah

❹ **la corda**
lah kordah

❺ **la presa di corrente**
lah praysah dee korrentay

❻ **i bagni**
ee banyee

2 CAMPSITE

Name these campsite items in Italian.

camper ❶   trash can ❷

❸ tent   guy rope ❹   ❺ electrical hook-up

3 AT THE HOTEL

4 minutes

You are booking a room in a hotel. Join in the conversation, replying in Italian, following the numbered English prompts.

Posso aiutarla?
❶ Do you have any rooms free?

Sì, abbiamo una matrimoniale.
❷ Do you accept pets?

Sì. Per quante notti?
❸ Three nights.

Sono duecentoquaranta euro.
❹ Is breakfast included?

Sì. Ecco la chiave.
❺ Thank you very much.

At the hotel

❶ **Avete una camera?**
avetay oonah kamayrah

❷ **Accettate animali domestici?**
acchayttatay aneemalee domesteechee

❸ **Tre notti.**
tray nottee

❹ **La colazione è compresa?**
lah kolatseeonay ay komprezah

❺ **Grazie.**
gratseeay

---

3 minutes

4 NEGATIVES

5 minutes

Make these sentences negative, using the correct form of the verb in brackets.

❶ **(io) _____ figli.** (avere)

❷ **(Lei) _____ a Genova domani.** (andare)

❸ **(lui) _____ vino.** (volere)

❹ **(io) _____ lo zucchero nel caffè.** (volere)

❺ **La camera _____ molto bella.** (essere)

Negatives

❶ **non ho**
non oh

❷ **non va**
non vah

❸ **non vuole**
non vwolay

❹ **non voglio**
non vollyoh

❺ **non è**
non ay

❻ toilets

1 WARM UP
1 minute

Ask "**How do I get to the station?**" (pp50–51).

Say "**Turn left at the traffic lights,**" "**Go straight on,**" and "**The station is across from the café**" (pp50–51).

I negozi
SHOPS

Small, traditional, specialized shops are still very common in Italian town centers, although you will see some chains as well. You can also find big supermarkets and shopping centers on the outskirts of major towns. Markets selling fresh local produce can be found everywhere. You can find out the market day at the tourist office.

2 ◀)) MATCH AND REPEAT

Match the numbered shops to the list, then test yourself, using the cover flap.

❶ **il panificio**
eel paneefeechoh

❷ **la pasticceria**
lah pastee-chayreeah

❸ **il tabaccaio**
eel tabakkaeeoh

❹ **la macelleria**
lah machayllay-reeah

❺ **la salumeria**
lah saloomay-reeah

❻ **la libreria**
lah leebrayreeah

❼ **la pescheria**
lah payskayreeah

❽ **gli alimentari**
lly aleementaree

❾ **la gelateria**
lah jaylatereeah

❶ **baker**

❷ **cake shop**

❹ **butcher**

❺ **delicatessen**

❼ **fishmonger**

❽ **grocery**

Cultural tip Although all Italian pharmacies sell cosmetics and toiletries, the best place for these is **la profumeria**, some of which are very high-end and offer a wide range of brands. The **tabaccaio** (*tobacconist*) is the only licensed outlet for cigarettes, and it also sells stamps (alongside the post office), newspapers, magazines, postcards, bus tickets, candy, cell phone minutes, and souvenirs, and sometimes it includes a café and bar.

Dov'è il fioraio?
dovay eel feeoraeeoh
Where is the florist?

3 🔊 USEFUL PHRASES

4 minutes

Learn these phrases, then test yourself, using the cover flap.

Where is the hairdresser?	**Dov'è il parrucchiere?** *dovay eel parrookyayray*
Where do I pay?	**Dove pago?** *dovay pagoh*
I'm just looking, thank you.	**Do solo un'occhiata, grazie.** *doh soloh oonokyatah, gratseeay*
Do you sell SIM cards?	**Avete carte SIM?** *avetay kartay seem*
I'd like to place an order.	**Vorrei fare un'ordinazione.** *vorray faray oonordeenatseeonay*
Can I exchange this?	**Posso cambiare questo?** *possoh kambeearay kwestoh*
Can you give me the receipt?	**Mi dà lo scontrino?** *mee dah loh skontreenoh*

4 minutes

❸ tobacconist

❻ bookshop

❾ ice cream parlor

4 🔊 WORDS TO REMEMBER

4 minutes

Familiarize yourself with these words, then test yourself, using the cover flap.

antiques shop	**l'antiquario** (m) *lanteekwareeoh*
hairdresser	**il parrucchiere** *eel parrookyayray*
jeweler	**la gioielleria** *la joyayllereeah*
post office	**le poste** *lay postay*
shoe repairer	**il calzolaio** *eel kaltsolaeeoh*
dairy	**la latteria** *lah lattereeah*
wine shop	**l'enoteca** (f) *laynotekah*
leather goods shop	**la pelletteria** *lah pellettereeah*
travel agent	**l'agenzia di viaggi** (f) *lajentseeah dee veeajjee*
bank	**la banca** *lah bankah*

5 SAY IT

2 minutes

Where is the bank?

Do you sell cheese?

Where do I pay?

1 | **WARM UP** | 1 minute

What is the Italian for "**40**," "**56**," "**77**," "**82**," and "**94**" (pp30–31)?

Say "**I'd like a big room**" (pp64–65).

Ask "**Do you have a small car?**" (pp64–65).

Al mercato
AT THE MARKET

Italy uses the metric system of weights and measures. You need to ask for produce in kilograms and grams. Some larger or more expensive items, such as melons or artichokes, may be sold as **l'uno** (*individually*). In many Italian markets, alongside foods, you will also find stalls selling clothing and household goods.

---

2 🔊 **MATCH AND REPEAT**

Match the numbered items to the list, then test yourself, using the cover flap.

❶ il finocchio
eel feenokeeoh

❷ la lattuga
lah lattoogah

❸ il cavolfiore
eel kavolfeeoray

❹ i peperoni
ee paypaironee

❺ le patate
lay patatay

❻ l'aglio (m)
lalyoh

❼ i pomodori
ee pomodoree

❽ gli asparagi
lly asparajee

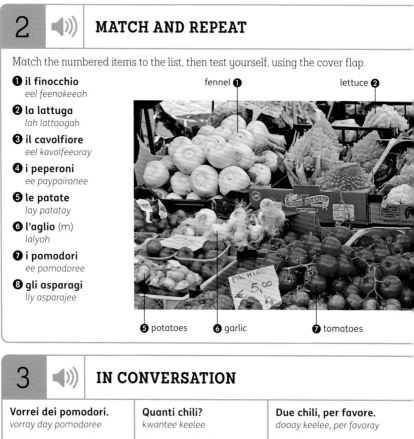

fennel ❶   lettuce ❷

❺ potatoes   ❻ garlic   ❼ tomatoes

---

3 🔊 **IN CONVERSATION**

Vorrei dei pomodori. *vorray day pomodoree*	**Quanti chili?** *kwantee keelee*	**Due chili, per favore.** *dooay keelee, per favoray*
I'd like some tomatoes.	How many kilos?	Two kilos, please.

5 SAY IT
2 minutes

Three kilos of bell peppers, please.

The asparagus is too expensive.

How much is the lettuce?

4 minutes

❸ cauliflower

❹ bell peppers

❽ asparagus

4 🔊 USEFUL PHRASES
5 minutes

Learn these phrases, then test yourself, using the cover flap.

Quel formaggio è troppo caro.
kwel formajjoh ay troppoh karoh

That cheese is too expensive.

Quanto costa quello lì?
kwantoh kostah kwelloh lee

How much is that one?

Basta così.
bastah kosee

That'll be all.

Cultural tip Italy uses the common European currency, the euro. This is divided into 100 cents, which the Italians call **centesimi**. You will usually hear the price given as **dieci euro e venti** (€10.20), **sei euro e novantanove** (€6.99), and so forth. Note that Italians, like many other Europeans, use a comma for the decimal point.

3 minutes

Altro, signora?
altroh, seennyorah

Anything else, madam?

Basta così, grazie. Quant'è?
bastah kozee, gratseeay. kwantay

That'll be all, thank you. How much?

Sei euro e cinquanta.
say ayooroh ay cheenkwantah

Six euros, fifty.

1 WARM UP
1 minute

What are these items you could buy in a supermarket (pp22–23)?

la carne
il pesce
il formaggio
il succo di frutta
il vino
l'acqua

Al supermercato
AT THE SUPERMARKET

Prices in supermarkets are usually lower than in smaller shops. They offer all kinds of products, with the larger **ipermercati** (*hypermarkets*) extending to clothes, household goods, garden furniture, DIY products, wine, full grocery lines, fresh produce, electronic items, and books. They may also stock regional products.

2 **MATCH AND REPEAT**
5 minutes

Match the numbered items to the list, then test yourself, using the cover flap.

❶ **gli articoli per la casa**
lly arteekolee per lah kazah

❷ **i cosmetici**
ee kosmeteechee

❸ **la frutta**
lah froottah

❹ **le bibite**
lay beebeetay

❺ **i piatti pronti**
ee pyattee prontee

❻ **la verdura**
lah verdoorah

❼ **i surgelati**
ee soorjelatee

❽ **i latticini**
ee latteecheenee

household products ❶
beauty products ❷
fruit ❸
drinks ❹
ready meals ❺
vegetables ❻
frozen foods ❼
dairy products ❽

Cultural tip For fruits and vegetables sold by the kilo, you will usually find a self-service scale next to or near the produce. Alternatively, there may occasionally be a separate counter to weigh and price the produce.

3 🔊 USEFUL PHRASES

3 minutes

Learn these phrases, then test yourself, using the cover flap.

May I have a bag please?	**Posso avere un sacchetto, per favore?** *possoh avayray oon sakkayttoh, per favoray*
Where is the drinks aisle?	**Qual è la corsia delle bibite?** *kwalay lah korseea dellay beebeetay*
Where is the checkout?	**Dov'è la cassa?** *dovay lah kassah*
Please type in your PIN.	**Può digitare il pin.** *pwoh deejeetaray eel pin*

4 🔊 WORDS TO REMEMBER

4 minutes

Familiarize yourself with these words, then test yourself, using the cover flap.

milk	**il latte** *eel lattay*
bread	**il pane** *eel panay*
butter	**il burro** *eel boorroh*
ham	**il prosciutto** *eel proshoottoh*
salt	**il sale** *eel salay*
pepper	**il pepe** *eel paypay*
laundry detergent	**il detersivo in polvere** *eel deterseevoh een polveray*
dishwashing liquid	**il detersivo per i piatti** *eel deterseevoh per ee peeattee*
toilet paper	**la carta igienica** *lah kartah eejeneekah*
hand sanitizer	**l'igienizzante per le mani** (m) *leejeneetsantay per lay manee*

5 SAY IT

2 minutes

Where is the dairy products aisle?

May I have some ham, please?

Where are the frozen foods?

1 WARM UP
1 minute

Say "**I'd like…**" (pp24–25).

Ask "**Do you have…?**" (pp12–13).

Say "**38**," "**42**," and "**46**" (pp30–31).

Say "**big**" and "**small**" (pp64–65).

Le scarpe e l'abbigliamento
CLOTHES AND SHOES

As in most of Europe, clothes and shoes in Italy are measured in metric sizes. Even allowing for conversion of sizes, Italian clothes tend to be cut smaller than American ones, and measurements may vary according to brand, cut, and style. Note that clothes size is **la taglia**, but shoe size is **il numero**.

2 ◀))) MATCH AND REPEAT

Match the numbered items to the list, then test yourself, using the cover flap.

❶ **la camicia**
   lah kameechah

❷ **la cravatta**
   lah kravattah

❸ **la giacca**
   lah jakkah

❹ **la manica**
   lah maneekah

❺ **la tasca**
   lah taskah

❻ **i pantaloni**
   ee pantalonee

❼ **le scarpe**
   lay skarpay

❽ **la gonna**
   lah gonnah

❾ **i collant**
   ee kollant

shirt ❶
tie ❷
jacket ❸
sleeve ❹
pocket ❺
pants ❻
skirt ❽
tights ❾
shoes ❼

Cultural tip Dress sizes usually range from 40 (US 4) to 48 (US 12) and shoe sizes from 37 (US 6½) to 46 (US 12). For men's shirts, a size 41 is a 16-inch collar, 43 is a 17-inch collar, and 45 is an 18-inch collar.

3 ◀)) USEFUL PHRASES

5 minutes

Learn these phrases, then test yourself, using the cover flap.

Do you have a larger size?	**Ha la taglia più grande?**
	ah lah tallyah peeoo granday

It's not what I want.	**Non è quello che cerco.**
	non ay kwelloh kay cherkoh

I'll take the pink one.	**Prendo quella rosa.** *prendoh kwellah rozah*

3 minutes

4 ◀)) WORDS TO REMEMBER

4 minutes

Colors are adjectives (pp64–65) and in most cases have a masculine, feminine, and plural form. The plurals are usually formed by changing the final **o** to an **i** (masculine) and the final **a** to an **e** (feminine). Familiarize yourself with these words, then test yourself, using the cover flap.

red	**rosso/rossa** *rossoh/rossah*
white	**bianco/bianca** *byankoh/byankah*
blue	**azzurro/azzurra** *adzoorroh/adzoorrah*
yellow	**giallo/gialla** *jalloh/jallah*
green	**verde** *verday*
black	**nero/nera** *neroh/nerah*

5 SAY IT

2 minutes

What shoe size?

I'll take the black one.

I'd like a 38.

Do you have a smaller size?

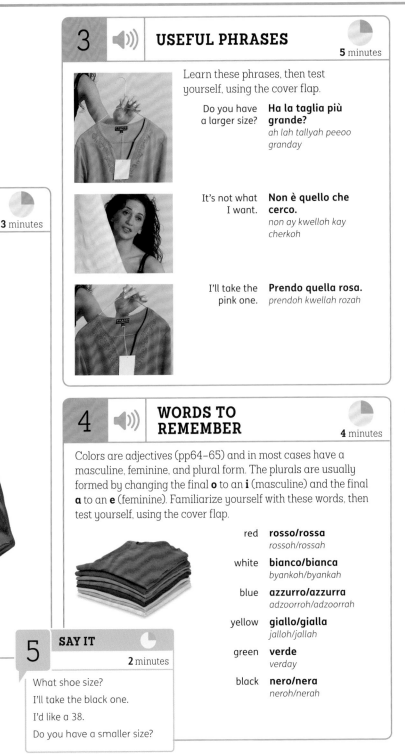

Ripassa e ripeti
REVIEW AND REPEAT

Market

❶ il finocchio
eel feenokkeeoh

❷ l'aglio
lalyoh

❸ i pomodori
ee pomodoree

❹ la lattuga
lah lattoogah

❺ il cavolfiore
eel kavolfeeoray

❻ gli asparagi
lly asparajee

Description

❶ These shoes are
too expensive.

❷ My room is very small.

❸ I'd like a bigger size.

Shops

❶ il panificio
eel paneefeechoh

❷ gli alimentari
lly aleementaree

❸ la libreria
lah leebrayreeah

❹ la pescheria
lah payskayreeah

❺ la pasticceria
lah pasteechayreeah

❻ la macelleria
lah machayllayreeah

1 MARKET

3 minutes

Name these vegetables in Italian.

❶ fennel ❸ tomatoes ❺ cauliflower

❷ garlic lettuce ❹ asparagus ❻

2 DESCRIPTION

2 minutes

What do these sentences mean?

❶ Queste scarpe sono troppo care.
❷ La mia camera è molto piccola.
❸ Vorrei una taglia più grande.

3 SHOPS

3 minutes

Name these shops in Italian.

❶ baker ❷ grocery ❸ bookshop

❹ fishmonger ❺ cake shop ❻ butcher

Risposte *Answers*
(Cover with flap)

4 SUPERMARKET

3 minutes

Name these products in Italian.

❶ household products

❷ beauty products

❸ drinks

❹ dairy products

❺ frozen foods

Supermarket

❶ **gli articoli per la casa**
lly arteekolee per lah kazah

❷ **i cosmetici**
ee kosmeteechee

❸ **le bibite**
lay beebeetay

❹ **i latticini**
ee latteecheenee

❺ **i surgelati**
ee soorjelatee

5 MUSEUM

4 minutes

You are buying entrance tickets at a museum. Join in the conversation, replying in Italian, following the numbered English prompts.

Buongiorno, desidera?
❶ I'd like five tickets.

Sono settanta euro.
❷ That's very expensive! Two are children.

Non ci sono riduzioni per bambini.
❸ How much is an audio guide?

Cinque euro.
❹ Five tickets and five audio guides, please.

Novantacinque euro.
❺ Here you are. Where are the toilets?

Là, a destra.
❻ Thank you.

Museum

❶ **Vorrei cinque biglietti.**
vorray cheenkway beellyettee

❷ **È molto caro! Due sono bambini.**
ay moltoh karoh. dooay sonoh bambeenee

❸ **Quanto costa l'audioguida?**
kwantoh kostah lah-oodeeo gweedah

❹ **Cinque biglietti e cinque audioguide, per favore.**
cheenkway beellyettee ay cheenkway ah-oodeeo gweeday, per favoray

❺ **Ecco a Lei. Dove sono i bagni?**
ekkoh ah lay. dovay sonoh ee banyee

❻ **Grazie.**
gratseeay

1 WARM UP
1 minute

Ask "**Which platform?**" (pp38–39).

What is the Italian for these family members: "**sister**," "**brother**," "**son**," "**daughter**," "**mother**," and "**father**" (pp10–11)?

Il lavoro
JOBS

Some occupations have a different form when the person is female—for example, **l'infermiere** (*male nurse*) and **l'infermiera** (*female nurse*). Others remain the same for both: **il/la giornalista** (*male/female journalist*). When you state your occupation, you don't need to use **un/una** (*a/an*), as in **sono redattore/redattrice** (*I'm an editor*).

2 **WORDS TO REMEMBER**: JOBS
7 minutes

Familiarize yourself with these words, then test yourself, using the cover flap. The feminine form is also shown.

il medico *eel medeekoh*	doctor
il/la dentista *eel/lah denteestah*	dentist
l'infermiere/a *leenfermyeray/ah*	nurse
l'insegnante *leensennyantay*	teacher
il/la ragioniere/a *eel/lah rajonyeray/ah*	accountant
l'avvocato *lavvokatoh*	lawyer
il/la grafico/a *eel/lah grafeekoh/ah*	designer
il/la consulente *eel/lah konsoolentay*	consultant
il/la segretario/a *segretaryoh/ah*	secretary
il/la commerciante *eel/lah kommerchantay*	shopkeeper
l'elettricista *lelettreecheestah*	electrician
l'idraulico *leedraooleekoh*	plumber
il/la cuoco/a *eel/lah kwokoh/ah*	cook/chef
l'ingegnere *leenjaynyeray*	engineer
il/la libero/a professionista *eel/lah leeberoh/ah professyoneestah*	self-employed

Sono un idraulico.
sonoh oon eedraooleekoh
I'm a plumber.

È studentessa.
ay stoodentessah
She is a student.

3 PUT INTO PRACTICE

4 minutes

Complete this dialogue, then test yourself, using the cover flap.

Che lavoro fa?
kay lavoroh fah

What do you do?

Say: I am a financial consultant.

Sono consulente finanziario.
sonoh konsoolentay feenantseearyoh

Per quale azienda lavora?
per kwalay adzyendah lavorah

What company do you work for?

Say: I'm self-employed.

Sono libero professionista.
sonoh leeberoh professyoneestah

Interessante!
eenteressantay

How interesting!

Ask: What do you do?

E Lei che lavoro fa?
ay lay kay lavoroh fah

Sono dentista.
sonoh denteestah

I'm a dentist.

Say: My sister is a dentist, too.

Anche mia sorella è dentista.
ankay mee-ah sorellah ay denteestah

4 WORDS TO REMEMBER: WORKPLACE

3 minutes

Familiarize yourself with these words, then test yourself, using the cover flap.

La sede centrale è a Napoli.
lah seday chentralay ay ah napolee
The head office is in Naples.

head office	**la sede centrale** *lah seday chentralay*
branch	**la filiale** *lah feelyalay*
department	**il reparto** *eel repartoh*
reception	**la reception** *lah raychepshown*
manager	**il direttore/la direttrice** *eel deerettoray/lah deerettreechay*
office worker	**l'impiegato/a** *leempyegatoh/ah*
trainee	**il/la tirocinante** *eel/lah teerocheenantay*

1 WARM UP
1 minute

Practice different ways of introducing yourself in different situations. Say your name, occupation, and any other information you'd like to give (pp8–9, pp14–15, and pp78–79).

L'ufficio
THE OFFICE

An office environment or business situation has its own vocabulary in any language, but there are many items for which the terminology is virtually universal. Most Italian computer keyboards use the standard English QWERTY convention, although note that some may have the QZERTY layout.

2 🔊 WORDS TO REMEMBER
5 minutes

Familiarize yourself with these words, then test yourself, using the cover flap.

la riunione *lah reeoonyonay*	meeting
la fotocopiatrice *lah fotokopyatreechay*	photocopier
il computer *eel komputer*	computer
lo schermo *loh skayrmoh*	monitor
il mouse *eel maoos*	mouse
internet (f) *eenternet*	Internet
l'email (f) *leemayl*	email
la password *lah password*	password
la password del Wi-Fi *lah password dell weefee*	Wi-Fi password
la conferenza *lah konferentsah*	conference
l'ordine del giorno (m) *lordeenay del jornoh*	agenda
l'agenda (f) *lajendah*	diary
il biglietto da visita *eel beellyettoh dah veeseetah*	business card
la segreteria telefonica *lah segretereeah telayfoneekah*	voicemail

3 🔊 MATCH

❶ wall clock

❹ telephone

❸ stapler   ❺ pen

notepad ❿   drawer ⓫

4 🔊 USEFUL PHRASES

2 minutes

Learn these phrases, then test yourself, using the cover flap.

I want to send an email.	**Voglio mandare un'email.**
	vollyoh mandaray oon eemayl

5 SAY IT

2 minutes

I'd like to arrange a conference.

Do you have a business card?

I have a laptop.

I need to make some photocopies.	**Ho bisogno di fare delle fotocopie.**
	oh beezonnyoh dee faray dellay fotokopyay

I'd like to schedule an appointment.	**Vorrei fissare un appuntamento.**
	vorray feessaray oon appoontamentoh

AND REPEAT

5 minutes

Match the numbered items to the list, then test yourself, using the cover flap.

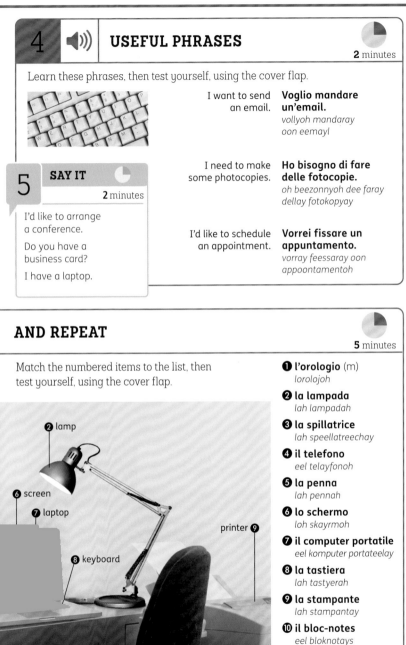

② lamp

⑥ screen
⑦ laptop

printer ⑨

⑧ keyboard

⑫ desk   ⑬ swivel chair

❶ l'orologio (m)
lorolojoh

❷ la lampada
lah lampadah

❸ la spillatrice
lah speellatreechay

❹ il telefono
eel telayfonoh

❺ la penna
lah pennah

❻ lo schermo
loh skayrmoh

❼ il computer portatile
eel komputer portateelay

❽ la tastiera
lah tastyerah

❾ la stampante
lah stampantay

❿ il bloc-notes
eel bloknotays

⓫ il cassetto
eel kassettoh

⓬ la scrivania
lah skreevaneeah

⓭ la sedia girevole
lah sedya jeerayvolay

1 WARM UP

1 minute

Say "**How interesting!**" (pp78–79), "**library**" (pp48–49), and "**appointment**" (pp32–33).

Ask "**What is your profession?**"; answer "**I'm an accountant**" (pp78–79).

Il mondo accademico
ACADEMIC WORLD

In Italy, as is now becoming standard across the EU, the first degree is **la laurea triennale** (*bachelor's*), followed by **la laurea magistrale** (*master's*), and then by **il dottorato di ricerca** (*PhD*). The title **dottore/dottoressa** is used by all graduates and most professionals.

2 USEFUL PHRASES

3 minutes

Learn these phrases, then test yourself, using the cover flap.

Di cosa si occupa?
dee kozah see okkoopah

What is your field?

Mi occupo di ricerca scientifica.
mee okkoopoh dee reecherkah shenteefeekah

I am doing scientific research.

Sono laureato/a in legge.
sonoh laooreatoh/ah een lejjay

I have a degree in law.

Tengo una conferenza sull'architettura moderna.
tayngoh oonah konferentsah soollarkeetettoorah modernah

I am giving a lecture on modern architecture.

3 IN CONVERSATION

Buongiorno, sono la professoressa Lanzi.
bwonjornoh, sonoh lah professoressah lantsee

Hello, I'm Professor Lanzi.

Dove insegna?
dovay eensennyah

Where do you teach?

Insegno all'università di Pisa.
eensennyoh allooneeverseetah dee pisah

I teach at the University of Pisa.

4 WORDS TO REMEMBER

4 minutes

Familiarize yourself with these words, then test yourself, using the cover flap.

Abbiamo uno stand alla fiera commerciale.
abbyamoh oonoh stend allah fyerah kommerchalay
We have a stand at the trade fair.

conference/ lecture	**la conferenza** *lah konferentsah*
trade fair	**la fiera commerciale** *lah fyerah kommerchalay*
seminar	**il seminario** *eel semeenaryoh*
lecture hall	**l'aula delle lezioni** (f) *la-oolah dellay letseeonee*
conference room	**la sala conferenze** *lah salah konferentsay*
exhibition	**la mostra** *lah mostrah*
university lecturer	**il professore universitario/ la professoressa universitaria** *eel professoray ooneeverseetareeoh/ lah professoressah ooneeverseetaryah*
medicine	**la medicina** *lah medeecheenah*
science	**la scienza** *lah schentsah*
literature	**la letteratura** *lah letteratoorah*
engineering	**l'ingegneria** (f) *leenjennyereeah*
information technology	**l'informatica** (f) *leenformateekah*

5 SAY IT

2 minutes

I'm doing research in medicine.

I have a degree in literature.

She's the professor.

---

5 minutes

Di cosa si occupa?
dee kozah see okkoopah

What's your field?

Di fisica. Mi occupo di ricerca.
dee feeseekah. mee okkoopoh dee reecherkah

Physics. I'm doing research.

Interessante!
eenteressantay

How interesting!

1 WARM UP

1 minute

Say "**I'm a trainee**" (pp78–79).

Say "**I want to send an email**" (pp80–81).

Say "**I'd like to schedule an appointment**" (pp80–81).

I contatti commerciali
IN BUSINESS

While on business trips to Italy, you will make a good impression and receive a more friendly reception if you make the effort to begin meetings with a short introduction in Italian, even if your vocabulary is limited. After that, everyone will probably be happy to continue the meeting in English.

2 🔊 **WORDS TO REMEMBER**

Familiarize yourself with these words, then test yourself, using the cover flap.

il programma *eel programmah*	schedule
la consegna *lah konsennyah*	delivery
il pagamento *eel pagamentoh*	payment
il budget *eel bajjet*	budget
il prezzo *eel pretsoh*	price
i documenti *ee dokoomentee*	documents
la fattura *lah fattoorah*	invoice
il preventivo *eel preventeevoh*	estimate
i profitti *ee profeettee*	profits
le vendite *lay vendeetay*	sales
le cifre *lay cheefray*	figures
l'ordine (m) *lordeenay*	order

Firmiamo il contratto?
feermyamoh eel kontrattoh
Shall we sign the contract?

il dirigente
eel deereejentay
executive

il contratto
eel kontrattoh
contract

Cultural tip In general, commercial dealings are formal, but a lunch with wine is still a feature of doing business in Italy. As a client, you can expect to be taken out to a restaurant, and as a supplier, you should consider entertaining your customers.

6 minutes

il cliente
eel klyentay
client

la relazione
lah relatseeyonay
report

4 SAY IT

2 minutes

Can you send me
the estimate?

Have we agreed on
a price?

What are the profits?

3 ◄)) USEFUL PHRASES

6 minutes

Learn these phrases, then test yourself, using the
cover flap. Notice the use of the word **può** (*can
you*) as a preface to polite requests.

**Può mandarmi il
contratto, per
favore?**
*pwoh mandarmee eel
kontrattoh, per favoray*

Can you send me the
contract, please?

**Abbiamo fissato
il prezzo?**
*abbeeamoh feessatoh
eel pretsoh*

Have we agreed
on a price?

**Quando può
effettuare la
consegna?**
*kwandoh pwoh
effettwaray lah
konsennyah*

When can you make
the delivery?

Quant'è il budget?
kwantay eel bajjet

What's the budget?

**Può mandarmi la
fattura?**
*pwoh mandarmee
lah fattoorah*

Can you send me
the invoice?

Ripassa e ripeti
REVIEW AND REPEAT

At the office

❶ l'orologio
lorolojoh

❷ il computer portatile
eel komputer portateelay

❸ la lampada
lah lampadah

❹ la stampante
lah stampantay

❺ la spillatrice
lah speellatreechay

❻ la penna
lah pennah

❼ il bloc-notes
eel bloknotays

❽ la scrivania
lah skreevaneeah

1 AT THE OFFICE

Name these items in Italian.

wall clock ❶　❷ laptop　❸ lamp

❺ stapler　pen ❻　❼ notepad　❽ desk

Jobs

❶ il medico
eel medeekoh

❷ l'idraulico
leedraooleekoh

❸ il/la commerciante
eel/lah kommerchantay

❹ il/la ragioniere/a
eel/lah rajonyeray/ah

❺ lo/la studente/essa
loh/lah stoodentay/essah

❻ l'avvocato
lavvokatoh

2 JOBS

3 minutes

Name these jobs in Italian.

❶ doctor
❷ plumber
❸ shopkeeper
❹ accountant
❺ student
❻ lawyer

4 minutes

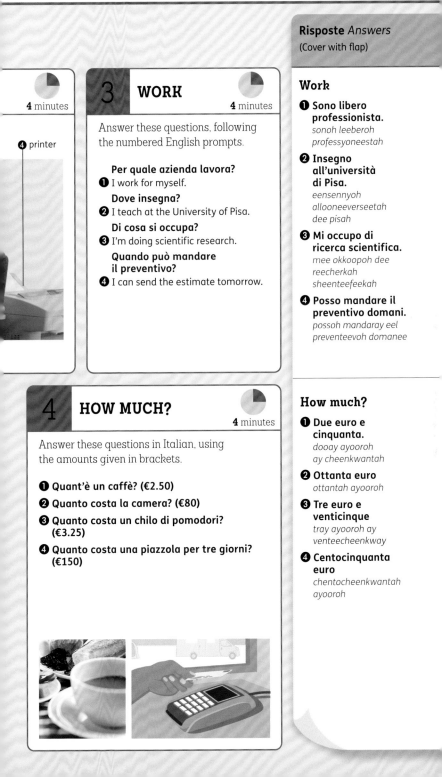

❹ printer

3 WORK

4 minutes

Answer these questions, following the numbered English prompts.

Per quale azienda lavora?
❶ I work for myself.
Dove insegna?
❷ I teach at the University of Pisa.
Di cosa si occupa?
❸ I'm doing scientific research.
Quando può mandare il preventivo?
❹ I can send the estimate tomorrow.

Work

❶ **Sono libero professionista.**
sonoh leeberoh professyoneestah

❷ **Insegno all'università di Pisa.**
eensennyoh allooneeverseetah dee pisah

❸ **Mi occupo di ricerca scientifica.**
mee okkoopoh dee reecherkah sheenteefeekah

❹ **Posso mandare il preventivo domani.**
possoh mandaray eel preventeevoh domanee

4 HOW MUCH?

4 minutes

Answer these questions in Italian, using the amounts given in brackets.

❶ **Quant'è un caffè? (€2.50)**
❷ **Quanto costa la camera? (€80)**
❸ **Quanto costa un chilo di pomodori? (€3.25)**
❹ **Quanto costa una piazzola per tre giorni? (€150)**

How much?

❶ **Due euro e cinquanta.**
dooay ayooroh ay cheenkwantah

❷ **Ottanta euro**
ottantah ayooroh

❸ **Tre euro e venticinque**
tray ayooroh ay venteecheenkway

❹ **Centocinquanta euro**
chentocheenkwantah ayooroh

1 WARM UP

1 minute

Say **"I'm allergic to nuts"** (pp22–23).

Say the verb **"avere"** (*to have*) in all its forms (**io, tu, Lei, lui/lei, noi, voi, loro**) (pp14–15).

Il corpo

THE BODY

A common phrase for talking about aches and pains is **mi fa male il/la...** (*my... hurts*). Another useful expression is **ho un dolore a...** (*I have a pain in...*). Note that **a** (*in*) joins with the definite article (*the*) to produce these combinations: **al (a + il)**, **allo (a + lo)**, **alla (a + la)**, **agli (a + gli)**, **ai (a + i)**, and **alle (a + le)**.

2 MATCH AND REPEAT: BODY

6 minutes

Match the numbered parts of the body to the list, then test yourself, using the cover flap.

1. **la mano**
   lah manoh
2. **il gomito**
   eel gomeetoh
3. **i capelli**
   ee kapellee
4. **la testa**
   lah testah
5. **il braccio**
   eel brachoh
6. **il collo**
   eel kolloh
7. **la spalla**
   la spallah
8. **il petto**
   eel pettoh
9. **lo stomaco**
   loh stomakoh
10. **la gamba**
    lah gambah
11. **il ginocchio**
    eel jeenokkyoh
12. **il piede**
    eel pyeday

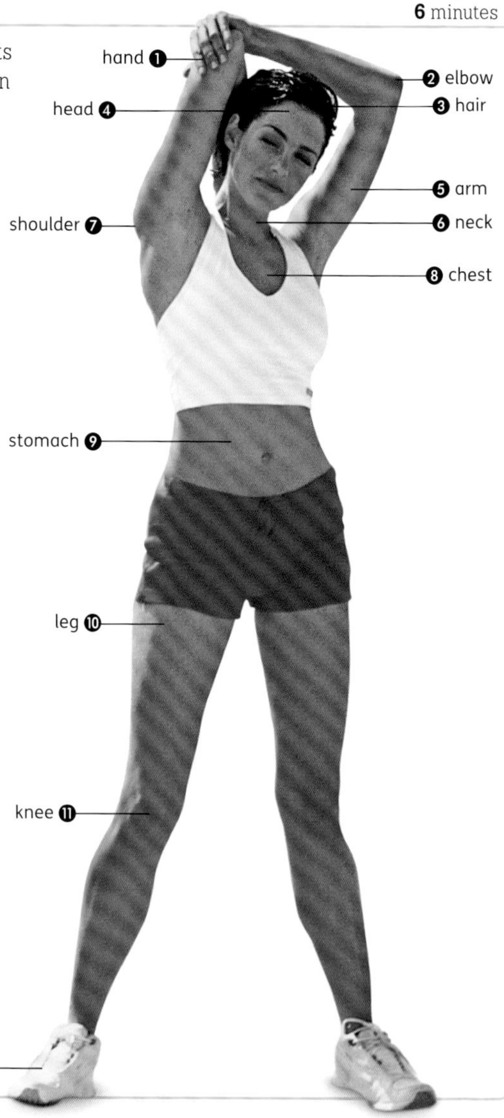

3 MATCH AND REPEAT: FACE

3 minutes

Match the numbered facial features to the list, then test yourself, using the cover flap.

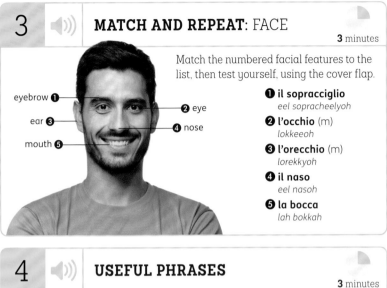

eyebrow **1**

2 eye

ear **3**

4 nose

mouth **5**

1 il sopracciglio
eel sopracheelyoh

2 l'occhio (m)
lokkeeoh

3 l'orecchio (m)
lorekkyoh

4 il naso
eel nasoh

5 la bocca
lah bokkah

4 USEFUL PHRASES

3 minutes

Learn these phrases, then test yourself, using the cover flap.

My back hurts. **Mi fa male la schiena.**
mee fah malay lah skyenah

I have a rash on my arm. **Ho un arrossamento sul braccio.**
oh oon arrossamentoh sool brachoh

I don't feel good. **Non mi sento bene.**
non mee sentoh benay

5 PUT INTO PRACTICE

2 minutes

Complete this dialogue, then test yourself, using the cover flap.

Cosa c'è? **Non mi sento bene.**
kozah chay *non mee sentoh benay*

What's the matter?

Say: I don't feel good.

Dove ti fa male? **Ho un dolore alla spalla.**
dovay ti fah malay *oh oon doloray allah spallah*

Where does it hurt?

Say: I have a pain in my shoulder.

1 WARM UP

1 minute

Say "**I have a rash**" and "**I don't feel good**" (pp88–89).

Say the Italian for "**red**," "**green**," "**black**," and "**yellow**" (pp74–75).

In farmacia
AT THE PHARMACY

Italian pharmacists study for at least five years before qualifying. They can give advice about minor health problems and are permitted to dispense a wide variety of medicines, even giving injections if necessary. There is a **farmacia di turno** (*24-hour duty pharmacy*) in most towns.

2 🔊 MATCH AND REPEAT

3 minutes

Match the numbered items to the list, then test yourself, using the cover flap.

❶ **la fascia**
lah fasheeah

❷ **lo sciroppo**
loh sheeroppoh

❸ **le gocce**
lay gocchay

❹ **la pomata**
lah pomatah

❺ **il cerotto**
eel chayrottoh

❻ **l'iniezione** (f)
leenyetsyonay

❼ **la supposta**
lah sooppostah

❽ **la compressa**
lah kompressah

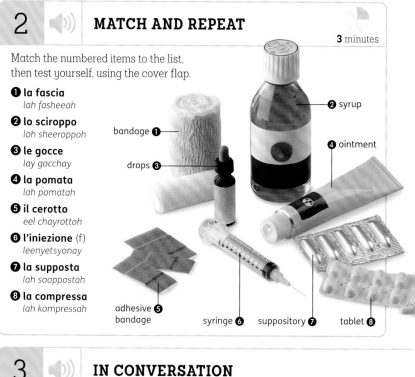

bandage ❶
syrup ❷
drops ❸
ointment ❹
adhesive ❺ bandage
syringe ❻
suppository ❼
tablet ❽

3 🔊 IN CONVERSATION

Buongiorno. Desidera?
bwonjornoh. dayseedayrah

Hello. What would you like?

Ho mal di pancia.
oh mal dee panchah

I have a stomachache.

Ha anche la diarrea?
ah ankay lah deearreah

Do you also have diarrhea?

4 🔊 WORDS TO REMEMBER

2 minutes

Familiarize yourself with these words, then test yourself, using the cover flap.

Ho mal di testa.
oh mal dee testah
I have a headache.

headache	**mal di testa** *mal dee testah*
stomachache	**mal di pancia** *mal dee panchah*
diarrhea	**la diarrea** *lah deearreah*
cold	**il raffreddore** *eel raffreddoray*
cough	**la tosse** *lah tossay*
sunburn	**l'eritema solare** (m) *lereetemah solaray*
toothache	**mal di denti** *mal dee dentee*

5 🔊 USEFUL PHRASES

4 minutes

Learn these phrases, then test yourself, using the cover flap.

Do you have face masks?	**Ha delle mascherine?** *ah dellay maskerinay*
Do you have that as a syrup?	**Lo ha in sciroppo?** *loh ah een sheeroppoh*
I'm allergic to penicillin.	**Sono allergico/a alla penicillina.** *sonoh allerjeekoh/ah allah peneecheelleenah*

6 SAY IT

2 minutes

I have a cold.

Do you have that as an ointment?

Do you have a cough?

3 minutes

No, ma ho mal di testa.
noh, mah oh mal dee testah

No, but I have a headache.

Prenda questo.
prendah kwestoh

Take this.

Lo ha in sciroppo?
loh ah een sheeroppoh

Do you have that as a syrup?

1 **WARM UP**
1 minute

Say "**I would like some tablets**" and "**He would like some ointment**" (pp24–25, pp90–91).

What is the Italian for "**I don't have a son**" (pp14–15)?

Dal medico
AT THE DOCTOR

In an emergency, dial 118 for an ambulance. If it isn't urgent, book an appointment with the doctor and pay when you leave. You can usually be reimbursed if you have comprehensive travel and medical insurance. You can find the names and addresses of local doctors at the town hall, tourist office, or pharmacy.

2 **USEFUL PHRASES YOU MAY HEAR**
3 minutes

Learn these phrases, then test yourself, using the cover flap.

Non è grave.
non ay gravay
It's not serious.

Fa qualche cura?
fah kwalkay koorah
Are you taking any medications?

Ha una frattura.
ah oonah frattoorah
You have a fracture.

Deve andare all'ospedale.
devay andaray allospedalay
You need to go to the hospital.

Apra la bocca.
aprah lah bokkah
Open your mouth.

Deve fare dei controlli.
devay faray day kontrollee
You need to have tests.

3 **IN CONVERSATION**

Cosa c'è?
kozah chay

What's the matter?

Ho un dolore al petto.
oh oon doloray al pettoh

I have a pain in my chest.

Ora la visito.
orah lah veezeetoh

Now I will examine you.

4  USEFUL PHRASES YOU MAY NEED TO SAY

4 minutes

Learn these phrases, then test yourself, using the cover flap.

Sono incinta.
sonoh eencheentah
I'm pregnant.

I'm diabetic.	**Sono diabetico/a.** *sonoh deeabeteekoh/ah*
I'm epileptic.	**Sono epilettico/a.** *sonoh epeeletteekoh/ah*
I'm asthmatic.	**Sono asmatico/a.** *sonoh asmateekoh/ah*
I have a heart condition.	**Ho disturbi cardiaci.** *oh deestoorbee kardeeachee*
I feel breathless.	**Faccio fatica a respirare.** *facchyoh fatikah ah respeeraray*
I have a fever.	**Ho la febbre.** *oh lah febbray*
It's urgent.	**È urgente.** *ay oorjentay*
I'm here for my vaccination.	**Sono qui per la vaccinazione.** *sonoh kwee per lah vaccheenatsyonay*

Cultural tip EU nationals can get free emergency medical treatment in Italy with a European Health Insurance Card (EHIC) or E111 form. For UK nationals, the Global Health Insurance Card (GHIC) has replaced the EHIC. Travelers from all other countries should make sure they have comprehensive travel and medical insurance.

5 SAY IT

2 minutes

Do I need tests?

My son needs to go to the hospital.

It's not urgent.

---

5 minutes

È grave?
ay gravay

Is it serious?

No, è solo un'indigestione.
noh, ay soloh oon eendeejestyonay

No, you only have indigestion.

Che sollievo!
kay soleeayvoh

What a relief!

1 WARM UP
1 minute

Ask "**How long is the journey?**" (pp42–43).

Ask "**Do I need…?**" (pp92–93).

What is the Italian for "**mouth**" and "**head**"? (pp88–89).

All'ospedale
AT THE HOSPITAL

Many big hospitals in Italy are attached to universities and are called **Aziende Ospedaliere Universitarie**. Emergency departments will treat all urgent cases free of charge, but non-EU citizens will need to sign a payment declaration. It is useful to know a few basic phrases relating to hospitals for use in an emergency or in case you need to visit a friend or colleague in hospital.

2 USEFUL PHRASES
5 minutes

Learn these phrases, then test yourself, using the cover flap.

Qual è l'orario di visita?
kwalay lorareeoh dee veezeetah
What are the visiting hours?

È disponibile un anello acustico?
ay deesponeebeelay oon anaylloh akoosteekoh
Is a hearing loop available?

Quanto ci vuole?
kwantoh chee vwolay
How long will it take?

Farà male?
farah malay
Will it hurt?

Si sdrai sul lettino.
see zdraee sool letteenoh
Please lie down on the bed.

Non deve mangiare.
non devay manjaray
You must not eat.

Non muova la testa.
non mwovah lah testah
Don't move your head.

Deve fare le analisi del sangue.
devay faray lay analeezee del sangway
You need a blood test.

Dov'è la sala d'aspetto?
dovay lah salah daspettoh
Where is the waiting room?

la flebo
lah flayboh
intravenous drip

Si sente meglio?
see sentay mellyoh
Are you feeling better?

3 WORDS TO REMEMBER

4 minutes

Familiarize yourself with these words, then test yourself, using the cover flap.

La radiografia è normale.
lah radeeografeeah ay normalay
The x-ray is normal.

emergency department	**il pronto soccorso** *eel prontoh sokkorsoh*
x-ray department	**il reparto di radiologia** *eel repartoh dee radeeolojyah*
children's ward	**il reparto di pediatria** *eel repartoh dee pedyatryah*
operating room	**la sala operatoria** *lah salah operatoreeah*
waiting room	**la sala d'aspetto** *lah salah daspettoh*
elevator	**l'ascensore** (m) *lashensoray*
stairs	**le scale** *lay skalay*

4 PUT INTO PRACTICE

3 minutes

Complete this dialogue, then test yourself, using the cover flap.

Forse c'è un'infezione.
forsay chay ooneenfetsyonay

You may have an infection.

Ask: Do I need tests?

Devo fare dei controlli?
devoh faray day kontrollee

Prima di tutto deve fare le analisi del sangue.
preemah dee toottoh devay faray lay analeezee del sangway

First, you will need a blood test.

Ask: Will it hurt?

Farà male?
farah malay

5 SAY IT

2 minutes

Does he need a blood test?

Where is the children's ward?

Do I need an x-ray?

No, non si preoccupi.
noh, non see prayokkoopee

No, don't worry.

Ask: How long will it take?

Quanto ci vuole?
kwantoh chee vwolay

Ripassa e ripeti
REVIEW AND REPEAT

Risposte *Answers*
(Cover with flap)

The body

❶ la testa
lah testah

❷ il braccio
eel brachoh

❸ il petto
eel pettoh

❹ lo stomaco
loh stomakoh

❺ la gamba
lah gambah

❻ il ginocchio
eel jeenokkyoh

❼ il piede
eel pyeday

1 THE BODY

4 minutes

Name these body parts in Italian.

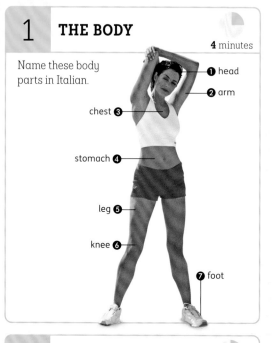

❶ head
❷ arm
chest ❸
stomach ❹
leg ❺
knee ❻
❼ foot

On the phone

❶ Vorrei parlare con il signor Salvetti.
vorray parlaray kon eel seennyor salvettee

❷ Sono il dottor Pieri della Bonanni.
sonoh eel dottor pyayree dellah bonannee

❸ Posso lasciare un messaggio?
possoh lasharay oon messajjoh?

❹ L'appuntamento è lunedì alle undici.
lappoontamentoh ay lunedee allay oondeechee

❺ Grazie, arrivederci.
gratseeay, arreevederchee

2 ON THE PHONE

4 minutes

You are arranging an appointment. Join in the conversation, replying in Italian, following the numbered English prompts.

Pronto? Tipografia Bartoli.
❶ I'd like to speak to Mr. Salvetti.

Chi parla, scusi?
❷ It's Dr. Pieri of Bonanni.

Mi dispiace, il signor Salvetti è in riunione.
❸ Can I leave a message?

Certo.
❹ The appointment is on Monday at 11am.

Benissimo.
❺ Thank you, goodbye.

Risposte *Answers*
(Cover with flap)

3 CLOTHING

3 minutes

Name these items of clothing in Italian.

tie ❶

❷ jacket

❸ skirt

pants ❹

❺ tights

shoes ❻

Clothing

❶ **la cravatta**
lah kravattah

❷ **la giacca**
lah jakkah

❸ **la gonna**
lah gonnah

❹ **i pantaloni**
ee pantalonee

❺ **le scarpe**
lay skarpay

❻ **i collant**
ee kollant

4 AT THE DOCTOR'S

4 minutes

Say these sentences in Italian.

❶ I don't feel good.

❷ Do I need tests?

❸ I have a heart condition.

❹ Do I need to go to the hospital?

❺ I'm pregnant.

❻ I'm here for my vaccination.

At the doctor's

❶ **Non mi sento bene.**
non mee sentoh benay

❷ **Devo fare dei controlli?**
devoh faray day kontrollee

❸ **Ho disturbi cardiaci.**
oh deestoorbee kardeeachee

❹ **Devo andare all'ospedale?**
devoh andaray allospedalay

❺ **Sono incinta.**
sonoh eencheentah

❻ **Sono qui per la vaccinazione.**
sonoh kwee per lah vaccheenatsyonay

1 | WARM UP

1 minute

Say the months of the year in Italian (pp28–29).

Ask "**Is there an art gallery?**" (pp48–49) and "**How many brothers do you have?**" (pp14–15).

Gli alloggi
AT HOME

Many city dwellers live in apartments (**i palazzi**), but in rural areas, the houses tend to be detached (**le villette**). If you ask "**quante camere?**," you will be told the number of bedrooms, whereas if you ask "**quante stanze?**," the answer will include the number of bedrooms plus the living room, but not the kitchen or bathrooms.

2 ◀)) | MATCH AND REPEAT

Match the numbered items to the list, then test yourself, using the cover flap.

❶ **la grondaia**
lah grondayah

❷ **la finestra**
lah feenestrah

❸ **il comignolo**
eel comeennyoloh

❹ **il tetto**
eel tettoh

❺ **il viale**
eel veealay

❻ **la porta**
lah portah

❼ **il muro**
eel mooroh

❽ **le persiane**
lay persyanay

gutter ❶   ❷ window   ❸ chimney

driveway ❺   shutters ❻   ❼ door

Cultural tip Most Italian houses have shutters (**le persiane**) or roller blinds at each window. These are closed at night and in the heat of the day. Curtains, where they are present, tend to be more for decoration. Most apartment blocks tend to have at least one balcony (**il balcone**) for each apartment. These are often filled with plants to make up for the lack of a yard.

Quant'è l'affitto al mese?
kwantay laffeettoh al mezay
What is the monthly rent?

5 minutes

roof **4**

wall **8**

3 ◀)) **USEFUL PHRASES**   **3** minutes

Learn these phrases, then test yourself, using the cover flap.

C'è il garage?
chay eel garadj

Is there a garage?

È libera subito?
ay leeberah soobeetoh

Is it available right away?

L'appartamento è ammobiliato?
lappartamayntoh ay ammobeelyatoh

Is the apartment furnished?

4 ◀)) **WORDS TO REMEMBER**   **4** minutes

Familiarize yourself with these words, then test yourself, using the cover flap.

room	**la stanza** *lah stantsah*
floor	**il pavimento** *eel paveementoh*
ceiling	**il soffitto** *eel soffeettoh*
cellar	**la cantina** *lah kanteenah*
attic	**la soffitta** *lah soffeettah*
bedroom	**la camera** *lah kamayrah*
bathroom	**il bagno** *eel bannyoh*
living room	**il soggiorno** *eel sojjornoh*
dining room	**la sala da pranzo** *lah salah dah pranzoh*
kitchen	**la cucina** *lah koocheenah*

5 **SAY IT**   **2** minutes

Is there a dining room?

Is it large?

Is it available in July?

1 WARM UP
1 minute

What is the Italian for "**room**" (pp58–59), "**desk**" (pp80–81), "**bed**" (pp60–61), and "**toilet(s)**" (pp52–53)?

How do you say "**soft**," "**beautiful**," and "**big**" (pp64–65)?

In casa
IN THE HOUSE

If you are renting an apartment or a house in Italy, it is usual to be asked to pay for utilities, such as electricity and heating, on top of the basic rent. However, for short vacation rentals, utilities might be included in the rent. Always check in advance with the homeowner or agent. You may be asked to pay a deposit (**versare una caparra** or **cauzione**) in case of damage.

2 ◀)) MATCH AND REPEAT
3 minutes

Match the numbered items to the list, then test yourself, using the cover flap.

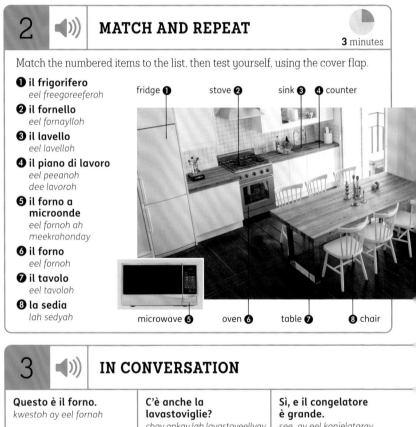

❶ **il frigorifero**
eel freegoreeferoh

❷ **il fornello**
eel fornaylloh

❸ **il lavello**
eel lavelloh

❹ **il piano di lavoro**
eel peeanoh dee lavoroh

❺ **il forno a microonde**
eel fornoh ah meekrohhonday

❻ **il forno**
eel fornoh

❼ **il tavolo**
eel tavoloh

❽ **la sedia**
lah sedyah

fridge ❶ stove ❷ sink ❸ ❹ counter

microwave ❺ oven ❻ table ❼ ❽ chair

3 ◀)) IN CONVERSATION

Questo è il forno.
kwestoh ay eel fornoh

This is the oven.

C'è anche la lavastoviglie?
chay ankay lah lavastoveellyay

Is there a dishwasher as well?

Sì, e il congelatore è grande.
see, ay eel konjelatoray ay granday

Yes, and there's a big freezer.

4 🔊 WORDS TO REMEMBER

2 minutes

Familiarize yourself with these words, then test yourself, using the cover flap.

wardrobe	**l'armadio** (m) *larmadeeoh*
armchair	**la poltrona** *lah poltronah*
fireplace	**il caminetto** *eel kameenettoh*
rug	**il tappeto** *eel tappaytoh*
bath	**la vasca** *lah vaskah*
toilet	**il bagno** *eel banyoh*
sink	**il lavandino** *eel lavandeenoh*
curtains	**le tende** *lay tenday*

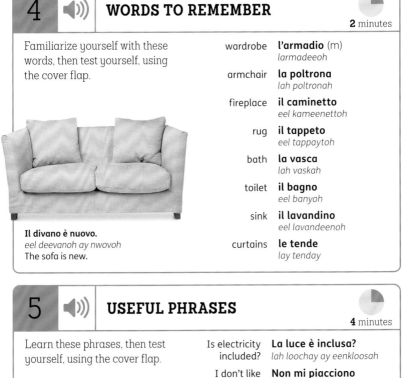

Il divano è nuovo.
eel deevanoh ay nwovoh
The sofa is new.

5 🔊 USEFUL PHRASES

4 minutes

Learn these phrases, then test yourself, using the cover flap.

Is electricity included?	**La luce è inclusa?** *lah loochay ay eenkloosah*
I don't like the curtains.	**Non mi piacciono le tende.** *non mee peeahchonoh lay tenday*
The fridge is broken.	**Il frigorifero è rotto.** *eel freegoreeferoh ay rottoh*

6 SAY IT

2 minutes

Is there a microwave?

I don't like the fireplace.

What a soft sofa!

---

3 minutes

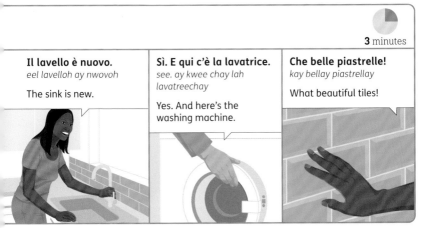

Il lavello è nuovo.
eel lavelloh ay nwovoh

The sink is new.

Sì. E qui c'è la lavatrice.
see. ay kwee chay lah lavatreechay

Yes. And here's the washing machine.

Che belle piastrelle!
kay bellay piastrellay

What beautiful tiles!

Il giardino
THE GARDEN

1 **WARM UP**
1 minute

Say "**I need**" and "**you need**" (pp80–81, pp92–95).

What is the Italian for "**day**," "**week**," and "**month**" (pp28–29)?

Ask "**Is the wardrobe included?**" (pp100–101).

The garden of a block of apartments may be communal, while houses generally have their own private yards. Check in advance with the estate agent or homeowner. Although not a traditional pastime among Italians, gardening for pleasure has become more popular in recent years. Garden centers and nurseries stock a wide range of plants.

2 🔊 **WORDS TO REMEMBER**

3 minutes

Familiarize yourself with these words, then test yourself, using the cover flap.

il tosaerba *eel tozaerbah*	lawnmower
la forchetta da giardino *lah forkettah dah jardeenoh*	fork
la vanga *lah vangah*	spade
il rastrello *eel rastrelloh*	rake
il vivaio *eel veevayoh*	garden center

3 🔊 **MATCH AND REPEAT**

Match the numbered items to the list, then test yourself, using the cover flap.

tree ❶

lawn ❷

path ❸　weeds ❹　terrace ❺

4 🔊 USEFUL PHRASES

4 minutes

Learn these phrases, then test yourself, using the cover flap.

Is the yard private?	**Il giardino è privato?** *eel jardeenoh ay preevatoh*
The gardener comes once a week.	**Il giardiniere viene una volta alla settimana.** *eel jardeenyeray vyenay oonah voltah allah setteemanah*
Can you mow the lawn?	**Può tagliare l'erba?** *pwoh tallyaray lerbah*
The garden needs watering.	**Bisogna annaffiare il giardino.** *beezonnyah annaffyaray eel jardeenoh*

5 SAY IT

2 minutes

The lawn needs water.

Are there any flowers?

The gardener comes on Fridays.

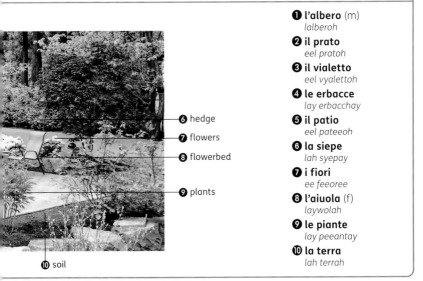

5 minutes

- ➊ **l'albero** (m) *lalberoh*
- ➋ **il prato** *eel pratoh*
- ➌ **il vialetto** *eel vyalettoh*
- ➍ **le erbacce** *lay erbacchay*
- ➎ **il patio** *eel pateeoh*
- ➏ **la siepe** *lah syepay*
- ➐ **i fiori** *ee feeoree*
- ➑ **l'aiuola** (f) *laywolah*
- ➒ **le piante** *lay peeantay*
- ➓ **la terra** *lah terrah*

➏ hedge
➐ flowers
➑ flowerbed
➒ plants
➓ soil

Gli animali
PETS

More than one-third of all Italian adults share their homes with at least one pet, which is often treated like a member of the family. Pet passports may be available to allow travelers to take their pets with them to Italy. Consult your vet for details of how to obtain the necessary vaccinations and paperwork.

---

2 🔊 **MATCH AND REPEAT**

Match the numbered animals to the list, then test yourself, using the cover flap.

❶ **il coniglio**
eel koneellyoh

❷ **il pesce**
eel peshay

❸ **l'uccello** (m)
loocchelloh

❹ **il gatto**
eel gattoh

❺ **il cane**
eel kanay

❻ **il criceto**
eel kreechetoh

❷ fish

❶ rabbit

dog ❺

❹ cat

---

3 🔊 **USEFUL PHRASES**

4 minutes

Learn these phrases, then test yourself, using the cover flap.

Questo cane è buono?
kwestoh kanay ay bwonoh
Is this dog friendly?

Posso portare il mio cane guida?
possoh portaray eel mee-oh kanay gweedah
Can I bring my guide dog?

Ho paura dei gatti.
oh paoorah day gattee
I'm frightened of cats.

Il mio cane non morde.
eel mee-oh kanay non morday
My dog doesn't bite.

Questo gatto ha le pulci.
kwestoh gattoh ah lay poolchee
This cat has fleas.

Cultural tip Many dogs in Italy are working or guard dogs, and you may encounter them tethered or roaming free. Approach farms and rural houses with care and keep away from the dog's territory. Look out for warning notices, such as **attenti al cane** (*beware of the dog*).

ATTENTI
AL CANE

4 ◀))) WORDS TO REMEMBER

4 minutes

Familiarize yourself with these words, then test yourself, using the cover flap.

bird **3**

hamster **6**

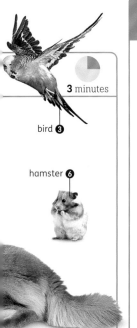

Il mio cane non sta bene.
eel mee-oh kanay non stah benay
My dog is not well.

vet	**il/la veterinario/a**
	eel/lah vetereenareeoh/ah
vaccination	**la vaccinazione**
	lah vaccheenatsyonay
pet passport	**il pet passport**
	eel pet passport
basket	**la cuccia**
	lah koocchah
cage	**la gabbia**
	lah gabbyah
bowl	**la ciotola del cane**
	lah chotolah del kanay
collar	**il collare**
	eel kollaray
leash	**il guinzaglio**
	eel gweentsallyoh
fleas	**le pulci**
	lay poolchee

5 ◀))) PUT INTO PRACTICE

3 minutes

Complete this dialogue, then test yourself, using the cover flap.

È suo il cane?
ay soo-oh eel kanay

Is this your dog?

Say: Yes, he's named Sandy.

Sì, si chiama Sandy.
see, see keeamah sendee

Ho paura dei cani.
oh paoorah day kanee

I'm frightened of dogs.

Say: Don't worry. He's friendly.

Non si preoccupi.
È buono.
non see preokkoopee.
ay bwonoh

Ripassa e ripeti
REVIEW AND REPEAT

Colors

❶ **nero**
neroh

❷ **azzurra**
azzoorrah

❸ **rosso**
rossoh

❹ **verde**
verday

❺ **gialli**
jallee

1 COLORS

◷ **4** minutes

Fill in the blanks with the correct Italian masculine or feminine form of the color given in brackets.

❶ **Questa giacca c'è in** _____ **?** (black)

❷ **Prendo la gonna** _____ **.** (blue)

❸ **Ha questa camicia in** _____ **?** (red)

❹ **No, ma c'è in** _____ **.** (green)

❺ **Ha pantaloni** _____ **?** (yellow)

Kitchen

❶ **il frigorifero**
eel freegoreeferoh

❷ **il fornello**
eel fornaylloh

❸ **il forno**
eel fornoh

❹ **il lavello**
eel lavelloh

❺ **il forno a microonde**
eel fornoh ah meekrohonday

❻ **il tavolo**
eel tavoloh

❼ **la sedia**
lah sedyah

2 KITCHEN

Name these items in Italian.

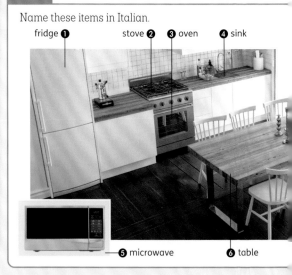

fridge ❶   stove ❷   ❸ oven   ❹ sink

❺ microwave   ❻ table

3 HOUSE

4 minutes

You are visiting a house in Italy. Join in the conversation, replying in Italian, following the numbered English prompts.

Questo è il soggiorno.
❶ What a lovely balcony!

E la cucina è molto bella.
❷ How many bedrooms?

Ci sono tre camere.
❸ Is there a garage?

No, ma c'è un giardino molto grande.
❹ Is the house available right away?

La casa è libera da luglio.
❺ What is the monthly rent?

House

❶ **Che bel balcone!**
kay bel balkonay

❷ **Quante camere ci sono?**
kwantay kameray chee sonoh

❸ **C'è il garage?**
chay eel garadj

❹ **La casa è libera subito?**
lah kazah ay leeberah soobeetoh

❺ **Quant'è l'affitto al mese?**
kwantay laffeettoh al mezay

---

4 minutes

4 AT HOME

3 minutes

Name these things in Italian.

❶ washing machine ❹ dining room
❷ sofa ❺ tree
❸ attic ❻ garden

❼ chair

At home

❶ **la lavatrice**
lah lavatreechay

❷ **il divano**
eel deevanoh

❸ **la soffitta**
lah soffeettah

❹ **la sala da pranzo**
lah salah dah pranzoh

❺ **l'albero**
lalberoh

❻ **il giardino**
eel jardeenoh

1 WARM UP

1 minute

Ask "**How do I get to the bank?**" and "**How do I get to the post office?**" (pp50–51, pp68–69).

What's the Italian for "**passport**" (pp54–55)?

Ask "**What time is the meeting?**" (pp30–31).

Il cambio, la banca e le poste
BUREAU DE CHANGE, BANK, AND MAIL

You can exchange one currency for another at a bureau de change. You can also get cash from a bank ATM but may be charged a fee. The post office also serves as a bank, usually with ATMs available outside the building. Stamps are sold at the post office as well as at **il tabaccaio** (p68).

2 ◀))) **WORDS TO REMEMBER**: MAIL

3 minutes

Familiarize yourself with these words, then test yourself, using the cover flap.

la cassetta delle lettere *lah kassettah dellay letteray*	mailbox
i francobolli *ee frankobollee*	stamps
via aerea *veeah a-ayreah*	air mail
la raccomandata *lah rakkomandatah*	registered mail
il codice postale *eel kodeechay postaleh*	post code
il/la postino/a *eel/lah posteenoh/ah*	mailman/ mailwoman

il pacco *eel pakkoh* package

la busta *lah boostah* envelope

la cartolina *lah kartoleenah* postcard

Quant'è per il Regno Unito? *kwantay per eel raynnyoh ooneetoh* How much is it for the United Kingdom?

3 ◀))) **IN CONVERSATION**: BUREAU DE CHANGE

Vorrei cambiare dei soldi. *vorray kambyaray day soldee*

I would like to change some money.

Cosa vuole cambiare? *kozah vwolay kambyaray*

What would you like to exchange?

Vorrei acquistare euro per cinquecento dollari. *vorray akweestaray ayooroh per cheenkwaychentoh dollaree*

I would like to buy euros for five hundred dollars.

4 🔊 WORDS TO REMEMBER: BANK

2 minutes

Familiarize yourself with these words, then test yourself, using the cover flap.

bank	**la banca** *lah bankah*
ATM/ cashpoint	**il bancomat** *eel bankomat*
PIN	**il pin** *eel pin*
cash	**il contante** *eel kontantay*
bills	**le banconote** *lay bankonotay*
coins	**le monete** *lay monetay*
credit card	**la carta di credito** *lah cartah dee kredeetoh*
contactless payment	**il pagamento contactless** *eel pagamayntoh contactless*

la carta di debito
lah kartah dee debeetoh
debit card

Come posso pagare?
komay possoh pagaray
How can I pay?

5 🔊 USEFUL PHRASES

4 minutes

Learn these phrases and then test yourself, using the cover flap.

I'd like to change some money.	**Vorrei cambiare dei soldi.** *vorray kambyaray day soldee*
What is the exchange rate?	**Quant'è il cambio?** *kwantay eel kambyoh*
What would you like to exchange?	**Cosa vuole cambiare?** *kozah vwolay kambyaray*

6 SAY IT

2 minutes

I'd like a stamp for the United States.

Can I pay by credit card?

Do I need my PIN?

3 minutes

Certo. Ha un documento d'identità? *chayrtoh. ah oon dokoomentoh deedenteetah*	**Sì, ecco il mio passaporto.** *see, ekkoh eel mee-oh passaportoh*	**Grazie, ecco i suoi euro.** *gratseeay ekkoh eeh swoy ayooroh*
Of course. Do you have any identification?	Yes, here's my passport.	Thank you, here are your euros.

1 WARM UP
1 minute

What is the Italian for "**It doesn't work**" (pp60–61)?

Say "**today**" and "**tomorrow**" in Italian (pp28–29).

Le riparazioni
REPAIRS

You can combine the Italian words on these pages with the vocabulary you learned in week 10 to help you explain basic problems and handle arranging most repairs. When organizing building work or a repair, it's a good idea to agree on the price and method of payment in advance.

2 ◀))) **WORDS TO REMEMBER:**
SERVICES

4 minutes

Familiarize yourself with these words, then test yourself, using the cover flap. The feminine form is also shown.

l'idraulico *leedraooleekoh*	plumber
l'elettricista *lelettreecheestah*	electrician
il/la meccanico/a *eel/lah mekkaneekoh/ah*	mechanic
il/la costruttore/trice *eel/lah kostroottoray/ treechay*	builder
l'imbianchino/a *leembyankeenoh/ah*	decorator
il/la falegname *eel/lah falennyamay*	carpenter
il/la muratore/trice *eel/lah mooratoray/ treechay*	bricklayer
il personale delle pulizie *eel payrsonalay dellay pooleetsyay*	cleaning staff

Non ho bisogno di un meccanico.
non oh beezonnyoh dee oon mekkaneekoh
I don't need a mechanic.

3 ◀))) **IN CONVERSATION**

La lavatrice non funziona.
lah lavatreechay non foontsyonah

The washing machine is not working.

Sì, il tubo è rotto.
see, eel tooboh ay rottoh

Yes, the hose is broken.

Può ripararlo?
pwoh reepararloh

Can you repair it?

4 USEFUL PHRASES

3 minutes

Learn these phrases, then test yourself, using the cover flap.

Dove posso farlo riparare?
dovay possoh farloh reepararay
Where can I get this repaired?

Can you clean the bathroom?	**Può pulire il bagno?** *pwoh pooleeray eel bannyoh*
Can you repair the boiler?	**Può riparare la caldaia?** *pwoh reepararay lah kaldayah*
Do you know a good electrician?	**Conosce un bravo elettricista?** *konoshay oon bravoh elettreecheestah*

5 PUT INTO PRACTICE

4 minutes

Complete this dialogue, then test yourself, using the cover flap.

Il suo muretto è rotto.
eel soo-oh mooray-ttoh ay rottoh

Your wall is broken.

Ask: Do you know a good bricklayer?

Conosce un bravo muratore?
konoshay oon bravoh mooratoray

Sì, ce n'è uno in paese.
see, chenay oonoh een paesay

Yes, there is one in the village.

Ask: Do you have his phone number?

Ha il suo numero di telefono?
ah eel soo-oh noomeroh dee telayfonoh

3 minutes

No, deve cambiarlo. *noh, devay kambeearloh*	**Può farlo oggi?** *pwoh farloh ojjee*	**No, torno domani.** *noh, tornoh domanee*
No, you need to change it.	Can you do it today?	No, I'll come back tomorrow.

1 **WARM UP**
1 minute

Ask "**How do I get to the library?**" (pp48–49).

How do you say "**cleaning staff**" (pp110–111)?

Say "**It's 9:30**," "**10:45**," and "**12:00**" (pp10–11 and pp30–31).

Venire
TO COME

The verb **venire** (*to come*) is another important verb that can be used to make a variety of useful idiomatic expressions—for example, **venire a capo** (*to solve something*), as in **sono venuto a capo del problema** (*I managed to solve the problem*). Other useful verbs are made up of **venire** with a prefix, such as **prevenire** (*to prevent*) and **divenire** (*to become*), formed in the same way as **venire** (below).

2 🔊 **VENIRE**: TO COME
6 minutes

Practice **venire** (*to come*) and the sample sentences, then test yourself, using the cover flap.

(io) vengo *(ee-oh) vengoh*	I come
(tu) vieni *(too) vyenee*	you come (informal singular)
(Lei) viene *(lay) vyenay*	you come (formal singular)
(lui/lei) viene *(loo-ee/lay) vyenay*	he/she/it comes
(noi) veniamo *(noy) veneeamoh*	we come
(voi) venite *(voy) veneetay*	you come (plural)
(loro) vengono *(loroh) vengonoh*	they come

Veniamo tutte le estati. *veneeamoh toottay lay estatee* — We come every summer.

Vengo anch'io. *vengoh ankeeoh* — I am coming too.

Lei viene dalla Nigeria. *lay vyenay dallah neejayreeah* — She comes from Nigeria.

Vengono in treno. *vengonoh een treno* They are coming by train.

Conversational tip In English, you say *come and see*, but in Italian, this translates to **vieni a vedere** (*come to see*). In the same way, *shall I come and pick you up?* translated into Italian is **vengo a prenderti?** (*shall I come to pick you up?*).

3 🔊 USEFUL PHRASES

4 minutes

Learn these phrases, then test yourself, using the cover flap.

Il personale delle pulizie viene il lunedì.
eel payrsonalay dellay pooleetsyay vyenay eel loonedee
The cleaning staff come every Monday.

When can I come? | **Quando posso venire?**
kwandoh possoh veneeray

Come and see. | **Vieni a vedere.**
vyenee ah vederay

Are you coming to my party? | **Venite alla mia festa?**
veneetay allah mee-ah festah

Come with me. (informal/formal) | **Vieni/venga con me.**
vyenee/vengah kon may

4 🔊 PUT INTO PRACTICE

4 minutes

Complete this dialogue, then test yourself, using the cover flap.

Buongiorno. Parrucchiere Leo.
bwonjornoh. parrookkyeray layo

Hello, this is Leo's hair salon.

Say: I'd like an appointment.

Vorrei un appuntamento.
vorray oon appoontamentoh

Quando vuol venire?
kwando vwol veneeray

When do you want to come?

Ask: Can I come today?

Posso venire oggi?
possoh veneeray ojjee

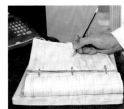

Sì certo, a che ora?
see chertoh, a kay orah

Yes of course, what time?

Say: At 10:30am.

Alle dieci e mezzo.
allay deeaychee ay metsoh

1 WARM UP
1 minute

What's the Italian for "**big/tall**" and "**small/short**" (pp64–65)?

Say "**The room is big**" and "**The bed is small**" (pp64–65).

Ask "**Is there a living room?**" (pp98–99).

La polizia e il crimine
POLICE AND CRIME

If you are the victim of a crime while in Italy, you should go to a police station to report it. In an emergency, you can dial 112 for the carabinieri or 113 for the police. You may have to explain your complaint in Italian, so some basic vocabulary is useful. In the event of a burglary, the police will usually come to the house.

2 WORDS TO REMEMBER: CRIME
4 minutes

Familiarize yourself with these words, then test yourself, using the cover flap.

il furto burglary
eel foortoh

il rapporto di polizia police report
eel rapportoh dee poleetseeah

il/la ladro/a thief
eel ladroh

la polizia police
lah poleetseeah

la denuncia statement
lah denoonchah

il/la testimone witness
eel/lah testeemonay

l'avvocato lawyer
lavvokatoh

Voglio un avvocato.
vollyoh oonavvokatoh
I want a lawyer.

3 USEFUL PHRASES
3 minutes

Learn these phrases, then test yourself, using the cover flap.

Sono stato/a derubato/a. I've been robbed.
sonoh statoh/ah deroobatoh/ah

Cosa hanno rubato? What was stolen?
kozah annoh roobatoh

Ha visto chi è stato? Did you see who did it?
ah veestoh kee ay statoh

Quando è successo? When did it happen?
kwandoh ay succhessoh

la macchina fotografica
lah makkeenah fotografeekah
camera

il portafoglio
eel portafollyoh
purse

4 🔊 WORDS TO REMEMBER: APPEARANCE

5 minutes

Familiarize yourself with these words, then test yourself, using the cover flap. Remember, some adjectives have a feminine form.

Ha i capelli lunghi e neri.
ah ee kapellee loongee ay nayree
She has long black hair.

È calvo e ha la barba
ay kalvoh ay ah lah barbah
He is bald and has a beard.

man/men	**l'uomo/gli uomini** *lwomoh/lly womeenee*
woman/ women	**la donna/le donne** *lah donnah/lay donnay*
tall	**alto/alta** *altoh/altah*
short	**basso/bassa** *bassoh/bassah*
young	**giovane** *jovanay*
old	**vecchio/vecchia** *vekkyoh/vekkyah*
fat	**grasso/grassa** *grassoh/grassah*
thin	**magro/magra** *magroh/magrah*
long/short hair	**i capelli lunghi/corti** *ee kapellee loongee/ kortee*
glasses	**gli occhiali** *lly okkyalee*
beard	**la barba** *lah barbah*

5 🔊 PUT INTO PRACTICE

2 minutes

Complete this dialogue, then test yourself, using the cover flap.

Lo può descrivere? **Basso e grasso.**
loh pwoh deskreeveray *bassoh ay grassoh*

Can you describe him?

Say: Short and fat.

E i capelli? **Capelli lunghi e barba.**
ay ee kapellee *kapellee loongee ay barbah*

And the hair?

Say: Long hair and a beard.

Cultural tip Italy has two main police forces: **la polizia** (*national police*, in blue uniforms) and **i carabinieri** (*military police*, in black). Both carry out policing duties, and if you are affected by a crime or other emergency, you can call either. Dial 112 for the carabinieri and 113 for the police.

Ripassa e ripeti
REVIEW AND REPEAT

Risposte *Answers*
(Cover with flap)

To come

1 **vengo**
vengoh

2 **viene**
vyenay

3 **veniamo**
veneeamoh

4 **venite**
veneetay

5 **vengono**
vengonoh

---

1 TO COME

3 minutes

Fill in the blanks with the correct form of
venire (*to come*).

1 (io) _____ alle quattro.

2 Il giardiniere _____ una volta alla settimana.

3 (noi) _____ in treno.

4 (voi) _____ con noi?

5 I miei genitori _____ lunedì.

Bank and mail

1 **il pacco**
eel pakkoh

2 **le cartoline**
lay kartoleenay

3 **i francobolli**
ee frankobollee

4 **la carta di debito**
lah cartah dee debeetoh

---

2 BANK AND MAIL

4 minutes

Name these items in Italian.

package **1**

2 postcards

3 stamps

debit card **4**

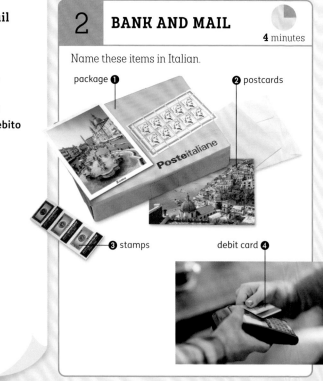

3 APPEARANCE

4 minutes

What do these sentences mean?

❶ Un uomo alto e magro.

❷ Una donna con i capelli corti e gli occhiali.

❸ Sono bassa e ho i capelli lunghi.

❹ È vecchia e grassa.

❺ Lui ha gli occhi azzurri e la barba.

Appearance

❶ A tall, thin man.

❷ A woman with short hair and glasses.

❸ I'm short, and I have long hair.

❹ She is old and fat.

❺ He has blue eyes and a beard.

4 THE PHARMACY

4 minutes

You are asking a pharmacist for advice. Join in the conversation, replying in Italian, following the numbered English prompts.

Buongiorno, desidera?
❶ I have a cough.

Ha anche il raffreddore?
❷ No, but I have a headache.

Prenda queste compresse.
❸ Do you have that as a syrup?

Certo. Ecco lo sciroppo.
❹ Thank you. How much is that?

Nove euro.
❺ Here you are. Goodbye.

The pharmacy

❶ **Ho la tosse.**
oh lah tossay

❷ **No, ma ho mal di testa.**
noh, mah oh mal dee testah

❸ **Le ha in sciroppo?**
lay ah een sheeroppoh

❹ **Grazie. Quant'è?**
gratseeay. kwantay

❺ **Ecco a Lei. Arrivederci.**
ekkoh ah lay. arreevederchee

1 WARM UP
1 minute

What is the Italian for "**museum**" and "**art gallery**" (pp48–49)?

Say "**I don't like the curtains**" (pp100–101).

Ask "**Do you want…?**' informally (pp24–25).

Il tempo libero
LEISURE TIME

Italy, with its long history and rich culture, provides many opportunities for cultural pursuits as well as modern leisure activities. Italians enjoy spending the weekends in historic cities, relaxing at the seaside in summer, or going skiing in winter. Be prepared for any of these topics to be the subject of conversation in social situations.

2 🔊 WORDS TO REMEMBER

Familiarize yourself with these words, then test yourself, using the cover flap.

il teatro *eel tayatroh*	theater
la musica *lah moozeekahh*	music
l'arte (f) *lartay*	art
il cinema *eel cheenemah*	cinema
i videogiochi *ee veedayohjokkee*	video games
il nightclub *eel naytclayb*	nightclub
lo sport *loh sport*	sports
fare un giro turistico *faray oon jeeroh turisticoh*	sightseeing

la galleria
lah gallayreeah
balcony ⎯

gli spettatori
lly spettatoree
audience ⎯

la platea
lah platayah
orchestra ⎯

Amo l'opera.
amoh lopayrah
I love opera.

3 🔊 IN CONVERSATION

Ciao Elena, vuoi giocare a tennis questa mattina?
chaw elayna, vwoee jokaray ah tennees kwaystah matteenah

Hi Elena, do you want to play tennis this morning?

No, grazie, ho altri programmi.
noh, gratseeay, oh altree programmee

No thank you, I have other plans.

Oh, cosa fai?
oh, kozah faee

Oh, what are you going to do?

5 SAY IT
2 minutes

I'm interested in music.

I prefer sports.

I like the theater.

Shopping is boring!

4 minutes

4))) USEFUL PHRASES
4 minutes

Learn these phrases, then test yourself, using the cover flap.

What do you do in your spare time? (formal/informal)
Cosa fa/fai nel tempo libero?
kozah fah/faee nel tempoh leeberoh

What do you plan to do this morning? (formal/informal)
Cosa farà/farai questa mattina?
koza farah/faraee kwaystah matteenah

I prefer the cinema.
Io preferisco il cinema.
ee-oh preferisko eel cheenemah

I'm interested in art.
Mi interessa l'arte.
mee eenteressah lartay

I hate shopping.
Odio fare shopping.
odeeoh faray shoppeeng

That's boring!
Che noia!
kay noeeah

Mi piacciono i videogiochi.
mee peeachonoh ee veedayohjokkee
I like video games.

4 minutes

Faccio un giro turistico! Vuoi venire con me?
facchoh oon jeeroh turisticoh. vwoee veneeray kon may

I am going sightseeing! Do you want to join me?

Sembra bello, ma voglio giocare a tennis.
sembrah belloh, mah vollyoh jokaray ah tennees

That sounds nice, but I want to play tennis.

Non c'è problema, divertiti!
non chay problemah, deeverteetee

No problem, enjoy your game!

Lo sport e gli hobby
SPORTS AND HOBBIES

1 WARM UP
1 minute

Ask "**Do you** (formal) **want to play tennis?**" (pp118–119).

Say "**I like the theater**" and "**I prefer sightseeing**" (pp118–119).

Say "**That doesn't interest me**" (pp118–119).

The verb **fare** (*to do* or *to make*) is a useful verb for talking about hobbies and is also used when describing the weather—for example, **fa freddo** (*it's cold*). **Giocare** (*to play*) is another handy verb for talking about sports—for example, **gioco a tennis** (*I play tennis*). Soccer is very popular in Italy, as are volleyball, basketball, swimming, cycling, and skiing.

2 ◀))) WORDS TO REMEMBER
5 minutes

Familiarize yourself with these words, then test yourself, using the cover flap.

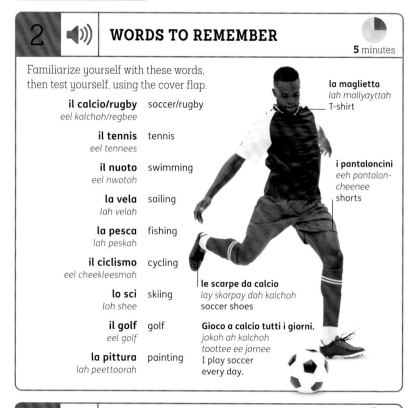

il calcio/rugby soccer/rugby
eel kalchoh/regbee

il tennis tennis
eel tennees

il nuoto swimming
eel nwotoh

la vela sailing
lah velah

la pesca fishing
lah peskah

il ciclismo cycling
eel cheekleesmoh

lo sci skiing
loh shee

il golf golf
eel golf

la pittura painting
lah peettoorah

la maglietta
lah mallyayttah
T-shirt

i pantaloncini
eeh pantalon-cheenee
shorts

le scarpe da calcio
lay skarpay dah kalchoh
soccer shoes

Gioco a calcio tutti i giorni.
jokoh ah kalchoh toottee ee jornee
I play soccer every day.

3 ◀))) USEFUL PHRASES
2 minutes

Learn these phrases, then test yourself, using the cover flap.

Gioco a pallacanestro. I play basketball.
jokoh ah pallakanaystroh

Gioca a tennis. He plays tennis.
jokah ah tennees

Fa un corso di pittura. She is in a
fah oon korsoh dee painting class.
peettoorah

4 FARE: TO DO OR TO MAKE

4 minutes

Practice **fare** (*to do or to make*) and the sample sentences, then test yourself, using the cover flap.

I do	**(io) faccio** *(ee-oh) facchoh*
you do (informal singular)	**(tu) fai** *(too) faee*
you do (formal singular)	**(Lei) fa** *(lay) fah*
he/she/it does	**(lui/lei) fa** *(loo-ee/lay) fah*
we do	**(noi) facciamo** *(noy) facchamoh*
you do (plural)	**(voi) fate** *(voy) fatay*
they do	**(loro) fanno** *(loroh) fannoh*

Oggi fa caldo, allora possiamo fare escursionismo.
ojjee fah caldoh, allorah possyamoh faray ayskursyoneesmoh
It's warm today, so we can go hiking.

What do you do? (formal/informal)	**Cosa fa/fai?** *kozah fah/faee*
I go hiking.	**Faccio escursionismo.** *facchoh ayskursyoneesmoh*
I like cycling and skiing.	**A me piace fare ciclismo e sciare.** *ah may peeachay faray ceekleesmoh ay sheearay*

5 PUT INTO PRACTICE

3 minutes

Complete this dialogue, then test yourself, using the cover flap.

Cosa ti piace fare?
kozah tee peeachay faray

What do you like doing?

Say: I like playing tennis.

Mi piace giocare a tennis.
mee peeachay jokaray ah tennees

Giochi anche a calcio?
jokee anchay ah kalchoh

Do you play soccer as well?

Say: No. I play rugby.

No. Gioco a rugby.
noh. jokoh ah regbee

Quando giochi?
kwandoh jokee

When do you play?

Say: I play every week.

Gioco tutte le settimane.
jokoh toottay lay setteemanay

1 WARM UP
1 minute

Say "**my husband**" and "**my wife**" (pp10–11).

How do you say "**lunch**" and "**dinner**" in Italian (pp20–21)?

Say "**Sorry, I'm busy**" (pp32–33).

I rapporti sociali
SOCIALIZING

The dinner table is the center of the Italian social world, and you can expect to do a lot of your socializing while enjoying good food and wine. It is best to use the more polite **Lei** form to talk to people you meet socially until they call you **tu**, at which point you can reciprocate.

2 🔊 USEFUL PHRASES

Learn these phrases, then test yourself, using the cover flap.

Vuol venire a cena con me?
vwol veneeray ah chenah con may
Would you like to come to dinner with me?

È libero/a mercoledì prossimo?
ay leeberoh/ah merkoledee prosseemoh
Are you free next Wednesday?

Magari un'altra volta.
magaree oonaltrah voltah
Perhaps another time.

Grazie dell'invito.
gratseeay delleenveetoh.
Thank you for inviting us.

la padrona di casa
lah padronah dee kazah
hostess

3 🔊 IN CONVERSATION

Vuol venire a cena da me martedì?
vwol veneeray ah chenah dah may martedee

Would you like to come to dinner on Tuesday?

Mi dispiace, martedì non posso.
mee deespeeachay, martedee non possoh

I'm sorry, I can't on Tuesday.

Facciamo giovedì?
facchamoh jovedee

What about Thursday?

Cultural tip When you visit someone for the first time, it is usual to take flowers or wine. Having seen their house, you can take a slightly more personal gift if invited again.

4 minutes

4 🔊 WORDS TO REMEMBER

3 minutes

Familiarize yourself with these words, then test yourself, using the cover flap.

party	**la festa**
	lah festah
dinner party	**la cena**
	lah chenah
cocktail party	**l'aperitivo** (m)
	lapayreeteevoh
reception	**il rinfresco**
	eel reenfreskoh
invitation	**l'invito** (m)
	leenveetoh

5 🔊 PUT INTO PRACTICE

3 minutes

Complete this dialogue, then test yourself, using the cover flap.

Facciamo una festa sabato. Siete liberi?
facchamoh oonah festah sabatoh. seeaytay leeberee

We are having a party on Saturday. Are you free?

Say: Yes, how nice!

Sì, che bello!
see, kay belloh

Benissimo.
beneesseemoh

That's great.

Ask: What time does it start?

A che ora comincia?
ah kay orah komeenchah

l'ospite
lospeetay
guest

4 minutes

Benissimo.
beneesseemoh

That's great.

Porti suo marito.
portee soo-oh mareetoh

Bring your husband.

Grazie. A che ora?
gratseeay. ah kay orah

Thank you. At what time?

Ripassa e ripeti
REVIEW AND REPEAT

Animals

❶ **il gatto**
eel gattoh

❷ **il criceto**
eel kreechetoh

❸ **il pesce**
eel peshay

❹ **l'uccello**
loocchelloh

❺ **il coniglio**
eel koneellyoh

❻ **il cane**
eel kanay

I like…

❶ **Gioco a pallacanestro.**
jokoh ah pallakanaystroh

❷ **Mi piace giocare a tennis.**
mee peeachay jokaray ah tennees

❸ **Non mi piace il calcio.**
non mee peeachay eel kalchoh

❹ **Mi piace la pittura.**
mee peeachay lah peettoorah

---

1 · ANIMALS

Name these animals in Italian.

❹ bird
❸ fish
❶ cat
❷ hamster

---

2 · I LIKE…

4 minutes

Say these sentences in Italian:

❶ I play basketball.
❷ I like playing tennis.
❸ I don't like soccer.
❹ I like painting.

3 minutes

5 rabbit

6 dog

---

3 TO DO

4 minutes

Fill in the blanks with the correct form of **fare** (*to do*).

1 Tu _____ vela?

2 Lei _____ un corso di pittura.

3 Cosa le piace _____ ?

4 _____ freddo oggi.

5 Voi _____ palestra?

6 Io _____ nuoto.

To do

1 fai
faee

2 fa
fah

3 fare
faray

4 fa
fah

5 fate
fatay

6 faccio
facchoh

---

4 AN INVITATION

4 minutes

You are invited for lunch. Join in the conversation, replying in Italian, following the numbered English prompts.

Vuol venire a pranzo da me sabato?
1 I am sorry, I can't on Saturday.

Facciamo domenica?
2 Great. I am free on Sunday.

Porti i bambini.
3 Thank you. What time?

All'una.
4 See you on Sunday.

An invitation

1 Mi dispiace, sabato non posso.
mee deespeeachay, sabatoh non possoh

2 Benissimo. Sono libera domenica.
beneesseemoh. sonoh leeberah domeneekah

3 Grazie. A che ora?
gratseeay. ah kay orah

4 A domenica.
ah domeneekah

Reinforce and progress

Regular practice is the key to maintaining and advancing your language skills. In this section, you will find a variety of suggestions for reinforcing and extending your knowledge of Italian. Many involve returning to exercises in the book and extending their scope by using the dictionaries. Go back through the lessons in a different order, mix and match activities to make up your own daily 15-minute program, or focus on topics that are of particular relevance to your current needs.

1 **WARM UP**

1 minute

Say "**He is**" and "**They are**" (pp14–15).

Say "**He is not**" and "**They are not**" (pp14–15).

What is Italian for "**my mother**" (pp10–11)?

Match, repeat, and extend
Remind yourself of words related to specific topics by returning to the Match and Repeat and Words to Remember exercises. Test yourself, using the cover flap. Discover new words in that area by referring to the dictionary and menu guide.

Keep warmed up
Revisit the Warm Up boxes to remind yourself of key words and phrases. Make sure that you work your way through all of them on a regular basis.

2 **MATCH AND REPEAT**

5 minutes

Match the numbered items to the list, then test yourself, using the cover flap.

❶ **la grondaia**
lah grondayah

❷ **la finestra**
lah feenestrah

❸ **il comignolo**
eel comeennyoloh

❹ **il tetto**
eel tettoh

❺ **il viale**
eel veealay

❻ **la porta**
lah portah

❼ **il muro**
eel mooroh

❽ **le persiane**
lay persyanay

gutter ❶   ❷ window   ❸ chimney   roof ❹

driveway ❺   shutters ❻ ❼ door   wall ❽

3 **IN CONVERSATION**

Carry on conversing
Reread the In Conversation panels. Say both parts of the conversation, paying attention to the pronunciation. Where possible, try incorporating new words from the dictionary.

Buongiorno, sono la professoressa Lanzi.
bwonjornoh, sonoh lah professoressah lantsee

Hello, I'm Professor Lanzi.

Dove insegna?
dovay eensennyah

Where do you teach?

Insegno all'università di Pisa.
eensennyoh allooneeverseetah dee pisah

I teach at the University of Pisa.

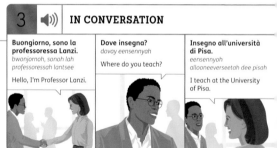

4 🔊 USEFUL PHRASES: MONTHS

2 minutes

Learn these phrases, then test yourself, using the cover flap.

My children are on vacation in August. **I miei bambini sono in vacanza in agosto.**
ee mee-ayee bambeenee sonoh een vakantsah een agostoh

My birthday is in June. **Il mio compleanno è in giugno.**
eel mee-oh kompleahnnoh ay een jooneeoh

Practice words and phrases
Return to the Words to Remember, Useful Phrases, and Put into Practice exercises. Test yourself, using the cover flap. When you are confident, devise your own versions of the phrases, using new words from the dictionary.

5 SAY IT

2 minutes

I'm doing research in medicine.

I have a degree in literature.

She's the professor.

Say it again
The Say It exercises are a useful instant reminder for each lesson. Practice these, using your own vocabulary variations from the dictionary or elsewhere in the lesson.

6 BE OR HAVE

5 minutes

Fill in the blanks with the correct form of **avere** (*to have*) or **essere** (*to be*).

❶ (noi) _____ italiani.
❷ (noi) _____ quattro figli.
❸ (lei) _____ inglese.
❹ (Lei) _____ un fratello?
❺ (io) _____ sposato/a.
❻ (voi) _____ figli?
❼ (io) non _____ il cellulare.
❽ (tu) _____ sicuro.

Review and repeat again
Work through a Review and Repeat lesson as a way of reinforcing words and phrases presented in the course. Return to the main lesson for any topic about which you are no longer confident.

Using other resources

As well as working with this book, try the following language extension ideas:

Visit Italy and try out your new skills with native speakers. Find out whether there is an Italian community near you. There may be shops, cafés, restaurants, and clubs. Try to visit some of these and use your Italian to order food and drink and strike up conversations. Most native speakers will be happy to speak Italian to you.

Join a language class or club. There are usually evening and day classes available at a variety of different levels. Or you could start a club yourself, if you have friends who are also interested in keeping up their Italian.

Look at Italian magazines and newspapers. The pictures will help you understand the text. Advertisements are also a useful way of expanding your vocabulary.

Use the Internet, where you can find all kinds of websites for learning languages, some of which offer free online help and activities. You can also find Italian websites for anything from renting a house to shampooing your pet. You can even access Italian radio and TV stations online. Start by going to a search engine and typing in a subject that interests you, or give yourself a challenge, such as finding a two-bedroom apartment for rent in Florence.

Menu guide

This guide lists the most common terms you may encounter on Italian menus or when shopping for food. If you can't find an exact phrase, try looking up its component parts.

A

abbacchio alla romana *Roman-style spring lamb*
acciughe sott'olio *anchovies in oil*
aceto *vinegar*
acqua *water*
acqua minerale gassata *sparkling mineral water*
acqua minerale non gassata *still mineral water*
acqua naturale *still mineral water, tap water*
affettato misto *variety of cold, sliced meats*
affogato al caffè *hot espresso on ice cream*
aglio *garlic*
agnello *lamb*
albicocche *apricots*
al forno *roast*
amatriciana *chopped bacon and tomato sauce*
ananas *pineapple*
anatra *duck*
anatra all'arancia *duck in orange sauce*
anguilla in umido *stewed eel*
anguria *watermelon*
antipasti *appetizers*
antipasti misti *mixed appetizers*
aperitivo *aperitif*
aragosta *lobster*
arancia *orange*
aranciata *orangeade*
aringa *herring*
arista di maiale al forno *roast chine of pork*
arrosto *roast*
arrosto di tacchino *roast turkey*
asparagi *asparagus*
avocado all'agro *avocado with dressing*

B

baccalà *dried cod*
baccalà alla vicentina *Vicentine-style dried cod*
bagnacauda *vegetables (often raw) in a sauce of oil, garlic, and anchovy*
Barbaresco *dry red wine from Piedmont*
Barbera *dry red wine from Piedmont*
Bardolino *dry red wine from the Veneto region*
Barolo *dark, dry red wine from Piedmont*
basilico *basil*
bavarese *ice-cream cake with cream*
bel paese *soft, white cheese*
besciamella *white sauce*
bignè *cream puff*
birra *beer*
birra chiara *light beer, lager*
birra grande *large beer*
birra piccola *small beer*
birra scura *dark beer*
bistecca ai ferri *grilled steak*
bistecca (di manzo) *steak*
braciola di maiale *pork steak*
branzino al forno *baked sea bass*
brasato *braised beef with herbs*
bresaola *dried, salted beef eaten with oil and lemon, or grana cheese and rocket, or balsamic vinegar, or by itself.*
brioche *type of croissant*
brodo *clear broth*
brodo di pollo *chicken broth*
brodo vegetale *clear vegetable broth*
budino *pudding*
burro *butter*
burro di acciughe *anchovy butter*

C

caciotta *tender, white cheese from Central Italy*
caffè *coffee*
caffè corretto *espresso with a dash of liqueur*
caffellatte *(caffè latte) half coffee, half hot milk*
caffè lungo *weak espresso*
caffè macchiato *espresso with a dash of milk*
caffè ristretto *strong espresso*
calamari in umido *stewed squid*
calamaro *squid*
calzone *folded pizza with tomato and cheese*
camomilla *camomile tea*
cannella *cinnamon*
cannelloni al forno *baked egg pasta rolls stuffed with meat*
cappuccino *espresso with foaming milk*
capretto al forno *roast kid*
carbonara *sauce of egg, bacon, and cheese*
carciofi *artichokes*
carciofini sott'olio *baby artichokes in oil*
carne *meat*
carote *carrots*
carpaccio *finely sliced beef fillets with oil, lemon, and parmesan*
carré di maiale al forno *roast pork loin*
cassata siciliana *ice-cream cake with chocolate, glacé fruit, and ricotta*
castagne *chestnuts*
cavoletti di Bruxelles *Brussels sprouts*
cavolfiore *cauliflower*
cavolo *cabbage*
cefalo *mullet*
cernia *grouper (fish)*
charlotte *ice-cream cake with cream, biscuits, and fruit*
Chianti *dark red Tuscan wine*
cicoria *chicory*
cicorino *small chicory plants*
ciliege *cherries*
cime di rapa *sprouting broccoli*
cioccolata *chocolate*
cioccolata calda *hot chocolate*
cipolle *onions*
cocktail di gamberetti *shrimp cocktail*
conchiglie alla marchigiana *pasta shells in tomato sauce with ham, celery, carrot, and parsley*
coniglio *rabbit*
coniglio in umido *stewed rabbit*
consommé *clear meat or chicken broth*
contorni *vegetables*
coperto *cover charge*

coppa *cured neck of pork*
costata alla fiorentina
T-bone veal/beef steak
costata di manzo
T-bone beef steak
cotechino *spiced pork sausage for boiling*
cotoletta *veal, pork, or lamb schnitzel*
costoletta ai ferri *grilled veal or pork chop*
cotoletta alla milanese *veal chop in breadcrumbs*
cotoletta alla valdostana *veal chop with ham and cheese, in breadcrumbs*
costolette di agnello *lamb chops*
costolette di maiale *pork chops*
cozze *mussels*
cozze alla marinara *mussels in white wine*
crema *custard dessert made with eggs and milk*
crema al caffè *coffee custard dessert*
crema al cioccolato *chocolate custard dessert*
crema di funghi *cream of mushroom soup*
crema di piselli *cream of pea soup*
crema pasticciera *confectioner's custard*
crêpes Suzette *pancakes flambéed with orange sauce*
crescente *fried bread made with flour, lard, and eggs*
crespelle *savory pancake*
crostata di frutta *fruit tart*

D, E

dadi *bouillon cubes*
datteri *dates*
degustazione *tasting*
degustazione di vini *wine tasting*
dentice al forno *baked dentex (type of sea bream)*
digestivo *digestive liqueur*
dolci *sweets, desserts, cakes*
entrecôte (di manzo) *beef entrecote*
espresso *strong, black coffee*

F

fagiano *pheasant*
fagioli *beans*
fagioli borlotti in umido *borlotti (kidney beans) in sauce of tomato, vegetables, and herbs*
fagiolini *long, green beans*

faraona *guinea fowl*
fegato *liver*
fegato alla veneta *liver in butter with onions*
fegato con salvia e burro *liver in butter and sage*
fettuccine *ribbon-shaped pasta*
fichi *figs*
filetto di pesce persico *fillets of perch*
filetto di sogliola *fillets of sole*
filetto ai ferri *grilled fillet of beef*
filetto al cognac *fillet of beef flambé*
filetto al pepe verde *fillet of beef with green peppercorns*
filetto al sangue *rare fillet of beef*
filetto ben cotto
well-done fillet of beef
filetto (di manzo)
fillet of beef
filetto medio *medium-cooked fillet of beef*
finocchi gratinati *fennel au gratin*
finocchio *fennel*
fonduta *cheese fondue*
formaggi misti *variety of cheeses*
fragole *strawberries*
fragole con gelato/panna *strawberries and ice cream/cream*
frappé *fruit or milk shake with crushed ice*
Frascati *dry white wine from area around Rome*
frittata *type of omelette*
frittata alle erbe *herb omelette*
fritto misto *mixed seafood in batter*
frittura di pesce *variety of fried fish*
frutta *fruit*
frutta alla fiamma *fruit flambé*
frutta secca *dried nuts and raisins*
frutti di bosco *mixture of strawberries, raspberries, mulberries, etc.*
frutti di mare *seafood*
funghi *mushrooms*
funghi trifolati *mushrooms fried in garlic and parsley*

G

gamberetti *shrimp*
gamberi *shrimp*
gamberoni *king shrimp*
gazzosa *clear lemonade*
gelatina *jelly*
gelato *ice cream*
gelato di crema *vanilla-flavored ice cream*
gelato di frutta *fruit-flavored ice cream*

gnocchetti verdi agli spinaci e al gorgonzola *small flour, potato, and spinach dumplings with melted gorgonzola*
gnocchi *small flour and potato dumplings*
gnocchi alla romana *small milk and semolina dumplings with butter*
Gorgonzola *strong blue cheese from Lombardy*
grancevola *spiny spider crab*
granchio *crab*
granita *crushed ice drink*
grigliata di pesce *grilled fish*
grigliata mista *mixed grill (meat or fish)*
grissini *thin, crisp breadsticks*
gruviera *Gruyère cheese*

I

indivia *endive*
indivia belga *white chicory*
insalata *salad*
insalata caprese *salad of tomatoes and mozzarella*
insalata di funghi porcini *boletus mushroom salad*
insalata di mare *seafood salad*
insalata di nervetti *boiled beef or veal served cold with beans and pickles*
insalata di pomodori *tomato salad*
insalata di riso *rice salad*
insalata mista *mixed salad*
insalata russa *Russian salad*
insalata verde *green salad*
involtini *meat rolls stuffed with ham and herbs*

L

lamponi *raspberries*
lasagne al forno *layers of pasta baked in meat sauce with cheese*
latte *milk*
latte macchiato *milk sprinkled with coffee*
latte macchiato con cioccolato *hot milk sprinkled with cocoa*
lattuga *lettuce*
leggero *light*
legumi *legumes or pulses*
lemonsoda *sparkling lemon drink*
lenticchie *lentils*
lepre *hare*
limonata *lemon-flavored fizzy drink*
limone *lemon*
lingua *tongue*

M

macedonia di frutta *fruit salad*
maiale *pork*
maionese *mayonnaise*
mandarino *mandarin*
mandorla *almond*
manzo *beef*
marroni *chestnuts*
Marsala *fortified wine*
marzapane *marzipan*
mascarpone *soft, mild cheese*
medaglioni di vitello *veal medallions*
mela *apple*
melanzane *aubergine*
melone *melon*
menta *mint*
meringata *meringue pie*
merluzzo *cod*
merluzzo alla pizzaiola *cod in tomato sauce with anchovies and capers*
merluzzo in bianco *cod with oil and lemon*
messicani in gelatina *rolls of veal in jelly*
millefoglie *pastry layered with custard*
minestra in brodo *noodle soup*
minestrone *vegetable soup with rice or pasta*
mirtilli *bilberries*
more *mulberries or blackberries*
moscato *sweet wine*
mousse al cioccolato *chocolate mousse*
mozzarella *cow cheese*
mozzarella di bufala *buffalo cheese*
mozzarella in carrozza *fried slices of bread and mozzarella*

N, O

nasello *hake*
nocciole *hazelnuts*
noce moscata *nutmeg*
noci *walnuts*
nodino *veal chop*
olio *oil*
origano *oregano*
ossobuco *stewed shin of veal*
ostriche *oysters*

P

paglia e fieno *mixed plain and green tagliatelle*
paillard di manzo *slices of grilled beef*
paillard di vitello *slices of grilled veal*
pane *bread*
panino *filled roll*
panna *cream*
parmigiana di melanzane *aubergines baked with cheese*
pasta al forno *pasta baked in white sauce and grated cheese*
pasta e fagioli *thick soup with puréed borlotti beans and pasta rings*
pasta e piselli *pasta with peas*
pasticcio di fegato d'oca *baked pasta dish with goose liver*
pasticcio di lepre *baked pasta dish with hare*
pasticcio di maccheroni *baked macaroni*
pastina in brodo *noodle soup*
patate *potatoes*
patate al forno/arrosto *roast potatoes*
patate fritte *chips*
patate in insalata *potato salad*
pecorino *strong, hard sheep's milk cheese*
penne *pasta quills*
penne ai quattro formaggi *pasta with four cheeses sauce*
penne all'arrabbiata *pasta with tomato and chili pepper sauce*
penne panna e prosciutto *pasta with cream and ham sauce*
pepe *pepper (spice)*
peperoncino *crushed chili pepper*
peperoni *peppers*
peperoni ripieni *stuffed peppers*
peperoni sott'olio *peppers in oil*
pera *pear*
pesca *peach*
pesce *fish*
pesce al cartoccio *fish baked in foil with herbs*
pesce in carpione *marinaded fish*
pesto *sauce of basil, pine nuts, Parmesan, garlic, and oil*
Pinot *dry white wine from the Veneto region*
pinzimonio *raw vegetables with oil and vinegar*
piselli *peas*
piselli al prosciutto *broth with peas, ham, and basil*
pizzaiola *slices of cooked beef in tomato sauce, oregano, and anchovies*
pizzoccheri alla Valtellinese *pasta strips with vegetables and cheese*
polenta *boiled cornmeal left to set and sliced*
polenta e osei *polenta with small birds*
polenta pasticciata *layers of polenta, tomato sauce, and cheese*
pollo *chicken*
pollo alla cacciatora *chicken in white wine and mushroom sauce*
pollo alla diavola *deep-fried chicken pieces*
polpette *meatballs*
polpettone *meatloaf*
pomodori *tomatoes*
pomodori ripieni *stuffed tomatoes*
pompelmo *grapefruit*
porri *leeks*
prezzemolo *parsley*
primi piatti *first courses*
prosciutto cotto *cooked ham*
prosciutto crudo *type of cured ham*
prugne *plums*
punte di asparagi all'agro *asparagus tips in oil and lemon*
purè di patate *mashed potatoes*
puttanesca *tomato sauce with anchovies, capers, and black olives*

Q, R

quaglie *quails*
radicchio *chicory*
ragù *meat-based sauce*
ragù alla bolognese *mince and tomato sauce*
rapanelli *radishes*
ravioli *stuffed pasta parcels*
ravioli al pomodoro *meat ravioli in tomato sauce*
razza *skate*
ricotta *type of cottage cheese*
risi e bisi *risotto with peas and ham*
riso *rice*
risotto *rice cooked in stock*
risotto alla castellana *risotto with mushroom, ham, cream, and cheese*
risotto alla milanese *risotto with saffron*
risotto al nero di seppia *risotto with cuttlefish ink*
risotto al tartufo *truffle risotto*
roast-beef all'inglese *thinly sliced cold roast beef*
robiola *type of soft cheese from Lombardy*
rognone trifolato *kidney in garlic, oil, and parsley*
rosatello/rosato *rosé wine*
rosmarino *rosemary*

S

salame *salami*
sale *salt*
salmone affumicato
smoked salmon
salsa cocktail/rosa
*mayonnaise and ketchup
sauce for fish and seafood*
salsa di pomodoro *tomato
sauce*
salsa tartara *tartar sauce*
salsa vellutata *white sauce
made with clear broth
instead of milk*
salsa verde *sauce for meat,
with parsley and oil*
salsiccia *sausage*
salsiccia di cinghiale *wild
boar sausage*
salsiccia di maiale *pork
sausage*
saltimbocca alla romana
*slices of veal stuffed with
ham and sage and fried*
salvia *sage*
sambuca (con la mosca)
*aniseed-flavor liqueur
served with a coffee bean*
sarde ai ferri *grilled sardines*
scaloppine *veal escalopes*
scaloppine al prezzemolo *veal
escalopes with parsley*
scamorza alla griglia *grilled
soft cheese*
scampi alla griglia *grilled
scampi*
secco *dry*
secondi piatti *second courses,
main courses*
sedano *celery*
selvaggina *game*
semifreddo *dessert of ice
cream and sponge fingers*
senape *mustard*
seppie in umido *stewed
cuttlefish*
servizio compreso *service
charge included*
servizio escluso *service
charge excluded*
Soave *dry white wine from the
Veneto region*
sogliola *sole*
sogliola ai ferri *grilled sole*
sogliola al burro *sole cooked
in butter*
sogliola alla mugnaia *sole
cooked in flour and butter*
sorbetto *sorbet, soft ice cream*
soufflé al formaggio *cheese
soufflé*
soufflé al prosciutto *ham
soufflé*
speck *cured, smoked ham*
spezzatino di vitello *veal stew*
spiedini *assorted chunks
of spit-cooked meat or fish*

spinaci *spinach*
spinaci all'agro *spinach with
oil and lemon*
spremuta di... *freshly
squeezed... juice*
spumante *sparkling wine*
stracchino *soft cheese from
Lombardy*
stracciatella *soup of beaten
eggs in clear broth*
strudel di mele *apple strudel*
succo di... *...juice*
sugo al tonno *tomato sauce
with garlic, tuna, and parsley*

T

tacchino ripieno *stuffed
turkey*
tagliata *finely cut beef fillet
cooked in the oven*
tagliatelle *thin pasta strips*
tagliatelle rosse *tagliatelle
with chopped red peppers*
tagliatelle verdi *tagliatelle
with spinach*
tagliolini *thin soup noodles*
tartine *small sandwiches*
tartufo *ice cream covered in
cocoa or chocolate; truffle*
tè *tea*
tiramisù *dessert with coffee-
soaked sponge, Marsala,
Mascarpone, and cocoa
powder*
tonno *tuna*
torta *tart, flan*
torta di ricotta *type of
cheesecake*
torta salata *savory flan*
tortellini *pasta shapes filled
with minced pork, ham,
Parmesan, and nutmeg*
trancio di palombo *smooth
dogfish steak*
trancio di pesce spada
swordfish steak
trenette col pesto *flat
spaghetti with pesto sauce*
triglie *mullet (fish)*
trippa *tripe*
trota *trout*
trota affumicata *smoked
trout*
trota al burro *trout cooked
in butter*
trota alle mandorle *trout
with almonds*
trota bollita *boiled trout*

U

uccelletti *cheese or meat
wrapped in bacon, baked, and
served on cocktail sticks; also
sweet bird-shaped stuffed
pastries*
uova *eggs*

uova alla coque *boiled eggs*
**uova al tegamino con
pancetta** *fried eggs and bacon*
uova farcite *eggs with tuna,
capers, and mayonnaise
filling*
uova sode *hard-boiled eggs*
uva *grapes*
uva bianca *white grapes*
uva nera *black grapes*

V

vellutata di asparagi *creamed
asparagus*
vellutata di piselli *creamed
peas*
verdura *vegetables*
vermicelli *very fine, thin pasta,
often used in soups*
vino *wine*
vino bianco *white wine*
vino da dessert *dessert wine*
vino da pasto *table wine*
vino da tavola *table wine*
vino rosso *red wine*
vitello *veal*
vitello tonnato *sliced veal in
tuna, anchovy, oil, and
lemon sauce*
vongole *clams*

W, Z

würstel *hot dog*
zabaione (zabaglione) *creamy
dessert of eggs, sugar, and
Marsala*
zafferano *saffron*
zucca *pumpkin*
zucchine *zucchini*
zucchine al pomodoro
*zucchini in tomato, garlic,
and parsley sauce*
zucchine ripiene *stuffed
zucchini*
zuccotto *ice-cream cake with
sponge fingers, cream, and
chocolate*
zuppa *soup*
zuppa di cipolle *onion soup*
zuppa di cozze *mussel soup*
zuppa di lenticchie *lentil soup*
zuppa di pesce *fish soup*
zuppa di verdura *vegetable
soup*
zuppa inglese *trifle*

Dictionary
ENGLISH TO ITALIAN

The gender of an Italian noun is shown by the word for *the*: **il** or **lo** (masculine), **la** (feminine), and their plural forms **i** or **gli** (masculine) and **le** (feminine). When **lo** or **la** are abbreviated to **l'** in front of a vowel or **h**, the gender is shown by the abbreviations (m) or (f). Italian adjectives (adj) vary according to the gender and number of the word they describe, and the masculine form is shown here. Adjectives that end in **-o** adopt an **-a** ending in the feminine form. Some adjectives end in **-e** for the masculine and the feminine, changing to **-i** in the plural. In general, plural endings are **-i** for masculine and **-e** for feminine. Those that do not follow this rule are described more fully here.

A

a **un/uno/una/un'**
about: about 16 **circa 16**;
a book about Venice **un libro su Venezia**
accelerator **l'acceleratore** (m)
accident **l'incidente** (m)
accommodations **l'alloggio** (m), **il posto**
accountant **il ragioniere/ la ragioniera**
ache **il dolore**
adaptor **il riduttore**
address **l'indirizzo** (m)
admission charge **il prezzo d'ingresso**
advance (on payment) **l'anticipo** (m); *in advance* (adj) **anticipato**
after **dopo**
afternoon **il pomeriggio**
aftershave **il dopobarba**
again **di nuovo**
against **contro**
agenda **l'ordine del giorno** (m)
AIDS **l'Aids** (f)
air **l'aria** (f)
air conditioning **l'aria condizionata** (f)
aircraft **l'aereo** (m)
airline **la linea aerea**
air mail **via aerea**
air mattress **il materassino gonfiabile**
airport **l'aeroporto** (m)
airport bus **l'autobus navetta** (m)
aisle (in supermarket, etc.) **la corsia**
alarm clock **la sveglia**
alcohol **l'alcol** (m)
all **tutto**; *all the streets* **tutte le strade**; *that's all* **questo è tutto**
allergic (adj) **allergico, allergici** (m pl), **allergiche** (f pl)
allow (verb) **permettere**; *allowed* **permesso**

almost **quasi**
alone (adj) **solo**
Alps **le Alpi**
already **già**
always **sempre**
am: I am (verb) **(io) sono**
ambulance **l'ambulanza** (f)
America **l'America** (f)
American (adj) **americano**
and **e**
ankle **la caviglia**
anniversary **l'anniversario** (m)
another **un altro, un'altra**
answering machine **la segreteria telefonica**
antiques shop **l'antiquario** (m)
antiseptic **l'antisettico** (m)
apartment **l'appartamento** (m)
aperitif **l'aperitivo** (m)
appetite **l'appetito** (m)
apple **la mela**
application form **il modulo per la domanda**
appointment **l'appuntamento** (m)
apricot **l'albicocca** (f)
April **aprile**
architecture **l'architettura** (f)
are: you are (singular, formal) **(Lei) è**; (singular, informal) **(tu) sei**; (plural) **(voi) siete**; *we are* **(noi) siamo**; *they are* **(loro) sono**
arm **il braccio, le braccia** (f pl)
armchair **la poltrona**
arrange (verb) (appointment etc) **fissare**
arrivals **gli arrivi**
arrive (verb) **arrivare**
art **l'arte** (f)
art gallery **la pinacoteca, la galleria d'arte**
artist **l'artista** (m/f)
as: as soon as possible **(il) più presto possibile**
ashtray **il portacenere**
asparagus **gli asparagi**
aspirin **l'aspirina** (f)

asthmatic (adj) **asmatico, asmatici** (m pl), **asmatiche** (f pl)
at: at the post office **all'ufficio postale**; *at night* **di notte**; *at 3 o'clock* **alle tre**
ATM **il bancomat**
attic **la soffitta**
attractive (adj) **attraente**
audience **gli spettatori/ le spettatrici**
August **agosto**
aunt **la zia**
Australia **l'Australia** (f)
Australian (adj) **australiano**
automatic (adj) **automatico, automatici** (m pl), **automatiche** (f pl)
autumn **l'autunno** (m)
away: is it far away? **è lontano?**; *go away!* **vattene!**
awful (adj) **terribile, orribile**

B

baby **il bambino/la bambina**
bachelor's degree **la laurea triennale**
back (not front) **la parte posteriore**; (body) **la schiena**; *to come back* (verb) **tornare**
backpack **lo zaino**
bacon **la pancetta**
bad (adj) **cattivo**
bag **la borsa, il sacchetto**
baggage claim **il ritiro bagagli**
bait **l'esca** (f)
bake (verb) **cuocere (al forno)**
baker **il panificio**
balcony **il balcone**
ball (soccer, etc.) **la palla, il pallone**; (tennis, etc.) **la pallina**
banana **la banana**
band (musicians) **la banda**
bandage **la fascia**

bandage (sticking) **il cerotto**
bank **la banca**
banknote **la banconota**
bar (drinks) **il bar**; *bar of chocolate* **la tavoletta di cioccolata**
barbecue **il barbecue**; (occasion) **la grigliata all'aperto**
barber's (shop) **il barbiere**
bargain **l'affare** (m)
basement **il seminterrato**
basket **il cestino**; (in supermarket) **il cestello**
basketball **la pallacanestro**
bath **il bagno**; (tub) **la vasca**; *to have a bath* (verb) **fare il bagno**
bathroom **il bagno**
battery **la batteria**
be (verb) **essere**
beach **la spiaggia**
beans **i fagioli**
beard **la barba**
beautiful (adj) **bello**
because **perché**
bed **il letto**
bed linen **le lenzuola**
bedroom **la camera (da letto)**
bedspread **il copriletto**
beef **il manzo**
beer **la birra**
before… **prima di…**
beginner **il/la principiante**
beginners' slope **la discesa per principianti**
behind **dietro**; *behind…* **dietro a…**
beige (adj) **beige**
bell (church) **la campana**; (door) **il campanello**
below **sotto**
belt **la cintura**
beside… **vicino a…**
best (adj) **il migliore**
better (than) (adj) **migliore (di)**
between… **fra…**
bicycle **la bicicletta**
big (adj) **grande**
bikini **il bikini**
bill **il conto**
bird **l'uccello** (m)
birthday **il compleanno**; *happy birthday!* **buon compleanno!**
biscuit **il biscotto**
bite (by dog) **il morso**; (by insect) **la puntura**; (verb: by dog) **mordere**; (verb: by insect) **pungere**
bitter (adj) **amaro**
black (adj) **nero**
black currant **il ribes nero**
blanket **la coperta**
bleach **la varechina**; (verb: hair) **ossigenare**

blind (adj) (cannot see) **cieco, ciechi** (m pl), **cieche** (f pl); (window blind) **la tenda avvolgibile**
blond (adj) **biondo**
blood **il sangue**; *blood test* **le analisi del sangue**
blouse **la camicetta**
blue (adj) **azzurro**; (navy blue) **blu**
boarding pass **la carta d'imbarco**
boat **la nave**; (small) **la barca**; (passenger) **il battello**
body **il corpo**
boil (verb: of water) **bollire**; (egg, etc.) **far bollire**
boiled (adj) **lesso**
boiler **la caldaia**
bolt (on door) **il catenaccio**; (verb) **chiudere con il catenaccio**
bone **l'osso** (m); (fish) **la lisca**
book **il libro**; (verb) **prenotare**
booking office **la biglietteria**
bookshop **la libreria**
boot (footware) **lo stivale**
border **il confine**
boring (adj) **noioso**; *that's boring!* **che noia!**
born, to be (verb) **nascere**; *I was born in London* **sono nato/a a Londra**
both of them **tutti e due**; *both… and…* **sia… che…**
bottle **la bottiglia**
bottle opener **l'apribottiglie** (m)
bottom **il fondo**; *at the bottom (of)* **in fondo (a)**
bowl **la scodella, la ciotola**; (mixing bowl) **la terrina**
box **la scatola**; (of wood, etc.) **la cassetta**
box office **il botteghino**
boy **il ragazzo**
bra **il reggiseno**
bracelet **il braccialetto**
brake **il freno**; (verb) **frenare**
branch (of company) **la filiale**
bread **il pane**
breakdown (car) **il guasto**; (nervous) **l'esaurimento nervoso** (m)
breakfast **la colazione**
breathe (verb) **respirare**
bricklayer **il muratore/ la muratrice**
bridge **il ponte**
briefcase **la cartella**
bring (verb) **portare**
British **britannico, britannici** (m pl), **britanniche** (f pl)
brochure **l'opuscolo** (m)
broken (adj) **rotto**; *broken leg* **la gamba rotta**

brooch **la spilla**
brother **il fratello**
brown (adj) **marrone**
bruise **il livido**
brush (hair) **la spazzola**; (paint) **il pennello**; (cleaning) **la scopa**; (verb: hair) **spazzolare**
bucket **il secchio**
budget **il budget**
builder **il costruttore/ la costruttrice**
building **l'edificio** (m)
bumper **il paraurti**
bunker (golf) **il bunker**
burglar **il ladro/la ladra**
burglary **il furto**
burn **la bruciatura**; (verb) **bruciare**
bus **l'autobus** (m)
business **l'affare** (m); *it's none of your business* **non sono affari tuoi**;
business card **il biglietto da visita**
bus station **la stazione degli autobus**
bus stop **la fermata dell'autobus**
busy (adj) (occupied) **occupato**; (bar etc) **animato**
but **ma**
butcher's (shop) **la macelleria**
butter **il burro**
button **il bottone**
buy (verb) **comprare**
by: by the window **vicino alla finestra**; *by Friday* **entro venerdì**; *by myself* **da solo/a**; *written by…* **scritto da…**

C

cabbage **il cavolo**
cable car **la funivia**
cable TV **la TV via cavo**
café **il caffè, il bar**
cage **la gabbia**
cake **la torta**
cake shop **la pasticceria**
calculator **la calcolatrice**
call **la chiamata**; *what's it called?/what are you called?* (formal) **come si chiama?**
camera **la macchina fotografica**
camper van **il camper**
campfire **il falò**
camping gas **il gas da campeggio**
campsite **il campeggio**
camshaft **l'albero a camme** (m)

can (vessel) **la lattina**;
(verb: to be able) *can I
have…?* **posso avere…?**;
can you…? **potreste…?**;
he/she can't… **non può…**
Canada **il Canada**
Canadian (adj) **canadese**
canal **il canale**
candle **la candela**
canoe **la canoa**
can opener **l'apriscatole** (m)
cap (bottle) **il tappo**;
(hat) **il berretto**
car **l'auto** (f), **la macchina**
caravan **la roulotte**
carburettor **il
carburatore**
card (greeting card)
il biglietto di auguri;
playing cards **le carte
da gioco**
careful (adj) **attento**; *be
careful!*; (verb) **stia
attento!**
caretaker **il portinaio/
la portinaia**
car park **il parcheggio**
carpenter **il/la falegname**
carpet **il tappeto**
carrot **la carota**
carry out (verb)
da portare via
car seat (for a baby)
**il seggiolino per la
macchina (per l'auto)**
cart **il carrello**
case (suitcase) **la valigia**
cash **il contante**; **il denaro,
gli spicci**; (verb) **riscuotere**;
to pay cash **pagare in
contanti**
cashier **il cassiere/
la cassiera**
cash machine **lo sportello
automatico**
cashpoint **il bancomat**
cassette **la cassetta**
cassette player **il
mangianastri**
castle **il castello**
cat **il gatto**
cathedral **il duomo,
la cattedrale**
Catholic **cattolico, cattolici**
(m pl), **cattoliche** (f pl)
cauliflower **il cavolfiore**
cave **la grotta**
ceiling **il soffitto**
cellar **la cantina**
cell phone **il cellulare,
il telefonino**
cemetery **il cimitero**
center **il centro**;
city center **il centro
città**
central heating **il
riscaldamento
centralizzato**

certificate
il certificato
certainly **certo**
chair **la sedia**; *swivel chair*
la sedia girevole
change (money) **il cambio,
gli spicci**; (verb: money,
trains) **cambiare**; (clothes)
cambiarsi
charger **il caricabatterie**
charging cable **il cavo di
ricarica**
charging point/station **la
colonnina di ricarica**
cheap (adj) **economico,
economici** (m pl),
economiche (f pl);
a buon mercato
check **l'assegno** (m)
checkbook **il libretto
degli assegni**
check in (verb) **fare il
check-in**
check-in **il check-in**;
check-in desk **lo sportello
del check-in**
checkout **la cassa**
cheers! (toast) **alla salute!,
cin cin!**
cheese **il formaggio**
chef/cook **il cuoco/la cuoca**
chemist **la farmacia**
cherry **la ciliegia**
chess **gli scacchi**
chest (part of body) **il petto**;
(furniture) **il baule**
chest of drawers **il
cassettone**
chewing gum **il chewing-gum,
la gomma da masticare**
chicken **il pollo**
child **il bambino**; (female)
la bambina
children **il bambini/le bambine**;
(own children) **i figli/le figlie**;
children's ward **il reparto
di pediatria**
chimney **il comignolo**
china **la porcellana**
chips **le patatine**
chocolate **la cioccolata**;
box of chocolates **la
scatola di cioccolatini**
chop (food) **la costoletta**;
(verb) **tagliare (a pezzetti)**
Christmas **il Natale**
church **la chiesa**
cigar **il sigaro**
cigarette **la sigaretta**
cinema **il cinema**
circle (in theatre) **la galleria**
city **la città**
city center **il centro città**
class **la classe**
classical music **la musica
classica**
clean (adj) **pulito**; (verb)
pulire

cleaning staff **il personale
delle pulizie**
clear (adj) (obvious) **chiaro**;
(water) **limpido**
clever (adj) **bravo,
intelligente**
client **il/la cliente**
clock **l'orologio** (m)
close (adj) (near) **vicino (a)**;
(stuffy) **soffocante**; (verb)
chiudere
closed (adj) **chiuso**
clothes **i vestiti**
clothespin **la molletta**
clubs (cards) **i fiori**
clutch **la frizione**
coach (long-distance bus)
il pullman
coat **il cappotto**
coat hanger
l'attaccapanni (m)
cocktail party **l'aperitivo** (m)
coffee **il caffè**
coin **la moneta**
cold (illness) **il raffreddore**;
(adj) **freddo**; *I have a cold*
ho un raffreddore
collar **il colletto**; (for dog)
il collare
colleague **il/la collega**
collection (stamps, etc.)
la collezione; (postal)
la levata
color **il colore**
color film **il rullino a colori**
comb **il pettine**; (verb)
pettinare
come (verb) **venire**;
I come from…
sono di…; *come here!*
(informal/formal) **vieni/
venga qui!**; *come with me*
(informal/formal) **vieni/
venga con me**
compact disc **il compact
disc**
compartment **lo
scompartimento**
complicated (adj)
complicato
computer **il computer**;
computer games
i videogiochi
concert **il concerto**
concessionary rate **la tariffa
ridotta**
conditioner (hair) **il balsamo**
condom **il preservativo**
conductor (bus) **il
bigliettaio/la bigliettaia**;
(orchestra) **il direttore/
la direttrice**
conference **la conferenza**;
conference room **la sala
conferenze**
congratulations!
congratulazioni!
connection **la coincidenza**

consulate **il consolato**

consultant **il/la consulente**

contact lenses **le lenti a contatto**

contactless payment **il pagamento contactless**

contraceptive **il contraccettivo**

contract **il contratto**

cook/chef **il cuoco/la cuoca**; (verb) **cucinare**

cooker **il fornello**

cool (adj) **fresco, freschi** (m pl), **fresche** (f pl)

cork **il tappo**

corkscrew **il cavatappi**

corner **l'angolo** (m)

corridor **il corridoio**

cosmetics **i cosmetici**

cost (verb) **costare**; what does it cost? **quanto costa?**

cot **il lettino**

cotton **il cotone**

cotton wool **il cotone idrofilo**

cough **la tosse**; (verb) **tossire**

countertop **il piano di lavoro**

country (state) **il paese**; (not town) **la campagna**

course (educational) **il corso**

cousin **il cugino/la cugina**

crab **il granchio**

cramp **il crampo**

crayfish **il gambero**

crazy (adj) **pazzo**

cream (dairy) **la crema, la panna**; (lotion) **la crema**

credit card **la carta di credito**

crew **l'equipaggio** (m)

croissant **la brioche**

crowded (adj) **affollato**

cruise **la crociera**

crutches **le stampelle**

cry (verb: weep) **piangere**; (verb: shout) **gridare**

cucumber **il cetriolo**

cuff links **i gemelli**

cup **la tazza**

cupboard **l'armadio** (m)

curlers **i bigodini**

curls **i ricci**

curtain **la tenda**

cushion **il cuscino**

customs **la dogana**

cut **il taglio**; (verb) **tagliare**

cycling **il ciclismo**

D

dad **il papà, il babbo**

dairy **la latteria**; dairy products **i latticini**

damp (adj) **umido**

dance **il ballo**; (verb) **ballare**

dangerous (adj) **pericoloso**

dark (adj) **scuro**

daughter **la figlia**

day **il giorno**

dead (adj) **morto**

deaf (adj) **sordo**

dear (adj) **caro**

debit card **la carta di debito**

December **dicembre**

decorator **l'imbianchino/a**

deep (adj) **profondo**

degree: I have a degree in… **sono laureato/a in…**

delayed (adj) **in ritardo**

deliberately **deliberatamente**

delicatessen **la salumeria**

delivery **la consegna**

dentist **il/la dentista**

dentures **la dentiera**

deodorant **il deodorante**

department **il reparto**

department store **il grande magazzino**

departure **la partenza**; departures **le partenze**; departure lounge **la sala d'attesa**

designer **il grafico/la grafica**

desk **la scrivania**

desserts **i dessert**

develop (verb) (film) **sviluppare**

diabetic (adj) **diabetico, diabetici** (m pl), **diabetiche** (f pl)

diamond (jewel) **il diamante**

diamonds (cards) **i quadri**

diapers **i pannolini**

diarrhea **la diarrea**

diary **l'agenda** (f)

dictionary **il dizionario**

die (verb) **morire**

diesel **il gasolio**

different (adj) **diverso**; that's different! **è diverso!**; I'd like a different one **ne vorrei un altro**

difficult (adj) **difficile**

dining room **la sala da pranzo**

dinner **la cena**

directory (telephone) **la guida telefonica**

dirty (adj) **sporco, sporchi** (m pl), **sporche** (f pl)

disabled (adj) (people) **le persone disabili**

discount **la riduzione**

dishtowel **lo strofinaccio**

dishwasher **la lavastoviglie**

dishwashing liquid **il detersivo per i piatti**

dive **il tuffo**; (verb) **tuffarsi**

diving board **il trampolino**

divorced (adj) **divorziato**

do (verb) **fare**; how do you do? **piacere di conoscerla**; what do you do? **che lavoro fa?**

dock **il molo**

doctor (academic) **il dottore/la dottoressa**; (medical) **il/la medico**

document **il documento**

dog **il cane**; dog basket **la cuccia**; dog bowl **la ciotola del cane**; guide dog **il cane guida**

doll **la bambola**

dollar **il dollaro**

door **la porta**; (of car) **lo sportello**

double room **la matrimoniale, la camera doppia**

doughnut **il krapfen**

down **giù**

drawer **il cassetto**

dress **il vestito**

drink **la bibita**; (verb) **bere**; would you like a drink? **vorresti qualcosa da bere?**

drinking water **l'acqua potabile** (f)

drive (verb) **guidare**

driver **il guidatore/la guidatrice**; (of bus, truck, etc.) **l'autista** (m/f)

driver's license **la patente (di guida)**

driveway **il viale**

drops **le gocce**

drunk (adj) **ubriaco, ubriachi** (m pl), **ubriache** (f pl)

dry (adj) **asciutto**; (wine) **secco** dry cleaner's **la lavanderia a secco**

during **durante**

dustbin **la pattumiera**

duster **lo straccio per la polvere**

duvet **il piumino**

E

each (every) **ogni**; twenty euros each **venti euro ciascuno**

ear **l'orecchio** (m); ears **le orecchie**

early **presto**; see you soon **a presto**

earphones **gli auricolari**

earrings **gli orecchini**

east **l'est** (m)

easy (adj) **facile**

eat (verb) **mangiare**

egg **l'uovo** (m), **le uova** (f pl)

eight **otto**

eighteen **diciotto**

eighty **ottanta**

either: either of them **l'uno/a o l'altro/a**

elastic (adj) **elastico**

elbow **il gomito**

electric (adj) **elettrico,
elettrici** (m pl)**, elettriche**
(f pl); electrical hook-up **la
presa di corrente**
electrician **il/la elettricista**
electricity **l'elettricità** (f)
eleven **undici**
else: something else
qualcos'altro; someone else
qualcun'altro; somewhere
else **da qualche altra parte**
e-mail **l'email** (f),
la posta elettronica
e-mail address **l'indirizzo
di posta elettronica** (m)
embarrassing (adj)
imbarazzante
embassy **l'ambasciata** (f)
emergency **l'emergenza** (f)
emergency exit **l'uscita
di sicurezza** (f)
emergency department
il pronto soccorso
empty (adj) **vuoto**
end **la fine**
engaged (adj) (to be married)
fidanzato/fidanzata;
(telephone, toilet) **occupato**
engine (car) **il motore**; (train)
la locomotiva
engineer **l'ingegnere** (m/f)
engineering **l'ingegneria** (f)
England **l'Inghilterra** (f)
English (adj) **inglese**
enlargement
l'ampliamento (m)
enough **abbastanza**
entrance **l'entrata** (f)
entrance ticket **il biglietto**
envelope **la busta**
epileptic (adj) **epilettico**
eraser **la gomma**
escalator **la scala mobile**
especially **particolarmente**
estate agent **l'agente
immobiliare** (m/f)
estimate **il preventivo**
evening **la sera**
every **ogni**; every day **tutti
i giorni**
everyone **ognuno, tutti**
everything **tutto**
everywhere **dappertutto**
example **l'esempio** (m);
for example **per esempio**
excellent (adj) **ottimo,
eccellente**
excess baggage **il bagaglio
in eccesso**
exchange (verb) **scambiare**
exchange rate **il** (**tasso di**)
cambio
excursion **l'escursione** (f)
excuse (verb) **scusare**; excuse
me! (to get attention)
mi scusi!; (when sneezing)
scusate!; (to get past)
permesso!

executive **il/la dirigente**
exhaust (car) **la marmitta**
exhibition **la mostra**
exit **l'uscita** (f)
expensive (adj) **caro, costoso**
extension lead **la prolunga**
eye **l'occhio** (m); eyes
gli occhi
eyebrow **il sopracciglio,
le sopracciglia** (f pl)

F

face **la faccia**
face mask **la maschera**
faint (adj) (unclear)
indistinto; (verb) **svenire**
fair (carnival) **il luna park**;
(trade) **la fiera**
(**commerciale**); (adj) it's
not fair **non è giusto**
false teeth **la dentiera**
family **la famiglia**
fan (ventilator) **il
ventilatore**; (enthusiast)
l'ammiratrice (f)
fan belt **la cinghia della
ventola**
fantastic (adj) **fantastico,
fantastici** (m pl)**,
fantastiche** (f pl)
far (adj) **lontano**; how far is it
to...? **quanto dista
da qui...?**
fare **il biglietto, la tariffa**
farm **la fattoria**
farmer **l'agricoltore** (m/f)
fashion **la moda**
fast (adj) **veloce**
fat **il grasso**; (adj) **grasso**
father **il padre**
February **febbraio**
feel (verb) (touch) **tastare**; I
feel hot **ho caldo**; I feel
like... **ho voglia di...**; I
don't feel good **non mi
sento bene**
fence **lo steccato**
fennel **il finocchio**
ferry **il traghetto**
fever **la febbre**
fiancé **il fidanzato**
fiancée **la fidanzata**
field **il campo**
fifteen **quindici**
fifty **cinquanta**
figures **le cifre**
filling (in tooth)
l'otturazione (f); (in
sandwich, cake, etc.)
il ripieno
film (for camera) **la pellicola**;
(at the cinema) **il film**
filter **il filtro**
fine! **benissimo!**
finger **il dito, le dita** (f pl)
fire **il fuoco**; (blaze)
l'incendio (m)

fire extinguisher
l'estintore (m)
fireplace **il caminetto**
fireworks **i fuochi d'artificio**
first **primo**; first class
prima classe
first aid **il pronto soccorso**
first floor **il primo piano**
first name **il nome
di battesimo**
fish **il pesce**
fishing **la pesca**; (verb) to go
fishing **andare a pesca**
fishmonger's (shop)
la pescheria
five **cinque**
fizzy (adj) **frizzante**
fizzy water **l'acqua
gassata** (f)
flag **la bandiera**
flash (camera) **il flash**
flat (adj) (level) **piatto**;
(apartment)
l'appartamento (m)
flavor **il gusto**
flea **la pulce**
flight **il volo**; flight number
il numero del volo
flip-flops **gli infradito**
flippers **le pinne**
floor (ground) **il pavimento**;
(story) **il piano**
Florence **Firenze**
flour **la farina**
flower **il fiore**; flower bed
l'aiuola (f)
flute **il flauto**
fly (insect) **la mosca**; (verb)
volare; I'm flying to
London **vado a Londra
in aereo**
flyover **il cavalcavia**
fly sheet **il telo protettivo**
fog **la nebbia**
folk music **la musica folk**
food **il cibo**
food poisoning **l'intossicazione
alimentare** (f)
foot **il piede**; on foot **a piedi**
for **per**; for me **per me**; what
for? **perché?**
forbidden (adj) **proibito**
foreigner **lo straniero/
la straniera, il forestiero/
la forestiera**
forest **la foresta**
forget (verb) **dimenticare**
fork (for food) **la forchetta**
forty **quaranta**
fountain **la fontana**
four **quattro**
fourteen **quattordici**
fourth **quarto**
fracture **la frattura**
France **la Francia**
free (adj) (not occupied)
libero; (no charge)
gratuito, gratis

freezer **il congelatore**
French (adj) **francese**
Friday **venerdì**
fridge **il frigorifero**
fried (adj) **fritto**
friend **l'amico**;
    (female) **l'amica**
friendly (adj) **cordiale**
frightened, to be (verb)
    avere paura; I'm
    frightened **ho paura**
front: in front of you **davanti**
    a te
frost **il gelo**
frozen foods **i surgelati**
fruit **la frutta**
fruit juice **il succo di frutta**
fry (verb) **friggere**
frying pan **la padella**
full (adj) **pieno**; I'm full (up)
    sono sazio/a
full board **la pensione**
    completa
funny (adj) **divertente**; (adj:
    odd) **strano**
furniture **i mobili**

G

garage **il garage**
garden **il giardino**; garden
    center **il vivaio**
gardener **il giardiniere** (m/f)
garlic **l'aglio** (m)
gas **la benzina**
gas-permeable lenses
    le lenti semi-rigide
gas station **il benzinaio,**
    la stazione di servizio
gate **il cancello**; (at airport)
    l'uscita (f)
gay (adj) (homosexual)
    omosessuale, gay
gear stick **la leva**
    del cambio
gel (hair) **il gel**
Genoa **Genova**
German (adj) **tedesco,**
    tedeschi (m pl), **tedesche**
    (f pl)
Germany **la Germania**
get (verb: obtain) **ricevere**;
    (verb: fetch: person)
    chiamare; (something)
    prendere; have you got...?
    ha...?; to get the train
    prendere il treno
get back: we get back
    tomorrow (verb) **torniamo**
    domani; to get something
    back **riavere indietro**
    qualcosa
get in (verb) **entrare**; (arrive)
    arrivare
get off (verb) (bus, etc.)
    scendere (**da**)
get on (verb) (bus, etc.)
    salire (**su**)

get out (verb) **uscire** (**da**)
get up (verb) **alzarsi**
gift **il regalo**
gin **il gin**
ginger (spice) **lo zenzero**
girl **la ragazza**
give (verb) **dare**; give way
    dare la precedenza
glad (adj) **contento**
glass (material) **il vetro**;
    (for drinking) **il bicchiere**
glasses **gli occhiali**
gloves **i guanti**
glue **la colla**
go (verb) **andare**; (depart)
    partire
go out (verb) **uscire**: he's
    gone out **è uscito**
gold **l'oro** (m)
golf **il golf**
golfer **il/la golfista**
good (adj) **buono**; good! **bene!**
goodbye **arrivederci**
good day **buongiorno**
good evening **buonasera**
good night **buonanotte**
government **il governo**
granddaughter **la nipote**
grandfather **il nonno**
grandmother **la nonna**
grandparents **i nonni**
grandson **il nipote**
grapes **l'uva** (f)
grass **l'erba** (f)
gray (adj) **grigio**
great! **benissimo!**
Great Britain **la Gran**
    Bretagna
Greece **la Grecia**
Greek (adj) **greco, greci**
    (m pl), **greche** (f pl)
green (adj) **verde**
grill **la griglia**
grilled (adj) **alla griglia**
grocery (shop) **gli**
    alimentari
ground floor **il pianterreno**
ground sheet **il telo per**
    campeggio
guarantee **la garanzia**;
    (verb) **garantire**
guard **la guardia**
guest **l'ospite** (m/f)
guide (person) **la guida**
guidebook **la guida**
guitar **la chitarra**
gun (rifle) **il fucile**; (pistol)
    la pistola
gutter **la grondaia**
guy rope **la corda**
gymnastics **la palestra**

H

hair **i capelli**
haircut **il taglio**
hairdresser **il parrucchiere/**
    la parrucchiera

hair dryer **il phon**
hairspray **la lacca**
    per i capelli
half **metà**; half an hour
    mezz'ora; half board
    mezza pensione;
    half past... **...e mezza**
ham **il prosciutto**
hamburger **l'hamburger** (m)
hammer **il martello**
hamster **il criceto**
hand **la mano**; hand luggage
    il bagaglio a mano
hand brake **il freno a mano**
hand sanitizer **l'igienizzante**
    per le mani (m)
handle (door) **la maniglia**
handshake **la stretta**
    di mano
handsome (adj) **bello,**
    attraente
hangover **i postumi**
    della sbornia
happy (adj) **felice, contento**
harbor **il porto**
hard (adj) **duro**; (difficult)
    difficile
hardware store **la**
    ferramenta
hat **il cappello**
have (verb) **avere**; I don't
    have... **non ho...**; do you
    have...? **ha...?**; I have to go
    now **devo andare adesso**
he **lui**
head **la testa**
headache **il mal di testa**
headlights **i fari**
headphones **le cuffie**
hear (verb) **udire, sentire**
hearing aid **l'apparecchio**
    acustico (m); hearing loop
    circuito uditivo (m)
heart **il cuore**
heart condition **il disturbi**
    cardiaci
hearts (cards) **i cuori**
heater **il termosifone**
heating **il riscaldamento**
heavy (adj) **pesante**
hedge **la siepe**
heel (of foot) **il tallone**;
    (of shoe) **il tacco**
hello **ciao, buongiorno**;
    (on phone) **pronto**
help **l'aiuto** (m); (verb)
    aiutare; can I help
    you? **dica?**
her **lei, suo, sua, suoi, sue**;
    it's for her **è per lei**; her
    book **il suo libro**; her
    house **la sua casa**; her
    shoes **le sue scarpe**; her
    dresses **i suoi vestiti**;
    it's hers **è suo**
herbal tea **la tisana**
here **qui**
here you are/here it is **ecco**

hi! **Ciao!**
high (adj) **alto**
hiking **l'escursionismo**
hill **la collina**
him: it's for him **è per lui**;
   give it to him
   daglielo
his **suo, sua, suoi, sue**; *his book*
   l suo libro; *his house* **la sua**
   casa; *his shoes* **le sue**
   scarpe; *his socks* **i suoi**
   calzini; *it's his* **è suo**
history **la storia**
hitchhike (verb) **fare l'autostop**
HIV-positive (adj) **HIV positivo**
hobby **il passatempo,**
   l'hobby (m)
holiday **la vacanza**; *public*
   holiday **il giorno festivo**
home: at home **a casa**
homeopathy **l'omeopatia** (f)
honest (adj) **onesto**
honey **il miele**
honeymoon **la luna di miele**
hood (car) **il cofano**
horn (car) **il clacson**;
   (animal) **il corno**
horrible (adj) **orribile**
hose **il tubo**
hospital **l'ospedale** (m);
   (attached to university)
   le Aziende Ospedaliere
   Universitarie
host **il padrone di casa**;
   hostess **la padrona**
   di casa
hot (adj) **caldo**
hour **l'ora** (f); *visiting hours*
   l'orario di visita (f)
house **la casa**
household products **gli**
   articoli per la casa
housekeeping **il personale**
   ai piani
how? **come?**
how much? **quanto costa?**;
   how much is that? **quant'è?**
hundred **cento**; *three*
   hundred **trecento**
hungry: I'm hungry (adj) **ho**
   fame
hurry (verb) **affrettarsi**; *I'm*
   in a hurry **ho fretta**
hurry up! **sbrigati!**
hurt (verb) **fare male**; *my...*
   hurts **mi fa male il/la...**; *will*
   it hurt? **farà male?**
husband **il marito**

I

I **io**
ice **il ghiaccio**
ice cream **il gelato**
ice cream parlour **la gelateria**
ice skates **i pattini da ghiaccio**
identification **il documento**
   d'identità

if **se**
ignition **l'accensione** (f)
ill (adj) **malato**
immediately
   immediatamente
impossible **impossibile**
in: in English **in inglese**;
   in the hotel **nell'albergo**;
   in Venice **a Venezia**
included (adj) **incluso**
indicator **la freccia,**
   l'indicatore di direzione (m)
indigestion **l'indigestione** (f)
infection **l'infezione** (f)
information **le informazioni**;
information technology
   l'informatica (f)
inhaler (for asthma, etc.)
   l'inalatore (m)
injection **l'iniezione** (f)
injury **la ferita**
ink **l'inchiostro** (m)
in-laws **i suoceri**
inner tube **la camera d'aria**
insect **l'insetto** (m)
insect repellent
   l'insettifugo (m)
insomnia **l'insonnia** (f)
instant coffee **il caffè**
   solubile
insurance **l'assicurazione** (f)
interesting (adj)
   interessante
internet **l'internet** (f)
interpret (verb) **interpretare**
interpreter **l'interprete** (m/f)
intravenous drip **la flebo**
invitation **l'invito** (m)
invoice **la fattura**
Ireland **l'Irlanda** (f)
Irish (adj) **irlandese**
iron (material) **il ferro**;
   (for clothes) **il ferro da**
   stiro; (verb) **stirare**
is: he/she/it is... **(lui/lei/**
   esso/a) è...
island **l'isola** (f)
it **esso/essa** (m/f)
Italian (adj) **italiano**
Italy **Italia**
its **suo/sua, suoi/sue**

J

jacket **la giacca**
jam **la marmellata**
January **gennaio**
jazz **il jazz**
jeans **i jeans**
jellyfish **la medusa**
jeweler **il gioielliere/**
   la gioielliera
job **il lavoro**
jog (verb) **fare jogging**;
   to go jogging **andare a**
   fare jogging
jogging **il jogging**
joke **lo scherzo**

journey **il viaggio**
July **luglio**
junction **l'incrocio** (m)
June **giugno**
just (only) **solo**; *it's just*
   arrived **è appena arrivato**

K

kettle **il bollitore**
key **la chiave**
keyboard **la tastiera**
kidney **il rene**
kilo **il chilo**
kilometer **il chilometro**
kitchen **la cucina**
knee **il ginocchio, i ginocchi**
   (m pl), **le ginocchia** (f pl)
knife **il coltello**
knit (verb) **lavorare a**
   maglia
knitwear **la maglieria**
know (verb) **sapere**; (person)
   conoscere; *I don't know*
   non so

L

label **l'etichetta** (f)
lace **il pizzo**
laces (of shoe) **i lacci**
lady **la signora**
lake **il lago**
lamb **l'agnello** (m)
lamp **la lampada**
lampshade **il paralume**
land **la terra**; (verb) **atterrare**
language **la lingua**
laptop (computer) **il**
   computer portatile
large (adj) **grande**
last (adj: final) **ultimo**;
   last week **la settimana**
   scorsa; *at last!*
   finalmente! *last name*
   il cognome
late: it's getting late (adj) **si**
   sta facendo tardi; *the bus*
   is late **l'autobus è**
   in ritardo
later **più tardi**
laugh (verb) **ridere**
laundry (place) **la lavanderia**;
   (dirty clothes) **la**
   biancheria
law **la legge**
lawn **il prato**; *lawnmower*
   il tosaerba
lawyer **l'avvocato** (m/f)
laxative **il lassativo**
lazy (adj) **pigro**
leaf **la foglia**
leaflet **il volantino**
learn (verb) **imparare**
leash (for dog) **il guinzaglio**
leather **la pelle, il cuoio**;
   leather goods shop **la**
   pelletteria

lecture hall **l'aula delle lezioni** (f)
left (adj: not right) **sinistra**; *there's nothing left* **non c'è rimasto più nulla**
left luggage locker **il deposito bagagli**
leg **la gamba**
lemon **il limone**
lemonade **la limonata**
length **la lunghezza**
lens **la lente**
less **meno**
lesson **la lezione**
letter **la lettera**
lettuce **la lattuga**
library **la biblioteca**
license **la patente**
license plate **la targa**
life **la vita**
lift **l'ascensore** (m)
light **la luce**; (adj) (not heavy) **leggero**; (not dark) **chiaro**
light bulb **la lampadina**
lighter **l'accendino** (m)
lighter fuel **il gas per accendini**
light meter **l'esposimetro** (m)
like (verb) **piacere**; *I like…* **mi piace…**; *it's like…* **assomiglia a…**; *like this one* **come questo**
lime (fruit) **il limoncello**
line (telephone, etc.) **la linea**; *outside line* **la linea esterna**
lipstick **il rossetto**
liqueur **il liquore**
list **l'elenco** (m)
literature **la letteratura**
litre **il litro**
litter (bin) **i rifiuti**
little (adj: small) **piccolo**; *it's a little big* **è un po' grande**; *just a little* **solo un po'**
liver **il fegato**
living room **il soggiorno**
lollipop **il lecca lecca**
long (adj) **lungo, lunghi** (m pl), **lunghe** (f pl); *how long does it take?* **quanto ci vuole?**
long-distance (call) **l'interurbana** (f)
lost: I'm lost (adj) **mi sono persa**
lost property **l'ufficio oggetti smarriti** (m)
lot: a lot **molto**
loud (adj) **forte**
love (verb) **amare**
low (adj) **basso**
luck **la fortuna**; *good luck!* **buona fortuna!**
luggage **i bagagli**
luggage rack **la reticella (per i bagagli)**
lunch **il pranzo**

M

madam **la signora**
magazine **la rivista**
mailbox **la cassetta delle lettere**
mailman/woman **il/la postino/a**
main courses **i secondi piatti**
make (verb) **fare**
makeup **il trucco**
man **l'uomo** (m); *men* **gli uomini**
manager **il direttore/la direttrice**
many (adj) **molti**; *not many* **non molti**
map **la carta (geografica)**; (of town) **la pianta**; (online) **le mappe online**
marble **il marmo**
March **marzo**
margarine **la margarina**
market **il mercato**
marmalade **la marmellata d'arance**
married (adj) **sposato**
mascara **il mascara**
Mass (church) **la messa**
mast **l'albero** (m)
master's degree **la laurea magistrale**
match (light) **il fiammifero**; (sport) **l'incontro** (m)
material (cloth) **la stoffa**
matter (verb) **importare**; *it doesn't matter* **non importa**; *what's the matter?* **cosa c'è?**
mattress **il materasso**
May **maggio**
maybe **forse**
me: it's me **sono io**; *it's for me* **è per me**
meal **il pasto**
mean (verb) **significare**; *what does this mean?* **che cosa significa?**
meat **la carne**
mechanic **il meccanico/la meccanica**
medicine **la medicina**
Mediterranean **il Mediterraneo**
meeting **la riunione, l'incontro** (m)
melon **il melone**
menu **il menù**
message **il messaggio**
microwave **il forno a microonde**
middle: in the middle of the square **in mezzo alla piazza**; *in the middle of the night* **nel cuore della notte**
midnight **mezzanotte**
Milan **Milano**
milk **il latte**

million **milione**
mine: it's mine (adj) **è mio/a miei/mie**
mineral water **l'acqua minerale** (f)
minute **il minuto**
mirror **lo specchio**
mistake **l'errore** (m)
modem **il modem**
Monday **lunedì**
money **i soldi**
monitor (computer) **il monitor, lo schermo**
month **il mese**
monument **il monumento**
moon **la luna**
moped **il motorino**
more **più**; *more than…* **più di…**
morning **la mattina**; *in the morning* **di mattina**
mosaic **il mosaico**
mosquito **la zanzara**
mother **la madre**
motorboat **il motoscafo**
motorcycle **la motocicletta**
motorway **l'autostrada** (f)
mountain **la montagna**
mountain bike **la mountain bike**
mouse (animal) **il topo**; (computer) **il mouse**
mousse (for hair) **la schiuma**
moustache **i baffi**
mouth **la bocca**
move (verb) **muovere**; *don't move!* **non muoverti!**
move house (verb) **traslocare**
Mr. **Signor**
Mrs. **Signora**
much **molto**; *much better* **molto meglio**; *much slower* **molto più lentamente**; *not much* **non molto**
mug **la tazza**
mum **la mamma**
museum **il museo**
mushroom **il fungo**
music **la musica**
musical instrument **lo strumento musicale**
musician **il/la musicista**
music system **lo stereo**
mussels **le cozze**
must (to have to) (verb) **dovere**; *I must* **devo**
mustard **la senape**
my **mio, mia, miei, mie**; *my book* **il mio libro**; *my bag* **la mia borsa**; *my dresses* **i miei vestiti**; *my keys* **le mie chiavi**

N

nail (metal) **il chiodo**; (finger) **l'unghia** (f)
nail clippers **il tagliaunghie**

nail file **la limetta per le unghie**
nail polish **lo smalto per le unghie**
name **il nome**; *what's your name?* **come si chiama/ti chiami?** *(formal/informal)*; *my name's...* **mi chiamo...**
napkin **il tovagliolo**
Naples **Napoli**
narrow *(adj)* **stretto**
near *(adj)* **vicino**; *near...* **vicino a...**
necessary *(adj)* **necessario, obbligatorio**
neck **il collo**
necklace **la collana**
need *(verb)* **avere bisogno**; *I need...* **ho bisogno di...**; *there's no need* **non c'è bisogno**
needle **l'ago** (m)
negative *(photo)* **il negativo**; *(adj)* **negativo**
nephew **il nipote**
never **mai**
new *(adj)* **nuovo**
news **le notizie**; *(on radio)* **il notiziario**
newsagent's *(shop)* **l'edicola** (f)
newspaper **il giornale**
New Zealand **la Nuova Zelanda**
New Zealander *(adj)* **neozelandese**
next *(adj)* **prossimo**; *next week* **la settimana prossima**; *what next?* **e poi?**; *who's next?* **a chi tocca?**
nice *(adj: attractive)* **carino, bello**; *(pleasant)* **simpatico, simpatici (m pl), simpatiche (f pl)**; *(to eat)* **buono**
niece **la nipote**
night **la notte**
nightclub **il nightclub**
nightdress **la camicia da notte**
nine **nove**
nineteen **diciannove**
ninety **novanta**
no *(negative response)* **no**; *I have no money* **non ho soldi**
nobody **nessuno**
no entry **il divieto di accesso**
noisy *(adj)* **rumoroso**
noon **il mezzogiorno**
north **il nord**
Northern Ireland **l'Irlanda del Nord** (f)
nose **il naso**
not **non**; *he's not...* **non è...**
notebook **il quaderno**
notepad **il bloc-notes**
nothing **niente**

novel **il romanzo**
November **novembre**
now **ora, adesso**
nowhere **da nessuna parte**
number **il numero**
nurse **l'infermiere/ l'infermiera**
nut **la noce, la nocciola**; *(for bolt)* **il dado**

O

oars **i remi**
occasionally **ogni tanto**
occupied *(adj)* **occupato**
o'clock: *one o'clock* **l'una**; *two o'clock* **le due**
October **ottobre**
octopus **la piovra, il polipo**
of **di**
office **l'ufficio** (m), **la direzione**; *office worker* **l'impiegato/a**; *head office* **la sede centrale**
often **spesso**
oil **l'olio** (m)
ointment **la pomata, l'unguento** (m)
OK **OK**
old *(adj)* **vecchio**; *how old are you?* **quanti anni hai?**
olive **l'oliva** (f)
olive oil **l'olio d'oliva** (m)
omelet **l'omelette** (f)
on **su**; *a book on Venice* **un libro su Venezia**; *on Monday* **di lunedì**
one **uno**
one way **il senso unico**
onion **la cipolla**
only **solo**
open *(adj)* **aperto**; *(verb)* **aprire**
opera **l'opera** (f)
operating room **la sala operatoria**
operation **l'operazione** (f)
operator **l'operatore/ l'operatrice** (m/f)
opposite **davanti a**
optician **l'ottico/a**
or **o**
orange *(fruit)* **l'arancia** (f); *(adj) (color)* **arancione**
orange juice **il succo d'arancia**
orchestra **l'orchestra** (f)
order *(for goods)* **l'ordinativo** (m), **l'ordine** (m)
ordinary *(adj)* **normale**
organ *(music)* **l'organo** (m)
other **altro** (m), **altra** (f), **altri** (m pl), **altre** (f pl); *the other (one)* **l'altro/a**
our **nostro/a nostri/e**; *our hotel* **il nostro albergo**; *our car* **la nostra macchina**; *it's ours* **è nostro**

outside **fuori**
oven **il forno**
over *(above)* **su, sopra**; *over 100* **più di cento**; *over the river* **al di là del fiume**; *it's over (finished)* **è finito**; *over there* **laggiù**

P

pacifier **il ciuccio**
pack *(of cards)* **il mazzo di carte**
package, packet **il pacchetto**
padlock **il lucchetto**
Padua **Padova**
page **la pagina**
pain **il dolore**
paint **la vernice**
painting **la pittura**
pair **il paio**
pajamas **il pigiama**
palace **il palazzo**
pale *(adj)* **pallido**
paper **la carta**; *(newspaper)* **il giornale**
pants **i pantaloni**
paraffin **la paraffina**
parcel **il pacco**
pardon? **prego?**
parents **i genitori**
park **il parco**; *(verb)* **parcheggiare**; *no parking* **la sosta vietata**
parking lights **le luci di posizione**
parsley **il prezzemolo**
parting *(hair)* **la riga**
party *(celebration)* **la festa**; *(group)* **il gruppo**; *(political)* **il partito**
pass *(verb) (driving)* **sorpassare**
passenger **il/la passeggero/a**
passport **il passaporto**; *passport control* **il controllo passaporti**
password **la password**
pasta **la pasta**
path **il vialetto, il sentiero**
pavement **il marciapiede**
pay *(verb)* **pagare**
payment **il pagamento**
peach **la pesca**
peanuts **le arachidi**
pear **la pera**
pearl **la perla**
peas **i piselli**
pedestrian **il pedone**
pedestrian zone **la zona pedonale**
peg *(tent)* **il picchetto**
pen **la penna**
pencil **la matita**
pencil sharpener **il temperamatite**
penicillin **la penicillina**

penknife **il temperino**
pen pal **il/la corrispondente**
people **la gente**
pepper (spice) **il pepe**; (vegetable) **il peperone**
peppermint **la menta piperita**
per: per person **a persona**; *per annum* **all'anno**
perfect (adj) **perfetto**
perfume **il profumo**
perhaps **magari, forse**
perm **la permanente**
PhD **il dottorato di ricerca**
photocopier **la fotocopiatrice**
photograph **la fotografia**; (verb) **fotografare**
photographer **il fotografo/ la fotografa**
phrase book **il vocabolarietto**
pickpocket **il borseggiatore/ la borseggiatrice**
picnic **il picnic**
piece **il pezzo**
pillow **il guanciale**
PIN **il pin, il codice segreto**
pin **lo spillo**
pineapple **l'ananas** (m)
pink (adj) **rosa**
pipe (for smoking) **la pipa**; (for water) **il tubo**
piston **il pistone**
pitch (in campsite, etc.) **la piazzola**
place **il posto**; *at your place* **a casa tua**
plans **i piani, i progetti**
plant **la pianta**
plastic **la plastica**
plastic bag **il sacchetto di plastica**
plate **il piatto**
platform **il binario**
play (theater) **la commedia**; (verb) **giocare, suonare**
please **per favore**
pleased to meet you **piacere**
plug (electrical) **la spina**; (sink) **il tappo**
plumber **l'idraulico** (m/f)
pocket **la tasca**
poison **il veleno**
police **la polizia**; *military police* **i carabinieri**
police officer **il poliziotto/ la poliziotta**
police report **il rapporto di polizia**
police station **la stazione di polizia**
politics **la politica**
poor (adj) **povero**
poor quality (adj) **di cattiva qualità**
pop music **la musica pop**
Pope **il Papa**

pork **la carne di maiale**
port **il porto**
porter (hotel) **il portiere** (m/f)
possible (adj) **possibile**
post **la posta**; (verb) **spedire per posta**
postcard **la cartolina**
post code **il codice postale**
post office **l'ufficio postale** (m)
potato **la patata**
poultry **il pollame**
potato chips **le patatine fritte**
pound (weight) **la libbra**; (currency) **la sterlina**
powdered detergent **il detersivo in polvere**
prefer (verb) **preferire**
pregnant **incinta, incinte** (f pl)
prescription **la ricetta**
presentation **la conferenza**
pretty (adj) (beautiful) **grazioso, carino**; (quite) **piuttosto**
price **il prezzo**
priest **il prete**
printer **la stampante**
private (adj) **privato**
problem **il problema**; *no problem* **non c'è problema**
profits **i profitti**
public (adj) **pubblico, pubblici** (m pl), **pubbliche** (f pl)
pull (verb) **tirare**
puncture **la foratura**
purple (adj) **viola**
purse **il portafoglio**
push (verb) **spingere**
put (verb) **mettere**

Q

quality **la qualità**
quarter **il quarto**; *quarter past…* **…e un quarto**
question **la domanda**
queue **la fila**; (verb) **fare la fila**
quick (adj) **veloce**
quiet (adj) **tranquillo**
quite (fairly) **abbastanza**; (fully) **molto**

R

rabbit **il coniglio**
radiator **il radiatore**
radio **la radio**
radish **il ravanello**
railway **la ferrovia**
rain **la pioggia**
raincoat **l'impermeabile** (m)
raisins **l'uvetta** (f)
rake **il rastrello**
rare ((adj) uncommon) **raro**; (meat) **al sangue**

rash **l'arrossamento** (m)
raspberry **il lampone**
rat **il ratto**
razor blades **le lamette**
read (verb) **leggere**
reading lamp **la lampada da studio**
ready (adj) **pronto**; *ready meals* **i piatti pronti**
rear lights **i fari posteriori**
receipt (restaurants, hotels) **la ricevuta**; (shops, bars) **lo scontrino**
reception (party) **il rinfresco**; (hotel) **la reception**
receptionist **il/la receptionist**
record (music) **il disco**; (sports, etc.) **il record**
record shop **il negozio di dischi**
red (adj) **rosso**
refreshments **i rinfreschi**
registered (post) **la raccomandata**
relax (verb) **rilassarsi**
relief: what a relief! **che sollievo!**
religion **la religione**
remember (verb) **ricordare**; *I don't remember* **non ricordo**
rent (verb) **affittare, noleggiare**
repair (verb) **riparare**
report **la relazione**
research **la ricerca**
reservation **la prenotazione**
rest (noun: remainder) **il resto**; (verb: to relax) **riposarsi**
restaurant **il ristorante**
return (verb) **ritornare**; (give back) **restituire**
return ticket **il biglietto di andata e ritorno**
rice **il riso**
rich (adj) **ricco, ricchi** (m pl), **ricche** (f pl)
right (adj) (correct) **giusto, esatto**; (not left) **destro**
ring (jewelry) **l'anello** (m)
ripe (adj) **maturo**
river **il fiume**
road **la strada**
roasted (adj) **arrosto**
rock (stone) **la roccia**; (music) **il rock**
roll (bread) **il panino**
Rome **Roma**
roof **il tetto**
room **la stanza, la camera**; (space) **lo spazio**; *room service* **il servizio in camera**
rope **la corda**
rose **la rosa**
round (adj) (circular) **rotondo**
roundabout **la rotatoria**

row (verb) **remare**
rubber band **l'elastico** (m)
ruby (gem) **il rubino**
rug (mat) **il tappeto**
rugby **il rugby**
ruins **le rovine, i resti**
ruler (for drawing) **la riga**
rum **il rum**
run (verb) **correre**

S

sad (adj) **triste**
safe (adj) (not dangerous)
   sicuro
safety pin **la spilla**
   di sicurezza
sailing **la vela**
salad **l'insalata** (f)
salami **il salame**
sale (at reduced prices)
   i saldi
sales (of goods, etc.)
   le vendite
saline solution (for contact
   lenses) **il liquido per lenti**
salmon **il salmone**
salt **Il sale**
same: the same dress **lo**
   stesso vestito; same
   again, please **un altro,**
   per favore
sand **la sabbia**
sandals **i sandali**
sand dunes **le dune**
sandwich **il panino**
sanitary towels **gli**
   assorbenti (igienici)
Sardinia **la Sardegna**
satellite TV **la TV satellitare**
Saturday **sabato**
sauce **la salsa**
saucepan **la pentola**
saucer **il piattino**
sauna **la sauna**
sausage **la salsiccia**
say (verb) **dire**; what did
   you say? **che cosa ha**
   detto?; how do you say...?
   come si dice...?
scarf **la sciarpa**; (head) **il**
   foulard
schedule **il programma**
school **la scuola**
science **la scienza**
scissors **le forbici**
Scotland **la Scozia**
Scotsman **lo scozzese**
Scotswoman **la scozzese**
Scottish (adj) **scozzese**
screen **lo schermo**
screw **la vite**
screwdriver **il cacciavite**
sea **il mare**
seafood **i frutti di mare**
seat **il posto**
seat belt **la cintura**
   di sicurezza

second **secondo**; second
   class **seconda classe**
secretary **il segretario/la**
   segretaria
see (verb) **vedere**; I can't
   see **non vedo**; I see
   (understand) **capisco,**
   vedo
self-employed **libero/a**
   professionista
sell (verb) **vendere**
seminar **il seminario**
send (verb) **mandare**
separate (adj) **separato**
separated (couple)
   separati
September **settembre**
serious (adj) **serio**; (illness)
   grave
server (waiter) **il cameriere/**
   la cameriera
seven **sette**
seventeen **diciassette**
seventy **settanta**
several **diversi/e**
sew (verb) **cucire**
shampoo **lo shampoo**
shave (verb) **radersi**
shaving cream **la schiuma**
   da barba
shawl **lo scialle**
she **lei**
sheers **le cesoie**
sheet **il lenzuolo**
shell **la conchiglia**
shellfish (crabs, etc.) **i**
   crostacei; (mollusks) **i**
   molluschi
sherry **lo sherry**
ship **la nave**
shirt **la camicia**
shoelaces **i lacci per**
   le scarpe
shoe polish **il lucido**
   per le scarpe
shoe repairer **il/la calzolaio/a**
shoes **le scarpe**; football
   shoes **le scarpe da calcio**
shop **il negozio**
shopkeeper **il/la**
   commerciante
shopping **lo shopping,**
   la spesa; (verb) to go
   shopping **andare a fare**
   acquisti; (for food) **andare**
   a fare la spesa
short (adj) **basso, corto**
shorts **i pantaloncini,**
   gli short
shoulder **la spalla**
shower **la doccia**; (rain)
   l'acquazzone (m)
shower gel **il docciaschiuma**
shutter (camera)
   l'otturatore (m); (window)
   l'imposta (f), **le persiane**
Sicily **la Sicilia**
side (edge) **il lato**

sightseeing **il giro turistico**
sign (in station, etc.) **il cartello**;
   (road, etc.) **l'insegna** (f)
sign (verb) **firmare**
silk **la seta**
silver (adj) (color)
   argentato; (metal)
   l'argento (m)
SIM card **la carta SIM**
simple (adj) **semplice**
sing (verb) **cantare**
single (adj: one) **solo**;
   (unmarried: man) **celibe**;
   (woman) **nubile**
single room **la camera singola**
single ticket **il biglietto di**
   sola andata
sink **il lavabo, il lavandino**;
   (kitchen) **il lavello**
sir **signore**
sister **la sorella**
six **sei**
sixteen **sedici**
sixty **sessanta**
size (clothes) **la taglia**;
   (shoe) **il numero**
skid (verb) **slittare**
skiing **lo sci**; (verb) to go
   skiing **andare a sciare**
skin cleanser **il latte**
   detergente
ski resort **la località**
   sciistica
skirt **la gonna**
skis **gli sci**
sky **il cielo**
sleep **il sonno**; (verb)
   dormire
sleeping bag **il sacco a pelo**
sleeping car **il vagone letto**
sleeping pill **il sonnifero**
sleeve **la manica**
slippers **le pantofole**
slow (adj) **lento**
small (adj) **piccolo**
smell **l'odore** (m);
   (verb: to stink) **puzzare**
smile **il sorriso**; (verb)
   sorridere
smoke **il fumo**; (verb) **fumare**
smoking (section) **fumatori**;
   nonsmoking **non**
   fumatori
snack **lo spuntino**
snorkel **il boccaglio**
snow **la neve**
so **così**; so good **così bene**;
   not so much **non così**
   tanto
soap **il sapone**
soccer (game) **il calcio**;
   (ball) **il pallone**
socks **i calzini**
soda water **l'acqua di**
   seltz (f)
sofa **il divano**
soft (adj) **morbido**
soil **la terra**

somebody **qualcuno**
somehow **in qualche modo**
something **qualcosa**
sometimes **qualche volta**
somewhere **da qualche parte**
son **il figlio**
song **la canzone**
sorry! **scusi!**; *I'm sorry* **mi dispiace, spiacente**; *sorry?* (pardon) **come?, scusi?**
soup **la minestra, la zuppa**
south **il sud**
souvenir **il souvenir**
spade (shovel) **la vanga**
spades (cards) **le picche**
Spain **la Spagna**
Spanish (adj) **spagnolo**
spare parts (car) **i pezzi di ricambio**
spark plug **la candela**
speak (verb) **parlare**; *do you speak...?* **parla...?**; *I don't speak...* **non parlo...**
spectacles **gli occhiali**
speed **la velocità**
SPF (sun protection factor) **il fattore di protezione**
spider **il ragno**
spinach **gli spinaci**
spoon **il cucchiaio**
sport **lo sport**
spring (mechanical) **la molla**; (season) **la primavera**
square (noun: in town) **la piazza**; (adj: shape) **quadrato**
staircase **la scala**
stairs **le scale**
stalls (in theatre) **la platea**
stamp **il francobollo**
stapler **la cucitrice, la spillatrice**
star **la stella**; (film) **la star**
start **l'inizio** (m); (verb) **cominciare**
starters **i primi piatti**
statement (to police) **la denuncia**
station **la stazione**
statue **la statua**
steal (verb) **rubare**; *it's been stolen* **è stato rubato**
steamed (adj) **a vapore**
steamer (boat) **la nave a vapore**; (for cooking) **la pentola a pressione**
still water **l'acqua naturale** (f)
stockings **le calze**
stomach **lo stomaco**
stomachache **il mal di pancia**
stop (noun: bus) **la fermata dell'autobus**; (verb) **fermare**; *stop!* **alt!, fermo!**

storm **la tempesta**
straight on **sempre dritto**
strawberry **la fragola**
stream **il ruscello**
street **la strada**
string (cord) **lo spago**; (guitar, etc.) **la corda**
stroller **il passegino**
stroller **la carrozzina**
strong (adj) **forte**
student **lo studente/la studentessa** (m/f)
stupid (adj) **stupido**
suburbs **la periferia**
sugar **lo zucchero**
suit **il completo**; *to suit* **stare bene**; *it suits you* **ti sta bene**
suitcase **la valigia**
summer **l'estate** (f)
sun **il sole**
sunbathe (verb) **prendere il sole**
sunburn **l'eritema solare** (m)
Sunday **domenica**
sunglasses **gli occhiali da sole**
sunny: it's sunny **c'è il sole**
sunshade **l'ombrellone** (m)
suntan **l'abbronzatura** (f); (verb) *to get a suntan* **abbronzarsi**
suntan lotion **la lozione solare**
suntanned (adj) **abbronzato**
supermarket **il supermercato**
supper **la cena**
supplement **il supplemento**
suppository **la supposta**
sure (adj) **sicuro**; *are you sure?* **sei sicuro?**
sweat **il sudore**; (verb) **sudare**
sweater **il maglione**
sweatshirt **la felpa**
sweet **la caramella**; (adj: not sour) **dolce**
swim (verb) **nuotare**
swimming **il nuoto**
swimming pool **la piscina**
swimming trunks **il costume da bagno (per uomo)**
swimsuit **il costume da bagno**
Swiss **lo svizzero/la svizzera**; (adj) **svizzero**
switch **l'interruttore** (m)
Switzerland **la Svizzera**
synagogue **la sinagoga**
syrup **lo sciroppo**

T

T-shirt **la maglietta**
table **il tavolo**; *bedside table* **il comodino**
tablet **la compressa**
take (verb) **prendere**
takeoff **il decollo**
talcum powder **il talco**
talk **la conversazione**; (verb) **parlare**
tall (adj) **alto**
tampons **i tamponi**
tangerine **il mandarino**
tap **il rubinetto**
tapestry **l'arazzo** (m)
taxi **il taxi**
taxi stand **il posteggio dei taxi**
tea **il tè**; *tea with milk* **il tè con latte**
teach (verb) **insegnare**
teacher **l'insegnante** (m/f)
technician **il tecnico** (m/f)
telephone **il telefono**; (verb) **telefonare**
telephone booth **la cabina telefonica**
telephone call **la telefonata**
telephone number **il numero di telefono**
television **la televisione**
temperature **la temperatura**; (fever) **la febbre**
ten **dieci**
tennis **il tennis**
tent **la tenda**
tent pole **il palo della tenda**
terminal (airport) **il terminal**
terrace **il patio**
test **il controllo**
than **di**
thank (verb) **ringraziare**; *thank you/thanks* **grazie**
that **quel, quello** (m); **quella** (f); **quelli, quegli** (m pl); **quelle** (f pl); *that one* **quello**; *that country* **quel paese**; *that man* **quell'uomo**; *that woman* **quella donna**; *what's that?* **cos'è quello?**; *I think that...* **penso che...**; *that'll be all* **basta così**
the **il/lo** (m); **la** (f); **i/gli** (m pl); **le** (f pl)
theatre **il teatro**
their: their room **la loro stanza**; *their friend* **il loro amico**; *their books* **i loro libri**; *their pens* **le loro penne**; *it's theirs* **è loro**
them: it's for them **è per loro**; *give it to them* **dallo a loro**

then **poi, allora**
there **là**; there is/are... **c'è/ci sono...**; is/are there...? **c'è/ci sono...?**
these **questi/queste**; these things **queste cose**; these boys **questi ragazzi**
they **loro**
thick (adj) **spesso**
thief **il/la ladro/a**
thin (adj) **magro**
think (verb) **pensare**; I think so **penso di sì**; I'll think about it **ci penserò**
third **terzo**
thirsty: I'm thirsty **ho sete**
thirteen **tredici**
thirty **trenta**
this **questo/questa**; this one **questo**; this picture **questo quadro**; this man **quest'uomo**; this woman **questa donna**; what's this? **cos'è questo?**; this is Mr... **(questo è) il signor...**
those **quelli/quelle**; those things **quelle cose**; those boys **quei ragazzi**
thousand **mille**
three **tre**
throat **la gola**
throat lozenges **le pasticche per la gola**
through **attraverso**
thumbtack **la puntina da disegno**
thunderstorm **il temporale**
Thursday **giovedì**
Tiber **il Tevere**
ticket **il biglietto**
ticket office **la biglietteria**
tide **la marea**
tie **la cravatta**; (verb) **legare**
tight (adj) (clothes) **stretto**
tights (sheer) **i collant**; (wool) **la calzamaglia**
tile **la piastrella**
time **il tempo**; what's the time? **che ore sono?**; opening times **l'orario di apertura** (m) ; leisure time **il tempo libero**
timetable **l'orario** (m)
tin **la scatola**
tip (money) **la mancia**; (end) **la punta**
tire **la gomma**; flat tire **la gomma a terra**
tired (adj) **stanco, stanchi** (m pl), **stanche** (f pl)
tissues **i fazzolettini di carta**
to: to England **in Inghilterra**; to the station **alla stazione**; to the doctor **dal dottore**; to the center **in centro**

toast **il pane tostato**
tobacco **il tabacco**
tobacconist (shop) **il tabaccaio**
today **oggi**
together **insieme**
toilet **il bagno, la toilette**
toilet paper **la carta igienica**
tomato **il pomodoro**
tomato juice **il succo di pomodoro**
tomorrow **domani**; see you tomorrow **a domani**
tongue **la lingua**
tonic **l'acqua tonica** (f)
tonight **stasera**
too (also) **anche**; (excessively) **troppo**
tooth **il dente**
toothache **il mal di denti**
toothbrush **lo spazzolino da denti**
toothpaste **il dentifricio**
torch **la torcia (elettrica)**
tour **il giro**; guided tour **la visita guidata**
tourist **il/la turista**
tourist information **l'azienda turistica** (f); (office) **l'ufficio turistico** (m)
towel **l'asciugamano** (m)
tower **la torre**; Leaning Tower of Pisa **la Torre di Pisa**
town **la città**
town hall **il municipio**
toy **il giocattolo**
toy shop **il negozio di giocattoli**
track suit **la tuta da ginnastica**
tractor **il trattore**
trade fair **la fiera commerciale**
tradition **la tradizione**
traffic **il traffico**
traffic jam **l'ingorgo** (m)
traffic lights **il semaforo**
trailer **il rimorchio, la roulotte**
train **il treno**
trainee **il/la tirocinante**
trainers **le scarpe da ginnastica**
translate (verb) **tradurre**
translator **il traduttore/ la traduttrice**
transmission (car) **il cambio**
trash **l'immondizia** (f), **la spazzatura**
trash bag **il sacchetto per la pattumiera**
travel (verb) **viaggiare**
travel agent **l'agenzia di viaggio** (f)
tray **il vassoio**
tree **l'albero** (m)
truck **il camion**

true (adj) **vero**
trunk (of car) **il bagagliaio**
try (verb) **provare**
Tuesday **martedì**
tunnel **il tunnel**
Turin **Torino**
turn: turn left/right (verb) **giri a sinistra/destra**
Tuscany **la Toscana**
tweezers **le pinzette**
twelve **dodici**
twenty **venti**
twin room **la camera a due letti**
twins **i gemelli**
two **due**
typewriter **la macchina da scrivere**

U

ugly (adj) **brutto**
umbrella **l'ombrello** (m)
uncle **lo zio**
under... **sotto...**
underground **la metro(politana)**
underpants **le mutande**
underskirt **la sottoveste**
understand (verb) **capire**; I don't understand **non capisco**
underwear **la biancheria intima**
university **l'università** (f)
university lecturer **il professore universitario/ la professoressa universitaria**
unleaded (adj) **senza piombo**
until **fino a**
unusual (adj) **insolito**
up **su**; (upward) **verso l'alto**; up there **lassù**
urgent (adj) **urgente**
us **noi**; it's for us **è per noi**
use **l'uso** (m); (verb) **usare**; it's no use **non serve a niente**
useful (adj) **utile**
usual (adj) **solito**
usually **di solito**

V

vacancy (room) **la stanza libera**
vacation **la vacanza**
vaccination **la vaccinazione**
valley **la valle**
valuables **gli oggetti di valore**
valve **la valvola**
vanilla **la vaniglia**
vase **il vaso**
Vatican **il Vaticano**; Vatican City **Città del Vaticano**
VCR **il videoregistratore**

veal **la carne di vitello**
vegetables **la verdura**
vegetarian (adj) **vegetariano**
vehicle **il veicolo**
Venice **Venezia**
very **molto**; *very much* **moltissimo**
vest **la canottiera**
vet **il/la veterinario/a**
video (tape/film) **la video cassetta**; *video games* **i videogiochi**
view **la vista**
viewfinder **il mirino**
villa **la villa**
village **il paese, il villaggio**
violin **il violino**
visit **la visita**; (verb) **andare a trovare**
visitor (guest) **l'ospite** (m/f)
vitamin pill **la compressa di vitamine**
vodka **la vodka**
voice **la voce**; *voicemail* **la segreteria telefonica**

W

wait (verb) **aspettare**; *wait!* **aspetta!**
waiter (server) **il cameriere**
waiting room **la sala d'aspetto**
waitress (server) **la cameriera**
Wales **il Galles**
walk **la passeggiata**; (verb) **camminare**; *to go for a walk* **andare a fare una passeggiata**
wall **il muro**
wallet **il portafoglio**
want (verb) **volere**; *I want* (**io**) **voglio**
war **la guerra**
wardrobe **il guardaroba, l'armadio** (m)
warm (adj) **caldo**
was: I was (verb) (**io**) **ero**; *he/she/it was* (**lui/lei/esso/a**) **era**
wash (verb) **lavare**
washing machine **la lavatrice**
wasp **la vespa**
watch **l'orologio** (m); (verb) **guardare**
water **l'acqua** (f)
water heater **lo scaldabagno**

waterfall **la cascata**
wave **l'onda** (f); (verb: with hand) **salutare**
wavy: wavy hair **i capelli ondulati**
we **noi**
weather **il tempo**
website **il sito internet**
wedding **il matrimonio**
Wednesday **mercoledì**
weed **l'erbaccia** (f)
week **la settimana**
welcome (adj) **benvenuto**; *you're welcome* **di niente, prego**
well done (adj: food) **ben cotta**
Wellington boots **gli stivali di gomma**
Welsh (adj) **gallese**
Welshman **il gallese**
Welshwoman **la gallese**
were: you were (**Lei**) **era**; (singular, familiar) (**tu**) **eri**; (plural) (**voi**) **eravate**; *we were* (**noi**) **eravamo**; *they were* (**loro**) **erano**
west **l'ovest** (m)
wet (adj) **bagnato**
what? **cosa?**
wheel **la ruota**; *wheel brace* **il girabacchino**
wheelchair **la sedia a rotelle**
when? **quando?**
where? **dove?**; *where are you from?* **di dov'è?/di dove sei?** (formal/informal)
whether **se**
which? **quale?**
white (adj) **bianco**
who? **chi?**
why? **perchè?**
wide (adj) **ampio**
wife **la moglie**
wind **il vento**
window **la finestra**
windscreen **il parabrezza**
wine **il vino**; *wine list* **la lista dei vini**; *wine shop* **l'enoteca** (f)
wing **l'ala** (f)
winter **l'inverno** (m)
with **con**
withdraw (verb) (money) **prelevare**
without **senza**
witness **il/la testimone**

woman **la donna**
wood (material) **il legno**
wool **la lana**
word **la parola**
work **il lavoro**; (verb) **lavorare**; (machine) **funzionare**
worry: don't worry **non si preoccupi**
worse (adj) **peggiore**
worst (adj) **il peggiore/ la peggiore**
wrapping paper **la carta da imballaggio**; (for presents) **la carta da regalo**
wrench **la chiave fissa**
wrist **il polso**
writing paper **la carta da scrivere**
wrong (adj) **sbagliato**

X, Y, Z

x-ray **la radiografia**; *x-ray department* **reparto di radiologia** (m)
year **l'anno** (m)
yellow (adj) **giallo**
yes **sì**
yesterday **ieri**
yet **ancora**; *not yet* **non ancora**
yogurt **lo yogurt**
you: (singular, formal) **Lei**; (singular, informal) **tu**; (plural) **voi**
young (adj) **giovane**
your (informal) **tuo, tua, tuoi, tue**; (formal) **suo, sua, suoi, sue**; (singular, formal) *your book* **il suo libro**; *your shirt* **la sua camicia**; *your shoes* **le sue scarpe**; (singular, informal) *your book* **il tuo libro**; *your shirt* **la tua camicia**; *your shoes* **le tue scarpe**
yours: is this yours? (singular, formal) **è suo?**; (singular, informal) **è tuo?**
youth hostel **l'ostello della gioventù** (m)
zip **la chiusura lampo**
zoo **lo zoo**

Dictionary
ITALIAN TO ENGLISH

The gender of Italian nouns listed here is indicated by the abbreviations (m) and (f), for masculine and feminine. Plural nouns are followed by the abbreviations (m pl) or (f pl). Italian adjectives (adj) vary according to the gender and number of the word they describe, and the masculine form is shown here. Adjectives that end in **-o** adopt an **-a** ending in the feminine form. Some adjectives end in **-e** for the masculine and the feminine, changing to **-i** in the plural. In general, plural endings are **-i** for masculine and **-e** for feminine. Those that do not follow this rule are mentioned here.

A

a *in, at, per;* **a casa** *at home;* **a Venezia** *in Venice;* **all'ufficio postale** *at the post office;* **alla stazione** *to the station;* **alle tre** *at 3 o'clock;* **a persona** *per person;* **all'anno** *per annum*

abbastanza *enough, quite (fairly)*

abbronzarsi (verb) *to get a suntan*

abbronzato (adj) *suntanned*

acceleratore (m) *accelerator*

accendino (m) *lighter*

accensione (f) *ignition*

acqua (f) *water;* **l'acqua di seltz** *soda water;* **l'acqua gassata** *fizzy water;* **l'acqua minerale** *mineral water;* **l'acqua naturale** *still water;* **l'acqua potabile** *drinking water;* **l'acqua tonica** *tonic water* **acquazzone** (m) *shower (rain)*

adesso *now*

aereo (m) *aircraft*

aeroporto (m) *airport*

affare (m) *business, bargain;* **non sono affari tuoi** *it's none of your business*

affittare (verb) *to rent*

affollato (adj) *crowded*

agenda (f) *diary*

agente immobiliare (m/f) *estate agent*

agenzia di viaggio (f) *travel agent*

aglio (m) *garlic*

agnello (m) *lamb*

ago (m) *needle*

agosto *August*

agricoltore (m/f) *farmer*

Aids (m) *AIDS*

aiuola (f) *flowerbed*

aiutare (verb) *to help*

aiuto (m) *help*

ala (f) *wing*

albero (m) *tree, mast;* **l'albero a camme** *camshaft*

albicocca (f) *apricot*

alcol (m) *alcohol*

alimentari (m pl) *grocer's*

alla salute! *cheers! (toast)*

allergico (adj) *allergic*

alloggio (m) *accommodations*

allora *then*

le Alpi (f pl) *the Alps*

al sangue (adj) *rare (steak)*

alt! *stop!*

alto (adj) *high, tall*

altro, altra, altri, altre *other;* **l'altro** *the other (one);* **un altro, un'altra** *another;* **l'uno o l'altro** *either of them;* **un altro, per favore** *same again, please;* **qualcos'altro** *something else;* **qualcun'altro** *someone else;* **da qualche altra parte** *somewhere else*

alzarsi (verb) *get up*

amare (verb) *to love*

amaro (adj) *bitter*

ambasciata (f) *embassy*

ambulanza (f) *ambulance*

America (f) *America*

americano (adj) *American*

amico/amica (m/f) *friend*

ammiratore/ammiratrice (m/f) *fan (enthusiast)*

ampio (adj) *wide*

ampliamento (m) *enlargement*

ananas (m) *pineapple*

anche *too (also)*

ancora *yet;* **non ancora** *not yet*

andare (verb) *to go;* **andare a trovare** (verb) *to visit*

anello (m) *ring (jewelry)*

anello acustico (m) *hearing loop*

angolo (m) *corner*

animato (adj) *busy (bar)*

anniversario (m) *anniversary*

anno (m) *year*

anticipo (m) *advance (on payment, etc.);* **anticipato** (adj) *in advance*

antiquario (m) *antiques shop*

antisettico (m) *antiseptic*

aperitivo (m) *aperitif, cocktail party*

aperto (adj) *open*

apparecchio acustico (m) *hearing aid*

appartamento (m) *apartment*

appetito (m) *appetite*

appuntamento (m) *appointment*

apribottiglie (m) *bottle opener*

aprile *April*

aprire (verb) *to open*

apriscatole (m) *can opener*

arachidi (f pl) *peanuts*

arancia (f) *orange (fruit)*

arancione (adj) *orange (color)*

arazzo (m) *tapestry*

architettura (f) *architecture*

argento (m) *silver (color);* **d'argento, argentato** *silver (metal)*

aria (f) *air*

aria condizionata (f) *air conditioning*

armadio (m) *cupboard, wardrobe*

arrivare (verb) *to arrive*

arrivederci *goodbye*

arrivi *arrivals*

arrossamento (m) *rash*

arrosto (adj) *roasted*

arte (f) *art*

articoli per la casa (m pl) *household products*

artista (m/f) *artist*

ascensore (m) *lift*

asciugamano (m) *towel*

asciutto (adj) *dry*

asmatico (adj) *asthmatic*

asparagi (m pl) *asparagus*

aspettare (verb) *to wait;* **aspetta!** *wait!*

aspirina (f) *aspirin*

assegno (m) *check*

assicurazione (f) *insurance*

assomiliare a (verb) *to be like;* **assomiglia a... it's like...**

assorbenti (igienici) (m pl) *sanitary napkins*

attaccapanni (m) *coat hanger*

attento (adj) *careful;* **stia attento!** *be careful!*

atterrare (verb) *to land*
attraente (adj) *attractive*
attraverso *through*
aula delle lezioni (f) *lecture hall*
auricolari (m pl) *earphones*
l'Australia (f) *Australia*
australiano (adj) *Australian*
autista (m/f) *driver* (of bus, truck, etc.)
auto (f) *car*
autobus (m) *bus;* **la stazione degli autobus** *bus station;* **la fermata dell'autobus** *bus stop*
automatico (adj) *automatic*
autostop: fare l'autostop (verb) *to hitchhike*
autostrada (f) *highway*
autunno (m) *autumn*
a vapore (adj) *steamed*
avere (verb) *to have;* **non ho...** *I don't have...;* **ha...?;** *do you have...?*
avvocato (m/f) *lawyer*
azienda turistica (f) *tourist informaion*
Aziende Ospedaliere Universitarie (f pl) *hospital* (attached to university)
azzurro (adj) *blue*

B

babbo (m) *dad*
baffi (m pl) *moustache*
bagagli (m pl) *luggage*
bagagliaio (m) *trunk* (of car)
bagaglio a mano (m) *hand luggage*
bagaglio in eccesso (m) *excess baggage*
bagnato (adj) *wet*
bagno (m) *bath, bathroom;* **fare il bagno** (verb) *to have a bath;* **i bagni** *toilets*
balcone (m) *balcony*
ballare (verb) *to dance*
ballo (m) *dance*
balsamo (m) *conditioner* (hair)
bambino (m), **bambina** (f) *baby, child*
bambola (f) *doll*
banana (f) *banana*
banca (f) *bank*
bancomat (m) *cashpoint, ATM*
banconota (f) *banknote*
banda (f) *band* (musicians)
bandiera (f) *flag*
bar (m) *bar* (drinks)
barba (f) *beard*
barbiere (m) *barber's*
barca (f) *boat* (small)
basso (adj) *low, short*
basta! *enough!;* **basta così** *that'll be all*
battello (m) *boat* (passenger)

batteria (f) *battery*
baule (m) *chest* (furniture)
beige (adj) *beige*
bello (adj) *beautiful, handsome, nice*
bene *good, well;* **bene!** (adj) *good!;* **benissimo!** *great!;* **ben cotta** *well done* (food); **non mi sento bene** *I don't feel well;* **ti sta bene** *it suits you*
benvenuto (adj) *welcome*
benzina (f) *gas*
benzinaio (m) *gas station*
bere (verb) *to drink*
berretto (m) *cap* (hat)
biancheria (f) *laundry* (dirty clothes)
biancheria intima (f) *underwear*
bianco (adj) *white*
bibita (f) *drink*
biblioteca (f) *library*
bicchiere (m) *glass* (for drinking)
bicicletta (f) *bicycle*
bigliettaio/bigliettaia (m/f) *conductor* (bus)
biglietteria (f) *ticket office, booking office*
biglietto (m) *ticket, card;* **il biglietto di andata e ritorno** *return ticket;* **il biglietto di sola andata** *single ticket;* **il biglietto da visita** (m) *business card;* **il biglietto di auguri** *greeting card;* **il biglietto entrance ticket***
bigodini (m pl) *curlers*
bikini (m) *bikini*
binario (m) *platform*
biondo (adj) *blond*
birra (f) *beer*
biscotto (m) *cookie*
bisogno (m) (verb) *need;* **ho bisogno di...** *I need...;* **non c'è bisogno** *there's no need*
bloc-notes (m) *notepad*
blu (adj) *navy blue*
bocca (f) *mouth*
boccaglio (m) *snorkel*
bollire (verb) *to boil* (water); (egg etc) **far bollire**
bollitore (m) *kettle*
borsa (f) *bag*
borseggiatore/borseggiatrice (m/f) *pickpocket*
botteghino (m) *box office*
bottiglia (f) *bottle*
bottone (m) *button*
braccialetto (m) *bracelet*
braccio (m) *arm;* **braccia** (f pl) *arms*
brandy (m) *brandy*
bravo (adj) *clever*
brioche (f) *croissant*

britannico (adj) *British*
bruciare (verb) *to burn*
bruciatura (f) *burn*
brutto (adj) *ugly*
budget (m) *budget*
bunker (m) *bunker* (golf)
buonanotte *good night*
buonasera *good evening*
buongiorno *good day, hello*
buono *good, nice* (adj: to eat); **a buon mercato** (adj) *cheap*
burro (m) *butter;* **il burro di cacao** *lip balm*
busta (f) *envelope*

C

c'è... *there is...;* **c'è...?** *is there...?*
cabina telefonica (f) *telephone booth*
cacciavite (m) *screwdriver*
caffè (m) *coffee, café;* **il caffè solubile** *instant coffee*
calcio (m) *football* (game)
calcolatrice (f) *calculator*
caldaia (f) *boiler*
caldo (adj) *hot, warm;* **ho caldo** *I feel hot*
calzamaglia (f) *tights* (wool)
calze (f pl) *stockings*
calzini (m pl) *socks*
calzolaio (m) *shoe repairer*
cambiare (verb) *to change* (money, trains)
cambiarsi (verb) *to change* (clothes)
cambio (m) *change* (money), *gear* (car); **il (tasso di) cambio** *exchange rate*
camera (f) *(bed)room;* **la camera a due letti** *twin room;* **la camera doppia** *double room;* **la camera singola** *single room* **camera d'aria** *inner tube*
cameriera (f) *waitress, server*
cameriere (m) *waiter, server*
camicetta (f) *blouse*
camicia (f) *shirt;* **la camicia da notte** *nightdress*
caminetto (m) *fireplace*
camion (m) *truck*
camminare (verb) *to walk*
campagna (f) *country* (not town)
campana (f) *bell* (church)
campanello (m) *bell* (door)
campeggio (m) *campsite*
camper (m) *camper van*
campo (m) *field*
Canada (m) *Canada*
canadese (adj) *Canadian*
canale (m) *canal*
cancello (m) *gate*
candela (f) *candle, spark plug*

cane (m) *dog;* **cane guida**
(m) *guide dog*
canoa (f) *canoe*
canottiera (f) *vest*
cantare (verb) *to sing*
cantina (f) *cellar*
canzone (f) *song*
capelli (m pl) *hair*
capire *to understand;* **non
capisco** *I don't understand*
cappotto (m) *coat*
cappello (m) *hat*
carabinieri (m pl) *military
police*
caramella (f) *sweet*
carburatore (m) *carburetor*
caricabatterie (m) *charger*
carino (adj) *nice, pretty*
carne (f) *meat*
caro (adj) *expensive*
carota (f) *carrot*
carrello (m) *cart*
carrozzina (f) *stroller*
carta (f) *paper, card;*
la carta (geografica)
map; **la carta di debito**
debit card; **la carta
d'imbarco** *boarding pass;*
la carta da imballaggio
wrapping paper; **la carta
da regalo** *wrapping paper*
(for presents); **la carta da
scrivere** *writing paper;* **la
carta di credito** *credit
card;* **la carta igienica**
toilet paper; **le carte da
gioco** *playing cards;* **la
carta SIM** *SIM card*
cartello (m) *sign*
(in station, etc.)
cartella (f) *briefcase*
cartolina (f) *postcard*
casa (f) *house, home*
cascata (f) *waterfall*
cassa (f) *checkout*
cassetta (f) *box* (of wood),
cassette; **la cassetta
delle lettere** *mailbox*
cassetto (m) *drawer*
cassettone (m) *chest
of drawers*
cassiere/cassiera (m/f) *cashier*
castello (m) *castle*
catenaccio (m) *bolt*
(on door)
cattedrale (f) *cathedral*
cattivo (adj) *bad*
cattolico (adj) *Catholic*
cavalcavia (m) *flyover*
cavatappi (m) *corkscrew*
caviglia (f) *ankle*
cavo di ricarica (m)
charging cable
cavolfiore (m) *cauliflower*
cavolo (m) *cabbage*
celibe (m) (adj: *unmarried)
single*
cellulare (m) *cell phone*

cena (f) *supper, dinner*
cento *hundred*
centro (m) *center;*
il centro città *city center*
cerotto (m) *bandage*
(sticking)
certificato (m) *certificate*
certo *certainly*
cesoie (f pl) *shears*
cestello (m) *basket*
(in supermarket)
cestino (m) *basket*
cetriolo (m) *cucumber*
check-in (m) *check-in;*
lo sportello del check-in
check-in desk; **fare il
check-in** (verb) *to check in*
chewing gum (m)
chewing gum
chi? *who?*
chiamare (verb) *to call*
chiaro *light* (adj: not dark),
clear (obvious)
chiave (f) *key;*
la chiave fissa *wheel
brace, wrench*
chiesa (f) *church*
chilo (m) *kilo*
chilometro (m) *kilometer*
chiodo (m) *nail* (metal)
chitarra (f) *guitar*
chiudere (verb) *to close;*
**chiudere con il
catenaccio** (verb) *to bolt*
chiuso (adj) *closed*
chiusura lampo (f) *zip*
ciao *hello, hi*
ciascuno *each;* **venti euro
ciascuno** *twenty euros each*
cibo (m) *food*
ciclismo (m) *cycling*
cieco (adj) *blind* (cannot see)
cielo (m) *sky*
cifre (f pl) *figures*
ciliegia (f) *cherry*
cimitero (m) *cemetery*
cin cin! *cheers!* (toast)
cinema (m) *cinema*
cinghia della ventola (f)
fan belt
cinquanta *fifty*
cinque *five*
cintura (f) *belt;* **la cintura
di sicurezza** *seat belt*
cioccolata (f) *chocolate;*
la scatola di cioccolatini
box of chocolates
ciotola (f) *bowl;* **la ciotola
del cane** *dog bowl*
cipolla (f) *onion*
cipria (f) *powder* (cosmetic)
circa 16 *about 16*
ci sono *there are…;*
ci sono? *are there…?*
città (f) *city, town*
ciuccio (m) *dummy* (for baby)
clacson (m) *horn* (car)
classe (f) *class*

cliente (m/f) *client*
codice segreto (m) *PIN*
codice postale (m) *post code*
cofano (m) *hood* (car)
cognome (m) *last name*
coincidenza (f) *connection*
colazione (f) *breakfast*
colla (f) *glue*
collana (f) *necklace*
collant (m pl) *tights* (sheer)
collare (m) *collar* (for dog)
collega (m/f) *colleague*
colletto (m) *collar*
collezione (f) *collection*
(stamps, etc.)
collina (f) *hill*
collo (m) *neck*
colonnina di ricarica (f)
charging point/station
colore (m) *color*
coltello (m) *knife*
come *like;* **come questo**
like this one
come? *how?, sorry?* (pardon);
come si chiama/ti chiami?
what's your name?
(formal/informal); **come si
chiama?** *what's it called?*
comignolo (m) *chimney*
cominciare (verb) *to start*
commedia (f) *play* (theater)
commerciante (m/f)
shopkeeper
comodino (m) *bedside table*
compact disc (m) *compact
disc*
compleanno (m) *birthday;*
buon compleanno!
happy birthday!
completo (m) *suit*
complicato (adj) *complicated*
comprare (verb) *buy*
compressa (f) *tablet;* **la
compressa di vitamine**
vitamin pill
computer (m) *computer;*
il computer portatile
laptop (computer)
con *with*
concerto (m) *concert*
conchiglia (f) *shell*
conferenza (f) *lecture,
conference;* **la sala
conferenze** (f) *conference room*
confine (m) *border*
congelatore (m) *freezer*
congratulazioni! (m pl)
congratulations!
coniglio (m) *rabbit*
conoscere *to know* (person)
consegna (f) *delivery*
consolato (m) *consulate*
consulente (m/f) *consultant*
contante (m) *cash*
contento (adj) *glad, happy*
conto (m) *bill*
contraccettivo (m)
contraceptive

contratto (m) *contract*
contro *against*
controllo (m) *test*
conversazione (f) *talk*
coperta (f) *blanket*
copriletto (m) *bedspread*
corda (f) *rope, guy rope, string* (guitar, etc.)
cordiale (adj) *friendly*
corno (m) *horn* (animal)
corpo (m) *body*
correre (verb) *to run*
corridoio (m) *corridor*
corrispondente (m/f) *pen pal*
corsia (f) *queue, aisle* (in supermarket, etc.)
corso (m) *course* (educational)
corto (adj) *short*
cosa? *what?;* **cosa c'è?** *what's the matter*
cosmetici (m pl) *cosmetics*
costare (verb) *to cost;* **quanto costa?** *what does it cost?*
costoletta (f) *chop* (food)
costoso (adj) *expensive*
costruttore/costruttrice (m/f) *builder*
costume da bagno (m) *swimsuit, swimming trunks*
cotone (m) *cotton;* **il cotone idrofilo** *cotton ball*
cozze (f pl) *mussels*
crampo (m) *cramp*
cravatta (f) *tie*
crema (f) *cream, lotion*
criceto (m) *hamster*
crociera (f) *cruise*
crostacei (m pl) *shellfish* (crabs, etc.)
cucchiaio (m) *spoon*
cuccia (f) *dog basket*
cucina (f) *kitchen, cooker*
cucinare (verb) *to cook*
cucire (verb) *to sew*
cucitrice (f) *stapler*
cuffie (f pl) *headphones*
cugino/cugina (m/f) *cousin*
cuocere (al forno) (verb) *to bake*
cuoco/cuoca (m/f) *cook/chef*
cuoio (m) *leather*
cuore (m) *heart;* **nel cuore della notte** *in the middle of the night*
cuori (m pl) *hearts* (cards)
curry (m) *curry*
cuscino (m) *cushion*

D

dado (m) *nut* (for bolt)
dappertutto *everywhere*
dare (verb) *to give;* **dare la precedenza** (verb) *to give way*
davanti a *opposite, in front of*

decollo (m) *takeoff*
deliberatamente *deliberately*
denaro (m) *cash*
dente (m) *tooth*
dentiera (f) *dentures, false teeth*
dentifricio (m) *toothpaste*
dentista (m/f) *dentist*
denuncia (f) *statement* (to police)
deodorante (m) *deodorant*
desposito bagagli (m) *left luggage locker*
dessert (m pl) *desserts*
destro *right* (adj: not left)
detersivo (m) *detergent;* **il detersivo in polvere** *powdered detergent;* **il detersivo per i piatti** *dishwashing liquid*
di *of, from, than, on, at:* **più di** *more than;* **di dov'è?/di dove sei?** *where are you from?* (formal/ informal); **di lunedì** *on Monday;* **di notte** *at night*
diabetico (adj) *diabetic*
diamante (m) *diamond* (gem)
diarrea (f) *diarrhea*
dica? *can I help you?*
dicembre *December*
diciannove *nineteen*
diciassette *seventeen*
diciotto *eighteen*
dieci *ten*
dietro *behind;* **dietro a...** *behind...*
difficile (adj) *difficult*
dimenticare (verb) *to forget*
dire (verb) *to say;* **che cosa ha detto?** *what did you say?;* **come si dice...?** *how do you say...?*
direttore (m) *conductor* (orchestra)
direttore/direttrice *manager*
direzione (f) *office*
dirigente (m/f) *executive*
discesa per principianti (f) *beginners' slope*
disco (m) *record* (music)
dito (m) *finger*
divano (m) *sofa*
diversi *several*
diverso (adj) *different;* **è diverso!** *that's different!*
divertente (adj) *funny*
divieto di accesso (m) *no entry*
divorziato (adj) *divorced*
dizionario (m) *dictionary*
doccia (f) *shower*
docciaschiuma (m) *shower gel*
documento (m) *document;* **il documento d'identità** *identification*
dodici *twelve*

dogana (f) *customs*
dolce (adj) *sweet* (not sour)
dollaro (m) *dollar*
dolore (m) *ache, pain*
domanda (f) *question*
domani *tomorrow;* **a domani** *see you tomorrow*
domenica *Sunday*
donna (f) *woman*
dopo *after*
dopobarba (m) *aftershave*
dormire (verb) *to sleep*
dottore/dottoressa (m/f) *doctor*
dottorato di ricerca (m) *PhD*
dove? *where?*
dovere (verb) *to have to (must);* **devo andare adesso** *I have to go now*
due *two;* **le due** *two o'clock*
dune (f pl) *sand dunes*
duomo (m) *cathedral*
durante *during*
duro (adj) *hard*
duty free (m) *duty-free*

E

e *and;* **e poi?** *what next?*
è *he/she/it is*
eccellente (adj) *excellent*
ecco *here you are, here it is*
economico (adj) *cheap*
edicola (f) *newsagent's (shop)*
edificio (m) *building*
elastico (m) *elastic, rubber band*
elettricista (m/f) *electrician*
elettricità (f) *electricity*
elettrico (adj) *electric*
email (f) *e-mail*
emergenza (f) *emergency*
enoteca (f) *wine shop*
entrare (verb) *to enter*
entrata (f) *entrance*
entro (venerdì) *by (Friday)*
epilettico (adj) *epileptic*
equipaggio (m) *crew*
era: (Lei) era *you were (singular, formal);* **(lui/lei/esso/a) era** *he/she/it was*
erano *they were*
eravamo *we were*
eravate *you were* (plural)
erba (f) *grass*
erbaccia (f) *weed*
eri *you were* (singular, informal)
eritema solare (m) *sunburn*
ero *I was*
errore (m) *mistake*
esatto (adj) *right* (correct)
esaurimento nervoso (m) *nervous breakdown*
esca (f) *bait*
escursione (f) *excursion*
escursionismo (m) *hiking*

esempio (m) *example;*
  per esempio *for example*
esposimetro (m) *light meter*
essere (verb) *to be*
esso/a (m/f) *it*
est (m) *east*
estate (f) *summer*
estintore (m) *fire*
  extinguisher
etichetta (f) *label*

F

faccia (f) *face*
facile (adj) *easy*
fagioli (m pl) *beans*
falegname (m/f) *carpenter*
falò (m) *campfire*
fame (f)**: ho fame** *I'm hungry*
famiglia (f) *family*
fantastico (adj) *fantastic*
fare (verb) *to do, to make;*
  che lavoro fa? *what*
  (work) do you do?
fare jogging (verb) *to jog;*
  andare a fare jogging
  (verb) *to go jogging*
fare la fila (verb) *to queue*
fari (m pl) *lights, headlights;*
  i fari posteriori *rear lights*
farina (f) *flour*
farmacia (f) *chemist (shop)*
fascia (f) (verb) *bandage*
fattore di protezione (m)
  SPF (sun protection factor)
fattoria (f) *farm*
fattura (f) *invoice*
favore: per favore *please*
fazzolettini di carta (m pl)
  tissues
febbraio *February*
febbre (f) *fever, temperature*
fegato (m) *liver*
felice (adj) *happy*
felpa (f) *sweatshirt*
ferita (f) *injury*
fermare (verb) *to stop;*
  fermo! *stop!*
fermata dell'autobus (f)
  bus stop
ferramenta (f) *hardware*
  store
ferro (m) *iron* (material);
  (for clothes) **il ferro da**
  stiro
ferrovia (f) *railway*
festa (f) *party* (celebration)
fiammifero (m) *match* (light)
fidanzata (f) (adj) *fiancée,*
  engaged
fidanzato (m) (adj) *fiancé,*
  engaged
fiera commerciale (f)
  trade fair
figlia (f) *daughter*
figlio (m) *son*
filiale (f) *branch* (of
  company)

film (m) *film* (cinema)
filtro (m) *filter*
finalmente! *at last!*
fine (f) *end*
finestra (f) *window*
finito *finished*
fino a *until*
finocchio (m) *fennel*
fiore (m) *flower*
fiori (m pl) *clubs* (cards)
Firenze *Florence*
firmare (verb) *to sign*
fissare (verb) *to arrange*
  (appointments, etc.)
fiume (m) *river*
flash (m) *flash* (camera)
flauto (m) *flute*
flebo (f) *intravenous drip*
foglia (f) *leaf*
fondo (m) *bottom;* **in fondo**
  (a) *at the bottom (of)*
fontana (f) *fountain*
foratura (f) *puncture*
forbici (f pl) *scissors*
forchetta (f) *fork* (for food)
foresta (f) *forest*
forestiero/forestiera
  (m/f) *foreigner*
formaggio (m) *cheese*
forno (m) *oven;* **il forno a**
  microonde *microwave*
forse *maybe, perhaps*
forte (adj) *loud, strong*
fortuna (f) *luck;* **buona**
  fortuna! *good luck!*
fotocopiatrice (f)
  photocopier
fotografare (verb) *to*
  photograph
fotografia (f) *photograph*
fotografo/fotografa (m/f)
  photographer
foulard (m) *headscarf*
fra… *between…*
fragola (f) *strawberry*
francese (adj) *French*
la Francia *France*
francobollo (m) *stamp*
fratello (m) *brother*
frattura (f) *fracture*
freccia (f) *indicator*
freddo (adj) *cold*
frenare (verb) *to brake*
freno (m) *brake;* **il freno**
  a mano *hand brake*
fresco (adj) *cool*
fretta (f)**: ho fretta** *I'm in*
  a hurry
friggere (verb) *to fry*
frigorifero (m) *fridge*
fritto (adj) *fried*
frizione (f) *clutch*
frizzante (adj) *fizzy*
frutta (f) *fruit*
frutti di mare (m pl)
  seafood
fucile (m) *gun* (rifle)
fumare (verb) *to smoke*

fumatori (m pl) *smoking*
  (section); **non fumatori**
  nonsmoking
fumo (m) *smoke*
fungo (m) *mushroom*
funivia (f) *cable car*
funzionare (verb) *to work*
  (machine)
fuochi d'artificio (m pl)
  fireworks
fuoco (m) *fire*
fuori *outside*
furto (m) *burglary*

G

gabbia (f) *cage*
galleria (f) *gallery, circle*
  (in theater); **la galleria**
  d'arte *art gallery*
il Galles *Wales*
gallese (adj) *Welsh*
gamba (f) *leg*
gambero (m) *crayfish*
garage (m) *garage*
garantire (verb) *to guarantee*
garanzia (f) *guarantee*
gas (m) *gas, fuel;* **il gas da**
  campeggio *camping gas;*
  il gas per accendini
  lighter fuel
gatto (m) *cat*
gay (adj) *gay* (homosexual)
gasolio (m) *diesel*
gel (m) *gel* (hair)
gelateria (f) *ice cream parlor*
gelato (m) *ice cream*
gelo (m) *frost*
gemelli/e (m/f pl) *cuff links;*
  twins
genitori (m pl) *parents*
gennaio *January*
Genova *Genoa*
gente (f) *people*
la Germania *Germany*
ghiaccio (m) *ice*
già *already*
giacca (f) *jacket*
giallo (adj) *yellow*
giardiniere (m) *gardener*
giardino (m) *garden*
gin (m) *gin*
ginocchio (ginocchi/
  ginocchia) *knee*
giocare (verb) *to play*
giocattolo (m) *toy*
gioielliere (m) *jeweler's*
  (shop)
giornale (m) *newspaper*
giorno (m) *day;* **il giorno**
  festivo *public holiday*
giovane (adj) *young*
giovedì *Thursday*
girabacchino (m) *wheel brace*
girare (verb) *to turn;* **giri a**
  sinistra/destra *turn left/right*
giro (m) *tour*
giro turistico (m) *sightseeing*

giù *down*
giugno *June*
giusto (adj) *right (correct)*;
 non è giusto *it's not fair*
gli *the* (m pl)
gocce (f pl) *drops*
gola (f) *throat*
golf (m) *golf*
golfista (m/f) *golfer*
gomito (m) *elbow*
gomma (f) *eraser, tire*;
 la gomma a terra *flat tire*
gonna (f) *skirt*
governo (m) *government*
grafico/grafica (m/f)
 designer
la Gran Bretagna *Great Britain*
granchio (m) *crab*
grande (adj) *big, large*
grande magazzino (m)
 department store
grasso (m) (adj) *fat*
gratis (adj) *free (no charge)*
gratuito (adj) *free (no charge)*
grave (adj) *serious (illness)*
grazie *thank you/thanks*
grazioso (adj) *pretty (beautiful)*
la Grecia *Greece*
greco (adj) *Greek*
gridare (verb) *to shout*
grigio (adj) *gray*
griglia (f) *grill*;
 alla griglia (adj) *grilled*
grondaia (f) *gutter*
grotta (f) *cave*
gruppo (m) *group*
guanciale (m) *pillow*
guanti (m pl) *gloves*
guardare (verb) *to watch*
guardaroba (m) *wardrobe*
guardia (f) *guard*
guasto (m) *breakdown (car)*
guerra (f) *war*
guida (f) *guide, guidebook*;
 la guida telefonica
 telephone directory
guidare (verb) *to drive*
guidatore/guidatrice (m/f)
 driver (car)
guinzaglio (m) *leash (for dog)*
gusto (m) *flavor*

H, I

ha…? *do you have…?*
hamburger (m) *hamburger*
HIV positivo (adj)
 HIV-positive
ho… (verb) *I have…*
hobby (m) *hobby*
i *the* (m pl)
idraulico (m/f) *plumber*
ieri *yesterday*
igienizzante per le mani
 (m) *hand sanitizer*
il *the* (m)
imbarazzante (adj)
 embarrassing

imbianchino/imbianchina
 (m/f) *decorator*
immediatamente
 immediately
immondizia (f) *rubbish*
imparare (verb) *to learn*
impermeabile (m) *raincoat*
impiegato/impiegata (m/f)
 office worker
importare (verb) *to matter*;
 non importa *it doesn't
 matter*
impossibile (adj) *impossible*
imposta (f) *shutter (window)*
in *in, to*: **in inglese** *in English*;
 in Inghilterra *to England*;
 in mezzo alla piazza *in the
 middle of the square*; **in
 centro** *to the center*
in ritardo (adj) *delayed*
inalatore (m) *inhaler
 (for asthma, etc.)*
incendio (m) *fire (blaze)*
inchiostro (m) *ink*
incidente (m) *accident*
incinta (f) (adj) *pregnant*
incluso (adj) *included*
incontro (m) *meeting,
 match (sport)*
incrocio (m) *junction*
indicatore di direzione (m)
 indicator
indigestione (f) *indigestion*
indirizzo (m) *address*;
 **l'indirizzo di posta
 elettronica** *e-mail
 address*
indistinto (adj: unclear) *faint*
infermiere/infermiera (m/f)
 nurse
infezione (f) *infection*
informatica (f) *information
 technology*
informazioni (f pl)
 information
infradito (m pl) *flip-flops*
ingegnere (m/f) *engineer*
ingegneria (f) *engineering*
l'Inghilterra (f) *England*
inglese (adj) *English*
ingorgo (m) *traffic jam*
iniezione (f) *injection*
inizio (m) *start*
insalata (f) *salad*
insegna (f) *sign (road, etc.)*
insegnante (m/f) *teacher*
insegnare *to teach*
insettifugo (m) *insect
 repellent*
insetto (m) *insect*
insieme *together*
insolito (adj) *unusual*
insonnia (f) *insomnia*
intelligente (adj) *clever*
interessante (adj) *interesting*
internet (f) *Internet*
interpretare (verb) *interpret*
interprete(m/f) *interpreter*

interruttore (m) *switch*
interurbana (f) *long-distance
 (call)*
intossicazione alimentare
 (f) *food poisoning*
inverno (m) *winter*
invito (m) *invitation*
io *I*
l'Irlanda (f) *Ireland*;
 l'Irlanda del Nord
 Northern Ireland
irlandese (adj) *Irish*
isola (f) *island*
Italia (f) *Italy*
italiano (adj) *Italian*

J, K

jazz (m) *jazz*
jeans (m pl) *jeans*
jogging (m) *jogging*
krapfen (m) *doughnut*

L

la *the* (f)
là *there*
lacca per i capelli (f)
 hairspray
lacci (m pl) *laces (of shoe)*
ladro/a (m/f) *burglar, thief*
laggiù *over there*
lago (m) *lake*
lamette (f pl) *razor blades*
lampada (f) *lamp*; **la
 lampada da studio**
 reading lamp
lampadina (f) *light bulb*
lampone (m) *raspberry*
lana (f) *wool*
lassativo (m) *laxative*
lassù *up there*
lato (m) *side* (adj: edge)
latte (m) *milk*; **il latte
 detergente** *skin cleanser*
latteria (f) *dairy*
latticini (m pl) *dairy products*
lattina (f) *can (vessel)*
lattuga (f) *lettuce*
laurea triennale (f)
 bachelor's degree
laurea magistrale (f)
 master's degree
**laureato/a: sono laureato/a
 in…** (m/f) *I have a degree in…*
lavabo (m) *sink*
lavanderia (f) *laundry
 (place)*; **la lavanderia a
 secco** *dry cleaner's*
lavandino (m) *sink, wash basin*
lavastoviglie (f) *dishwasher*
lavatrice (f) *washing
 machine*
lavello (m) *sink (kitchen)*
lavorare (verb) *to work*
lavorare a maglia (verb) *knit*
lavoro (m) *job, work*
le *the* (f pl)

lecca lecca (m) *lollipop*
legare (verb) *to tie*
legge (f) *law*
leggere (verb) *to read*
leggero (adj) *light* (not heavy)
legno (m) *wood* (material)
lei *she*
Lei *you* (singular, formal)
lente (f) *lens*; **le lenti a contatto** *contact lenses*; **le lenti semi-rigide** *gas-permeable lenses*
lento (adj) *slow*
lenzuola (f pl) *bed linen*
lenzuolo (m) *sheet*
lesso (adj) *boiled*
lettera (f) *letter*
letteratura (f) *literature*
lettino (m) *cot*
letto (m) *bed*
leva del cambio (f) *gear stick*
levata (f) *collection* (postal)
lezione (f) *lesson*
libbra (f) *pound* (weight)
libero (adj) *free* (not occupied)
libero/a professionista (m/f) *self-employed*
libreria (f) *bookshop*
libretto degli assegni (m) *checkbook*
libro (m) *book*
limetta per le unghie (f) *nail file*
limonata (f) *lemonade*
limoncello (m) *lime* (fruit)
limone (m) *lemon*
limpido (adj) *clear* (water)
linea (f) *line* (telephone, etc.); **la linea aerea** *airline*; **la linea esterna** *outside line*
lingua (f) *language, tongue*
liquido per lenti (m) *saline solution* (for contact lenses)
liquore (m) *liqueur*
lisca (f) *fishbone*
litro (m) *liter*
livido (m) *bruise*
lo (m) *the*
località sciistica (f) *ski resort*
locomotiva (f) *engine* (train)
lontano (adj) *far*; **è lontano?** *is it far away?*
loro *they, their, them*; **la loro stanza** *their room*; **il loro amico** *their friend*; **i loro libri** *their books*; **le loro penne** *their pens*; **è loro** *it's theirs*; **è per loro** *it's for them*; **dallo a loro** *give it to them*
lozione solare (f) *suntan lotion*
lucchetto (m) *padlock*
luce (f) (adj) *light*
luci di posizione (f pl) *parking lights*
lucido per le scarpe (m) *shoe polish*
luglio *July*

lui *he, him*; **è per lui** *it's for him*
luna (f) *moon*; **la luna di miele** *honeymoon*
luna park (m) *fair* (funfair)
lunedì *Monday*
lunghezza (f) *length*
lungo (adj) *long*

M

ma *but*
macchina (f) *car*
macchina da scrivere (f) *typewriter*
macchina fotografica (f) *camera*
macelleria (f) *butcher's* (shop)
madre (f) *mother*
magari *perhaps*
maggio *May*
maglieria (f) *knitwear*
maglietta (f) *T-shirt*
maglione (m) *sweater*
magro (adj) *thin*
mai *never*; **non fumo mai** *I never smoke*
mal di denti (m) *toothache*
mal di pancia (m) *stomachache*
mal di testa (m) *headache*
malato (adj) *ill*
male: mi fa male il/la... *my... hurts*; **farà male?** *will it hurt?*
mamma (f) *mom*
mancia (f) *tip* (money)
mandare (verb) *to send*
mandarino (m) *tangerine*
mangianastri (m) *cassette player*
mangiare (verb) *to eat*
manica (f) *sleeve*
maniglia (f) *handle* (door)
mano (f) *hand*
manzo (m) *beef*
mappe online (f pl) *online maps*
marciapiede (m) *pavement*
mare (m) *sea*
marea (f) *tide*
margarina (f) *margarine*
marito (m) *husband*
marmellata (f) *jam*; **la marmellata d'arance** *marmalade*
marmitta (f) *exhaust* (car)
marmo (m) *marble*
marrone (adj) *brown*
martedì *Tuesday*
martello (m) *hammer*
marzo *March*
mascara (m) *mascara*
maschera (f) *face mask*
materassino gonfiabile (m) *air mattress*
materasso (m) *mattress*
matita (f) *pencil*
matrimoniale (f) *double room*

matrimonio (m) *wedding*
mattina (f) *morning*; **di mattina** *in the morning*
maturo (adj) *ripe*
meccanico (m) *mechanic*
medicina (f) *medicine*
medico (m/f) *doctor*
il Mediterraneo *the Mediterranean*
medusa (f) *jellyfish*
mela (f) *apple*
melone (m) *melon*
meno *less*
menta piperita (f) *peppermint*
menù (m) *menu*
mercato (m) *market*
mercoledì *Wednesday*
mese (m) *month*
messa (f) *Mass* (church)
messaggio (m) *message*
metà *half*
metro(politana) (f) *underground*
mettere (verb) *to put*
mezzanotte (f) *midnight*
mezzo *half*: **...e mezzo** *half past...*; **mezz'ora** *half an hour*; **mezzo pensione** *half board*
mezzogiorno (m) *noon*
mia (f) *my, mine*; **la mia borsa** *my bag*; **la borsa è mia** *the bag is mine*
mi chiamo... *my name's...*
mi dispiace *I'm sorry*
mie (f pl) *my, mine*; **le mie chiavi** *my keys*; **le chiavi sono mie** *the keys are mine*
miei (m pl) *my, mine*; **i miei vestiti** *my dresses*
miele (m) *honey*
migliore (adj) *best, better*; **migliore di** *better than*
Milano *Milan*
milione *million*
mille *thousand*
minestra (f) *soup*
minuto (m) *minute*
mio (m) *my, mine*; **il mio libro** *my book*; **è mio** *it's mine*
mirino (m) *viewfinder*
mi scusi! *excuse me!* (to get attention)
mobili (m pl) *furniture*
moda (f) *fashion*
modem (m) *modem*
modulo per la domanda (m) *application form*
moglie (f) *wife*
molla (f) *spring* (mechanical)
molletta (f) *clothespin*
molluschi (m pl) *shellfish* (mollusks)
molo (m) *dock*
molto *a lot*; **molto meglio** *much better*; **molto più lentamente** *much slower*; **non molto** *not much*

moltissimo *very much*
moneta (f) *coin*
monitor (m) *monitor* (computer)
montagna (f) *mountain*
monumento (m) *monument*
mora (f) *blackberry*
morbido (adj) *soft*
mordere (verb: by dog) *bite*
morire (verb) *to die*
morso (m) (noun: by dog) *bite*
morto (adj) *dead*
mosaico (m) *mosaic*
mosca (f) *fly* (insect)
mostra (f) *exhibition*
motocicletta (f) *motorcycle*
motore (m) *engine* (car)
motorino (m) *moped*
motoscafo (m) *motorboat*
mountain bike (f) *mountain bike*
mouse (m) *mouse* (computer)
municipio (m) *town hall*
muovere (verb) *to move;* **non muoverti!** *don't move!*
muratore/muratrice (m/f) *bricklayer*
muro (m) *wall*
museo (m) *museum*
musica (f) *music;* **la musica classica** *classical music;* **la musica folk** *folk music;* **la musica pop** *pop music*
musicista (m/f) *musician*
mutande (f pl) *underpants*

N

Napoli *Naples*
nascere (verb) *to be born;* **sono nato/a a Londra** *I was born in London*
naso (m) *nose*
Natale (m) *Christmas*
nave (f) *boat, ship;* **la nave a vapore** *steamer* (boat)
nebbia (f) *fog*
necessario (adj) *necessary*
negativo (m) *negative* (photo); (adj) **negativo**
negozio (m) *shop;* **il negozio di dischi** *record shop;* **il negozio di giocattoli** (m) *toy shop*
neozelandese (m/f) (adj) *New Zealander; New Zealand*
nero (adj) *black*
nessuno *nobody;* **da nessuna parte** *nowhere*
neve (f) *snow*
niente *nothing;* **di niente** *you're welcome;* **non serve a niente** *it's no use*
nightclub (m) *nightclub*
nipote (f) *granddaughter, niece*
nipote (m) *grandson, nephew*

no *no* (negative response)
nocciola (f) *nut*
noce (f) *nut*
noi *we, us;* **è per noi** *it's for us*
noioso (adj) *boring;* **che noia!** *that's boring!*
noleggiare (verb) *to rent*
nome (m) *name;* **il nome di battesimo** *first name*
non *not;* **non è...** *he's not...*
nonna (f) *grandmother*
nonni (m pl) *grandparents*
nonno (m) *grandfather*
nord (m) *north*
normale (adj) *ordinary*
nostro/a *our;* **il nostro albergo** *our hotel;* **la nostra macchina** *our car;* **è nostro** *it's ours*
notizie (f pl) *news;* (on radio) **il notiziario**
notte (f) *night*
novanta *ninety*
nove *nine*
novembre *November*
nubile (f) (adj: unmarried woman) *single*
numero (m) *number, shoe size;* **il numero di telefono** *telephone number*
nuotare (verb) *to swim*
nuoto (m) *swimming*
la Nuova Zelanda *New Zealand*
nuovo (adj) *new;* **di nuovo** *again*

O

o *or;* **o... o...** *either... or...*
obbligatorio (adj) *necessary*
occhiali (m pl) *eyeglasses,* **occhiali da sole** (m pl) *sunglasses*
occhio (m) *eye;* **gli occhi** *eyes*
occupato (adj) *busy, occupied*
odore (m) *smell*
oggetti di valore (m pl) *valuables*
oggi *today*
ogni *each, every;* **ogni tanto** *occasionally*
ognuno *everyone*
olio (m) *oil;* **olio d'oliva** (m) *olive oil*
oliva (f) *olive*
ombrello (m) *umbrella*
ombrellone (m) *sunshade*
omelette (f) *omelet*
omeopatia (f) *homeopathy*
omosessuale (adj) *gay* (homosexual)
onda (f) *wave;* **i capelli ondulati** (m pl) *wavy hair*
onesto (adj) *honest*
opera (f) *work (of art), opera*
operatore/operatrice (m/f) *operator*

operazione (f) *operation*
opuscolo (m) *brochure*
ora (f) *hour;* **ora sono occupato** *I'm busy now*
orario (m) *timetable;* **l'orario di apertura** *opening times;* **l'orario di visita** (m) *visiting hours*
orchestra (f) *orchestra*
ordinativo (m) *order* (for goods)
ordine del giorno (m) *agenda*
ore: che ore sono? *what's the time?*
orecchini (m pl) *earrings*
orecchio (m) *ear;* **le orecchie** (f pl) *ears*
organo (m) *organ* (music)
oro (m) *gold*
orologio (m) *clock, watch*
orribile (adj) *awful, horrible*
ospedale (m) *hospital*
ospite (m/f) *guest*
ossigenare (verb) *to bleach* (hair)
osso (m) *bone*
ostello della gioventù (m) *youth hostel*
ottanta *eighty*
ottico (m) *optician*
ottimo (adj) *excellent*
otto *eight*
ottobre *October*
otturatore (m) *shutter* (camera)
otturazione (f) *filling* (in tooth)
ovest (m) *west*

P

pacchetto (m) *package, packet*
pacco (m) *parcel*
padella (f) *frying pan*
Padova *Padua*
padre (m) *father*
padrona di casa (f) *hostess*
padrone di casa (m) *host*
paese (m) *country* (state), *village*
pagamento (m) *payment*
pagamento contactless (m) *contactless payment*
pagare (verb) *to pay;* **pagare in contanti** (verb) *to pay cash*
pagina (f) *page*
paio (m) *pair;* **paia** (f pl) *pairs*
palazzo (m) *palace*
palestra (f) *gymnastics*
palla (f) *ball* (football, etc.)
pallacanestro (f) *basketball*
pallido (adj) *pale*
pallina (f) *ball* (tennis, etc.)
pallone (m) *ball, football*
palo della tenda (m) *tent pole*

pancetta (f) *bacon*
pane (m) *bread;* **il pane tostato** (m) *toast*
panificio (m) *baker*
panino (m) *sandwich; rock* (music)
panna (f) *cream* (dairy)
pannolini (m pl) *diapers*
pantaloncini (m pl) *shorts*
pantaloni (m pl) *trousers*
pantofole (m pl) *slippers*
papà (m) *dad*
Papa: il Papa *Pope*
parabrezza (m) *windshield*
paraffina (f) *paraffin*
paralume (m) *lampshade*
paraurti (m) *bumper*
parcheggiare (verb) *to park*
parcheggio (m) *car park*
parco (m) *park*
parlare (verb) *to talk, speak;* **parla... ?** *do you speak... ?;* **non parlo...** *I don't speak...*
parola (f) *word*
parrucchiere/parrucchiera (m/f) *hairdresser's*
parte posteriore (f) *back* (not front)
partenza (f) *departure;* **le partenze** *departures*
particolarmente *especially*
partire (verb) *to depart, leave*
partito (m) *party* (political)
passaporto (m) *passport;* **il controllo passaporti** *passport control*
passatempo (m) *hobby*
passeggero/passeggera (m/f) *passenger*
passeggiata (f) *walk;* **andare a fare una passeggiata** (verb) *to go for a walk*
passegino (m) *stroller*
password (f) *password*
pasta (f) *pasta*
pasticceria (f) *cake shop*
pasticche per la gola (f pl) *throat lozenges*
pasto (m) *meal*
patata (f) *potato*
patatine (f pl) *chips*
patatine fritte (f pl) *potato chips*
patente (f) *license;* **patente di guida** *driver's license*
patio (m) *terrace*
pattini da ghiaccio (m pl) *ice skates*
pattumiera (f) *dustbin*
paura: (f) ho paura *I'm frightened*
pavimento (m) *floor* (ground)
pazzo (adj) *crazy*
pedone (m) *pedestrian;* **la zona pedonale** *pedestrian zone*

peggiore (adj) *worst, worse*
pelle (f) *leather*
pelletteria (f) *leather goods shop*
pellicola (f) *film* (for camera)
penicillina (f) *penicillin*
penna (f) *pen*
pennello (m) *paintbrush*
pensare (verb) *to think;* **penso di sì** *I think so;* **ci penserò** *I'll think about it*
pensione completa (f) *full board*
pentola (f) *saucepan;* **la pentola a pressione** *steamer* (for cooking)
pepe (m) *pepper* (spice)
peperone (m) *pepper* (red, green)
per *for;* **per me** *for me*
pera (f) *pear*
perché *because*
perché? *why?, what for?*
perfetto (adj) *perfect*
pericoloso (adj) *dangerous*
periferia (f) *suburbs*
perla (f) *pearl*
permanente (f) *perm*
permesso *allowed;* **permesso!** *excuse me!* (to get past)
persiane (f pl) *shutters* (window)
personale ai piani (m) *housekeeping*
personale delle pulizie (m/f) *cleaning staff*
persone disabili (m pl) *the disabled*
pesante (adj) *heavy*
pesca (f) *peach, fishing;* **andare a pesca** *to go fishing*
pesce (m) *fish*
pescheria (f) *fishmonger's* (shop)
pettinare (verb) *to comb*
pettine (m) *comb*
petto (m) *chest* (part of body)
pezzi di ricambio (m pl) *spare parts* (car)
pezzo (m) *piece*
phon (m) *hair dryer*
piacere (verb) *to like;* **mi piace...** *I like...;* **mi piace nuotare** *I like swimming*
piacere *pleased to meet you*
piacere di conoscerla *how do you do?*
piangere (verb: weep) *cry*
piano (m) *floor* (story); **piano di lavoro** *countertop*
pianta (f) *map* (of town), *plan; plant*
pianterreno (m) *ground floor*
piastrella (f) *tile*
piattino (m) *saucer*
piatto (m) *plate, meal;* **i piatti pronti** *ready meals*

piatto (adj) *flat* (level)
piazza (f) *square*
piazzola (f) *pitch* (in campsite, etc.)
picche (m pl) *spades* (cards)
picchetto (m) *tent peg*
piccolo (adj) *little, small*
picnic (m) *picnic*
piede (m) *foot;* **a piedi** *on foot*
pieno (adj) *full*
pigiama (m) *pajamas*
pigro (adj) *lazy*
pin (m) *PIN*
pinacoteca (f) *art gallery*
pinne (f pl) *flippers*
pinzette (f pl) *tweezers*
pioggia (f) *rain*
piovra (f) *octopus*
pipa (f) *pipe* (for smoking)
piscina (f) *swimming pool*
piselli (m pl) *peas*
pistola (f) *gun* (pistol)
pistone (m) *piston*
pittura (f) *painting*
più *more;* **più di...** *more than...;* **più presto possibile** *as soon as possible*
piumino (m) *duvet*
piuttosto *pretty, quite*
pizzo (m) *lace*
plastica (f) *plastic*
platea (f) *seats* (in theater)
po' *a little;* **è un po' grande** *it's a little big;* **solo un po'** *just a little*
poi *then*
polipo (m) *octopus*
politica (f) *politics*
polizia (f) *police*
poliziotto/poliziotta (m/f) *police officer*
pollame (m) *poultry*
pollo (m) *chicken*
polso (m) *wrist*
poltrona (f) *armchair*
pomata (f) *ointment*
pomeriggio (m) *afternoon*
pomodoro (m) *tomato*
ponte (m) *bridge*
porcellana (f) *china*
porta (f) *door*
portacenere (m) *ashtray*
portafoglio (m) *wallet, purse*
portare (verb) *to bring;* **portare via** (verb) *to carry out*
portiere (m/f) *porter* (hotel); **il portiere di notte** *night porter*
portinaio/portinaia (m/f) *caretaker*
porto (m) *harbor, port*
possibile (adj) *possible*
posso avere...? *can I have...?*
posta (f) *post;* **la posta elettronica** *email*
posteggio dei taxi (m) *taxi rank*
postino/a (m/f) *mailman/ mailwoman*

posto (m) *place, accommodations, seat*
postumi della sbornia (m pl) *hangover*
potreste...? *could you...?*
povero (adj) *poor*
pranzo (m) *lunch*
prato (m) *lawn*
preferire *to prefer*
prego *you're welcome;*
prego? *pardon?*
prelevare (verb) *to withdraw* (money)
prendere (verb) *to fetch* (something)
prendere (verb) *to take;* **prendere il sole** *to sunbathe;* **prendere il treno** *to catch the train*
prenotare (verb) *to book*
prenotazione (f) *reservation*
preoccuparsi (verb) *to worry;* **non si preoccupi!** *don't worry!*
presa di corrente (f) *electrical hook-up*
preservativo (m) *condom*
presto *early;* **a presto** *see you soon*
prete (m) *priest*
preventivo (m) *estimate*
prezzemolo (m) *parsley*
prezzo (m) *price;* **il prezzo d'ingresso** *admission charge*
prima di... *before...*
primavera (f) *spring* (season)
primi piatti (m pl) *starters*
primo *first;* **il primo piano** *first floor;* **la prima classe** *first class*
principiante (m/f) *beginner*
privato (adj) *private*
problema (m) *problem;* **non c'è problema** *no problem*
professore/professoressa (m/f) *teacher;* **il professore universitario** *university lecturer*
profitti (m pl) *profits*
profondo (adj) *deep*
profumo (m) *perfume*
programma (m) *schedule*
proibito (adj) *forbidden*
prolunga (f) *extension lead*
pronto (adj) *ready, hello* (on phone)
pronto soccorso (m) *emergency department, first aid*
prosciutto (m) *ham*
prossimo (adj) *next;* **la settimana prossima** *next week*
provare (verb) *to try*
pubblico (adj) *public*
pulce (f) *flea*
pulire (verb) *to clean*
pulito (adj) *clean*

pullman (m) *coach* (long-distance bus)
pungere (verb) *to bite* (by insect)
punta (f) *tip* (end)
puntina da disegno (f) *thumbtack*
puntura (f) *bite* (by insect)
può *he/she can;* **non può...** *he/she can't...*
puzzare (verb: stink) *to smell*

Q

quaderno (m) *notebook*
quadrato (adj) *square* (shape)
quadri (m pl) (cards) *diamonds*
qualche modo *somehow*
qualche parte *somewhere*
qualche volta *sometimes*
qualcosa *something*
qualcuno *somebody*
quale? *which?*
qualità (f) *quality*
quando? *when?*
quant'è? *how much is that?*
quanti anni hai? *how old are you?*
quanto ci vuole? *how long does it take?*
quanto costa? *how much?*
quanto dista da qui...? *how far is it to...?*
quaranta *forty*
quarto (m) *quarter;* **...e un quarto** *quarter past...*
quarto *fourth*
quasi *almost*
quattordici *fourteen*
quattro *four*
quei (m pl) *those;* **quei ragazzi** *those boys*
quella (f) *that;* **quella donna** *that woman*
quelle (f pl) *those;* **quelle cose** *those things*
quelli (m pl) *those;* **prendo quelli** *I'll take those*
quello (m) *that;* **quell'uomo** *that man;* **cos'è quello?** *what's that?*
questa (f) *this;* **questa donna** *this woman*
queste (f pl) *these;* **queste cose** *these things*
questi (m pl) *these;* **questi ragazzi** *these boys*
questo (m) *this;* **questo quadro** *this picture;* **quest'uomo** *this man;* **cos'è questo?** *what's this?;* **questo è il signor...** *this is Mr....*
quindici *fifteen*

R

raccomandata (f) *registered* (post)
radersi (verb) *to shave*
radiatore (m) *radiator*
radio (f) *radio*
radiografia (f) *x-ray*
raffreddore (m) *cold* (illness); **ho un raffreddore** *I have a cold*
ragazza (f) *girl*
ragazzo (m) *boy*
ragioniere/ragioniera (m/f) *accountant*
ragno (m) *spider*
rapporto di polizia (m) *police report*
raro (adj) *rare* (uncommon)
rastrello (m) *rake*
ratto (m) *rat*
ravanello (m) *radish*
reception (f) *reception* (hotel)
receptionist (m/f) *receptionist*
record (m) *record* (sports, etc.)
regalo (m) *gift*
reggiseno (m) *bra*
relazione (f) *report*
religione (f) *religion*
remare (verb) *to row*
remi (m pl) *oars*
rene (m) *kidney*
reparto (m) *department, ward;* **il reparto di pediatria** *children's ward;* **il reparto di radiologia** *x-ray department*
respirare (verb) *to breathe*
resti (m pl) *ruins*
restituire (verb: give back) *to return*
resto (m) (noun: remainder) *rest*
reticella (per i bagagli) (f) *luggage rack*
riavere indietro qualcosa (verb) *to get something back*
ribes nero (m) *black currant*
ricci (m pl) *curls*
ricco (adj) *rich*
ricerca (f) *research*
ricetta (f) *prescription*
ricevere (verb: obtain) *to get*
ricevuta (f) *receipt* (restaurants, hotels)
ricordare (verb) *to remember;* **non ricordo** *I don't remember*
ridere (verb) *to laugh*
riduttore (m) *adaptor*
riduzione (f) *discount*
rifiuti (m pl) *trash (bin)*
riga (f) *ruler* (for drawing)
rilassarsi (verb) *to relax*
rimorchio (m) *trailer*
rinfreschi (m pl) *refreshments*
rinfresco (m) *reception* (party)
ringraziare (verb) *to thank*

riparare (verb) *to repair*
ripieno (m) *filling (in sandwich, cake, etc.)*
riposarsi (verb) *to rest*
riscaldamento (m) *heating;* **il riscaldamento centralizzato** *central heating*
riscuotere (verb) *to cash*
riso (m) *rice*
ristorante (m) *restaurant*
ritardo: (m) **l'autobus è in ritardo** *the bus is late*
ritiro bagagli (m) *baggage claim*
ritornare (verb) *to return*
riunione (f) *meeting*
rivista (f) *magazine*
roccia (f) *rock (stone)*
Roma *Rome*
romanzo (m) *novel*
rosa (f) *rose;* *pink* (adj: color)
rossetto (m) *lipstick*
rosso (adj) *red*
rotatoria (f) *roundabout*
rotondo (adj) *round (circular)*
rotto (adj) *broken;* **la gamba rotta** *broken leg*
roulotte (f) *trailer, caravan*
rovine (f pl) *ruins*
rubare (verb) *steal;* **è stato rubato** *it's been stolen*
rubinetto (m) *tap*
rubino (m) *ruby (gem)*
rugby (m) *rugby*
rullino a colori (m) *color film*
rum (m) *rum*
rumoroso (adj) *noisy*
ruota (f) *wheel*
ruscello (m) *stream*

S

sabato *Saturday*
sabbia (f) *sand*
sacchetto (m) *bag;* **il sacchetto di plastica** *plastic bag;* **il sacchetto per la pattumiera** *trash bag;* **sacco a pelo** *sleeping bag*
sala (f) *room;* **la sala d'aspetto** *waiting room;* **la sala da pranzo** *dining room;* **la sala operatoria** *operating room*
salame (m) *salami*
saldi (m pl) *sale (at reduced prices)*
sale (m) *salt*
salire (verb) *to go up;* **salire su** (verb: bus, etc.) *to get on*
salmone (m) *salmon*
salsa (f) *sauce*
salsiccia (f) *sausage*
salumeria (f) *delicatessen*
salutare (verb) *to wave*

sandali (m pl) *sandals*
sangue (m) *blood;* **le analisi del sangue** (f pl) *blood test*
sapere (verb) *know (fact);* **non so** *I don't know*
sapone (m) *soap*
la Sardegna *Sardinia*
sauna (f) *sauna*
sazio (adj) *full (up):* **sono sazio** *I'm full (up) (after a meal)*
sbagliato (adj) *wrong*
sbrigati! *hurry up!*
scacchi (m pl) *chess*
scala (f) *staircase;* **le scale** *stairs;* **la scala mobile** *escalator*
scaldabagno (m) *water heater*
scambiare (verb) *to exchange*
scarpe (f pl) *shoes;* **le scarpe da calcio** *football shoes;* **le scarpe da ginnastica** *trainers*
scatola (f) *box, tin*
scendere (verb) *to go down;* **scendere da** (verb: bus, etc.) *to get off*
schermo (m) *screen, monitor*
scherzo (m) *joke*
schiena (f) *back (body)*
schiuma (f) *foam, mousse, cream (for hair);* **la schiuma da barba** *shaving cream*
sci (m pl) *skis*
scialle (m) *shawl*
sci (m) *skiing;* **andare a sciare** (verb) *to go skiing*
sciarpa (f) *scarf*
scienza (f) *science*
sciroppo (m) *syrup*
scodella (f) *bowl*
scompartimento (m) *compartment*
scontrino (m) *receipt (shops, bars)*
scopa (f) *brush (cleaning)*
la Scozia *Scotland*
scozzese (adj) *Scottish*
scritto da... *written by...*
scrivania (f) *desk*
scuola (f) *school*
scuro (adj) *dark*
scusate! *excuse me! (when sneezing, etc.)*
scusi! sorry!; scusi? *pardon?*
se *if, whether*
secchio (m) *bucket*
secco (adj) *dry (wine)*
secondi piatti (m pl) *main courses*
secondo *second;* **seconda classe** *second class*
sede centrale (f) *head office*
sedia (f) *chair;* **la sedia girevole** *swivel chair;* **la sedia a rotelle** *wheelchair*
sedici *sixteen*

seggiolino per la macchina (m) *car seat (for a baby)*
segretario/segretaria (m/f) *secretary;* **la segreteria telefonica** *answering machine, voicemail*
sei *six*
sei *you are (singular, informal)*
semaforo (m) *traffic lights*
seminario (m) *seminar*
seminterrato (m) *basement*
semplice (adj) *simple*
sempre *always;* **sempre dritto** *straight on*
senape (f) *mustard*
senso unico (m) *one way*
sentiero (m) *path*
sentire (verb) *to hear*
senza *without;* **senza piombo** *unleaded*
separati (m pl) *separated (couple)*
separato (adj) *separate*
sera (f) *evening*
serio (adj) *serious*
servizio in camera (m) *room service*
sessanta *sixty*
seta (f) *silk*
sete (f) *thirsty;* **ho sete** *I'm thirsty*
settanta *seventy*
sette *seven*
settembre *September*
settimana (f) *week;* **la settimana scorsa** *last week*
shampoo (m) *shampoo*
sherry (m) *sherry*
shopping (m) *shopping*
short (m pl) *shorts*
sì *yes*
sia... che... *both... and...*
siamo *we are*
Sicilia (f) *Sicily*
sicuro (adj) *safe (not dangerous);* *sure (certain);* **sei sicuro?** *are you sure?*
siepe (f) *hedge*
siete *you are (plural, informal)*
sigaretta (f) *cigarette*
sigaro (m) *cigar*
significare (verb) *to mean;* **che cosa significa?** *what does this mean?*
Signor (m) *Mr.*
signora (f) *lady, madam*
Signora *Mrs.*
signore (m) *sir*
simpatico (adj) *nice (pleasant)*
sinagoga (f) *synagogue*
sinistra *left (adj: not right)*
sito internet (m) *website*
slittare (verb) *to skid*
smalto per le unghie (m) *nail polish*
soffitta (f) *attic*
soffitto (m) *ceiling*
soffocante (adj) *close (stuffy)*

soggiorno (m) *living room*
soldi (m pl) *money*
sole (m) *sun;* **c'è il sole** (adj) *it's sunny*
solito (adj) *usual;* **di solito** *usually*
sollievo: (m) **che sollievo!** *what a relief!*
solo (adj) *alone, single (one), only;* **da solo** *by oneself*
sonnifero (m) *sleeping pill*
sonno (m) *sleep*
sono *I am;* **sono di...** *I come from...*
sopra *over (above)*
sopracciglio (m) *eyebrow;* **sopracciglia** (f pl) *eyebrows*
sordo (adj) *deaf*
sorella (f) *sister*
sorpassare (verb) *to pass (driving)*
sorridere (verb) *to smile*
sorriso (m) *smile*
sosta vietata (f) *no parking*
sotto *below, under*
sottoveste (f) *underskirt*
souvenir (m) *souvenir*
Spagna (f) *Spain*
spagnolo (adj) *Spanish*
spago (m) *string (cord)*
spalla (f) *shoulder*
spazio (m) *room (space)*
spazzatura (f) *rubbish*
spazzola (f) *hairbrush*
spazzolare (verb) *to brush (hair)*
spazzolino da denti (m) *toothbrush*
specchio (m) *mirror*
spedire per posta (verb) *to post*
spesa (f) *shopping;* **andare a fare la spesa** (verb) *to go shopping*
spesso *often;* (adj) *thick*
spettatori/spettatrici (m pl/ f pl) *audience*
spiacente (adj) *I'm sorry*
spiaggia (f) *beach*
spicci (m pl) *cash, change*
spilla (f) *brooch;* **la spilla di sicurezza** *safety pin*
spillatrice (f) *stapler*
spillo (m) *pin*
spina (f) *plug (electrical)*
spinaci (m pl) *spinach*
spingere (verb) *to push*
sporco (adj) *dirty*
sport (m) *sport*
sportello (m) *door (of car);* **lo sportello automatico** *cash machine*
sposato (adj) *married*
spuntino (m) *snack*
stampante (f) *printer*
stampelle (f pl) *crutches*
stanco (m) (adj) *tired*

stanza (f) *room;* **stanza libera** *vacancy (room)*
star (f) *star (film)*
stasera *tonight*
statua (f) *statue*
stazione (f) *station;* **la stazione di polizia** *police station;* **la stazione di servizio** *gas station*
steccato (m) *fence*
stella (f) *star*
stereo (m) *music system*
sterlina (f) *pounds sterling*
stesso *same;* **lo stesso vestito** *the same dress*
stirare (verb) *to iron*
stivale (m) *boot (footwear);* **gli stivali di gomma** *Wellington boots*
stoffa (f) *fabric*
stomaco (m) *stomach*
storia (f) *history*
straccio per la polvere (m) *duster*
strada (f) *road, street*
straniero/straniera (m/f) *foreigner*
strano (adj) *odd, funny*
stretta di mano (f) *handshake*
stretto (adj) *narrow, tight (clothes)*
strofinaccio (m) *dishcloth*
strumento musicale (m) *musical instrument*
studente/studentessa (m/f) *student*
stupido (adj) *stupid*
su *on, over (above);* **sul tavolo** *on the table;* **un libro su Venezia** *a book on Venice*
succo (m) *juice;* **il succo d'arancia** *orange juice;* **il succo di frutta** *fruit juice;* **il succo di pomodoro** *tomato juice*
sud (m) *south*
sudare (verb) *to sweat*
sudore (m) *sweat*
suo (m) *her/his/your (singular, formal):* **il suo libro** *her/his/your book;* **la sua casa** *her/his/your house;* **le sue scarpe** *her/his/your shoes;* **i suoi vestiti** *her/his/your dresses;* **è suo** *it's hers/his/ yours*
suoceri (m pl) *in-laws*
supermercato (m) *supermarket*
supplemento (m) *supplement*
supposta (f) *suppository*
surgelati (m pl) *frozen foods*
sveglia (f) *alarm clock*
svenire (verb) *to faint*
sviluppare (verb: film) *to develop*
la Svizzera *Switzerland*
svizzero (adj) *Swiss*

T

tabaccaio (m) *tobacconist (shop)*
tabacco (m) *tobacco*
tacco (m) *heel (of shoe)*
taglia (f) *size (clothes)*
tagliare (verb) *to cut, chop*
tagliaunghie (m) *nail clippers*
taglio (m) *cut, haircut*
talco (m) *talcum powder*
tallone (m) *heel (of foot)*
tamponi (m pl) *tampons*
tappeto (m) *carpet, rug*
tappo (m) *cap (bottle), cork, plug (sink)*
tardi *late;* **si sta facendo tardi** *it's getting late;* **più tardi** *later*
targa (f) *license plate*
tariffa (f) *fare, rate;* **la tariffa ridotta** *concessionary rate*
tasca (f) *pocket*
tastare (verb) *to feel (touch)*
tastiera (f) *keyboard*
tavoletta di cioccolata (f) *bar of chocolate*
tavolo (m) *table*
taxi (m) *taxi*
tazza (f) *cup, mug*
tè (m) *tea;* **il tè con latte** *tea with milk*
teatro (m) *theater*
tecnico (m) *technician*
tedesco (adj) *German*
telefonare (verb) *to telephone*
telefonata (f) *telephone call*
telefonino (m) *cell phone*
telefono (m) *telephone*
televisione (f) *television*
telo per campeggio (m) *ground sheet*
telo protettivo (m) *fly sheet*
temperamatite (m) *pencil sharpener*
temperatura (f) *temperature*
temperino (m) *penknife*
tempesta (f) *storm*
tempo (m) *time, weather;* **il tempo libero** *leisure time*
temporale (m) *thunderstorm*
tenda (f) *curtain, tent;* **la tenda avvolgibile** *blind (on window)*
tennis (m) *tennis*
terminal (m) *terminal (airport)*
termosifone (m) *heater*
terra (f) *soil, land*
terribile (adj) *awful, terrible*
terrina (f) *mixing bowl*
terzo *third*
testa (f) *head*
testimone (m/f) *witness*
tetto (m) *roof*
il Tevere *the Tiber*
tirare (verb) *to pull*
tirocinante (m/f) *trainee*

tisana (f) *herbal tea*
toilette (f) *toilet;* (men's)
  la toilette degli uomini;
  (women's) **la toilette**
  delle donne
topo (m) *mouse* (animal)
torcia (elettrica) (f) *flashlight*
Torino *Turin*
tornare (verb) *to come back*
torre (f) *tower*
torta (f) *cake*
tosaerba (m) *lawnmower*
la Toscana *Tuscany*
tosse (f) *cough*
tossire (verb) *to cough*
tovagliolo (m) *napkin*
tradizione (f) *tradition*
tradurre (verb) *to translate*
traduttore/traduttrice
  (m/f) *translator*
traffico (m) *traffic*
traghetto (m) *ferry*
trampolino (m) *diving board*
tranquillo (adj) *quiet*
traslocare (verb) *to move
  house*
trattore (m) *tractor*
tre *three*
trecento *three hundred*
tredici *thirteen*
treno (m) *train*
trenta *thirty*
triste (adj) *sad*
troppo *too* (excessively)
trucco (m) *makeup*
tu *you* (singular, informal)
tubo (m) *hose, pipe* (for water)
tuffarsi (verb) *to dive*
tuffo (m) *dive*
tunnel (m) *tunnel*
tuo, tua, tuoi, tue *your*
  (singular, informal);
  il tuo libro *your book;*
  la tua camicia *your shirt;*
  le tue scarpe *your shoes;*
  è tuo? *is this yours?*
turista (m/f) *tourist*
tuta da ginnastica (f) *track suit*
tutto, tutta, tutti, tutte
  all; everything; **tutte le
  strade** *all the streets;*
  questo è tutto *that's all;*
  tutti *everyone;* **tutti i
  giorni** *every day*
TV via cavo (f) *cable TV*
TV satellitare *satellite TV*

U

ubriaco (adj) *drunk*
uccello (m) *bird*
udire (verb) *to hear*
ufficio (m) *office;* **l'ufficio
  oggetti smarriti** *lost
  property office;* **l'ufficio
  postale** *post office;*
  l'ufficio turistico *tourist
  office*

ultimo (adj) *last* (final)
umido (adj) *damp*
un, uno, una, un' *a*
undici *eleven*
unghia (f) *nail* (finger)
unguento (m) *ointment*
università (f) *university*
uno *one;* **l'una** *one o'clock*
uomo (m) *man;* **gli
  uomini** *men*
uovo (m) *egg*
urgente (adj) *urgent*
usare (verb) *to use*
uscire (verb) *to go out*
uscita (f) *exit, gate*
  (at airport)
uso (m) *use*
utile (adj) *useful*
uva (f) *grapes*
uvetta (f) *raisins*

V

vacanza (f) *vacation*
vaccinazione (f) *vaccination*
vagone letto (m) *sleeping car*
valigia (f) *case, suitcase*
valle (f) *valley*
valvola (f) *valve*
vanga (f) *spade* (shovel)
vaniglia (f) *vanilla*
varecchina (f) *bleach*
vasca (f) *bath* (tub)
vaso (m) *vase*
vassoio (m) *tray*
vattene! (verb) *go away!*
Vaticano (m) *Vatican;* **Città
  del Vaticano** *Vatican City*
vecchio (adj) *old*
vedere (verb) *to see*
vegetariano (adj) *vegetarian*
veicolo (m) *vehicle*
vela (f) *sailing*
veleno (m) *poison*
veloce (adj) *fast, quick*
velocità (f) *speed*
vendere (verb) *to sell*
vendite (f pl) *sales* (of
  goods, etc.)
venerdì *Friday*
Venezia *Venice*
venga qui! (verb) *come here!*
  (formal); **venga con me**
  come with me (formal)
venire (verb) *to come*
venti *twenty*
ventilatore (m) *fan*
  (ventilator)
vento (m) *wind*
verde (adj) *green*
verdura (f) *vegetables*
vernice (f) *paint*
vero (adj) *true*
vespa (f) *wasp*
vestito (m) *dress;* **i vestiti**
  (m pl) *clothes*
veterinario/veterinaria
  (m/f) *vet*

vetro (m) *glass* (material)
via aerea (f) *air mail*
viaggiare (verb) *to travel*
viaggio (m) *journey*
viale (m) *driveway*
vialetto (m) *path*
vicino (a) *close, near (to);*
  vicino alla finestra *near
  the window;* **vicino alla
  porta** *near the door*
video cassetta (f) *video*
  (tape/film)
videogiochi (m pl) *video
  games*
videoregistratore (m) *VCR*
vieni qui! (verb) *come here!*
  (informal); **vieni con me**
  come with me (informal)
villa (f) *villa*
villaggio (m) *village*
vino (m) *wine;* **la lista dei
  vini** *wine list*
viola (adj) *purple*
violino (m) *violin*
visita (f) *visit;* **la visita
  guidata** *guided tour*
vista (f) *view*
vita (f) *life*
vite (f) *screw*
vivaio (m) *garden center*
vocabolarietto (m) *phrase
  book*
voce (f) *voice*
vodka (f) *vodka*
voi *you* (plural)
volantino (m) *leaflet*
volare (verb) *to fly*
volere (verb) *to want*
volo (m) *flight;* **il numero del
  volo** (m) *flight number*
vorrei *I'd like*
vuoto (adj) *empty*

W, Y, Z

whisky (m) *whisky*
yogurt (m) *yogurt*
zaino (m) *backpack*
zanzara (f) *mosquito*
zenzero (m) *ginger* (spice)
zia (f) *aunt*
zio (m) *uncle*
zoo (m) *zoo*
zucchero (m) *sugar*
zuppa (f) *soup*

Acknowledgments

FOURTH EDITION (2023)
For this edition, the publisher would like to thank Ankita Gupta for editorial assistance, Manpreet Kaur for picture research assistance, Karen Constanti for assistance with artwork commissioning, and Andiamo! Language Services Ltd. for the editorial review and foreign language proofreading.

THIRD EDITION (2018)
Senior Editors Angeles Gavira, Christine Stroyan
Project Art Editor Vanessa Marr
DTP Designer John Goldsmid
Jacket Design Development Manager Sophia MTT
Jacket Designer Juhi Sheth
Pre-Producer David Almond
Senior Producer Ana Vallarino
Associate Publisher Liz Wheeler
Publishing Director Jonathan Metcalf

FIRST EDITION (2005)
The publisher would like to thank the following for their help in the preparation of this book: Fiorella Elviri and Anna Mazzotti for the organization of location photography in Italy; Farmacia Gaoni, Rome; La Taverna del Borgia, Rome; Treni Italia, Tuscolana, Rome; Coolhurst Tennis Club, London; Magnet Showroom, Enfield, MyHotel, London; Kathy Gammon; Juliette Meeus and Harry.

Produced for Dorling Kindersley by Schermuly Design Co.
Language content for Dorling Kindersley by g-and-w publishing
Managed by Jane Wightwick
Editing and additional input Paula Tite
Additional design assistance Phil Gamble, Lee Riches, Fehmi Cömert, Sally Geeve
Additional editorial assistance Kajal Mistry, Paul Docherty, Lynn Bresler
Picture research Louise Thomas

PICTURE CREDITS

The publisher would like to thank the following for their kind permission to reproduce their photographs.

Key: a-above; b-below/bottom; c-centre; f-far; l-left; r-right; t-top

1 Getty Images: Suttipong Sutiratanachai. **2 Getty Images / iStock:** krblokhin (br). **3 Alamy Stock Photo:** imageBROKER / Daniel Meissner (bl). **Dreamstime.com:** Diego Vito Cervo (tl). **Getty Images / iStock:** IvanZivkovic (tr); nullplus (br). **9 Getty Images:** Maskot (tl). **10 Getty Images / iStock:** E+ / Morsa Images (cr). **Shutterstock.com:** Africa Studio (bl). **11 Getty Images / iStock:** pixdeluxe (tl). **12 Getty Images / iStock:** stocknroll (r). **13 Dreamstime.com:** Monkey Business Images (br). **Getty Images / iStock:** E+ / kali9 (cla); monkeybusinessimages (cl); E+ / Orbon Alija (clb). **14 Ingram Image Library:** (tr); **Dreamstime.com:** Diego Vito Cervo (br); Nyul (crb/woman). **Getty Images / iStock:** Prostock-Studio (crb). **15 Dreamstime.com:** Arne9001 (cla). **Getty Images / iStock:** agrobacter (cl); nd3000 (tl); **Ingram Image Library:** (cbl, bl). **17 Getty Images / iStock:** E+ / Morsa Images (b); pixdeluxe (ca). **18-19 Getty Images / iStock:** IvanZivkovic (c). **18 Dreamstime.com:** Billyfoto (clb). **19 Alamy Stock Photo:** Foodfolio (c); nito (cb). **21 Getty Images:** DigitalVision / 10'000 Hours (tl). **22 Getty Images / iStock:** gmevi (crb). **23 DK Images:** Dave king (tcl). **24 Getty Images:** Stuart Snelling / EyeEm (r); **Ingram Image Library:** (bl). **25 Ingram Image Library:** (tl). **Getty Images / iStock:** monkeybusinessimages (clb); ShotShare (cl); monkeybusinessimages (bl). **26 Dreamstime.com:** Billyfoto (br); Monkey Business Images (crb). **Getty Images / iStock:** IvanZivkovic (bc); kuppa_rock (tr). **27 Getty Images / iStock:** gmevi (tl). **28 Dreamstime.com:** Robert Kneschke (br); Laupri (cra). **29 Alamy Stock Photo:** PhotoAlto / Michele Constantini (bl). **Shutterstock.com:** Africa Studio (clb); by-studio (cl). **30 DK Images:** (cr), (bcr). **31 Getty Images / iStock:** E+ / AsiaVision (l). **32 Getty Images / iStock:** E+ / kupicoo (cr). **33 Getty Images / iStock:** Moon Safari (tl); Moon Safari (cla); Moon Safari (cl/x2). **34 Dreamstime.com:** Roman Egorov (cl). **Getty Images:** fStop / Halfdark (cr). **Shutterstock.com:** Araddara (cb). **34-35 Dreamstime.**

com: Jiri Hera (c). **35 Dreamstime.com:** Oleg Dudko (cl). **36 Dreamstime.com:** Oleg Dudko (cra); Roman Egorov (ca). **36-37 Dreamstime.com:** Jiri Hera (t). **37 Getty Images:** Stuart Snelling / EyeEm (b); fStop / Halfdark (cla); **Ingram Image Library:** (c). **38 Dreamstime.com:** Scaliger (cr). **39 Getty Images / iStock:** tommaso79 (tl). **40 Dreamstime.com:** Msalena (cr); Vitalyedush (bl). **41 Dreamstime.com:** Libux77 (tl); Yingko (cla). **Getty Images / iStock:** Tramino (bl). **42 Shutterstock.com:** Massimo Todaro (cr). **43 Alamy Stock Photo:** Cultura RM / IS703 (cla). **Dreamstime.com:** Libux77 (cb). **Shutterstock.com:** Samnata (cl). **44-45 Shutterstock.com:** Nerthuz (c). **46 Dreamstime.com:** Msalena (br); Vitalyedush (ca); Yingko (tr). **Shutterstock. com:** Nerthuz (tc). **46-47 Getty Images / iStock:** Tramino (tc). **47 Dreamstime.com:** Libux77 (cla); Scaliger (bl). **48 Dreamstime.com:** Leonid Andronov (bc); Rostislav Glinsky (cb); Danflcreativo (cb/Museum); Konstantinos Papaioannou (br). **48-49 Getty Images / iStock:** Fani Kurti (c). **49 Dreamstime.com:** A1977 (bl); Saiko3p (tl). **50-51 Dreamstime.com:** Nicolaforenza (c). **50 Dreamstime.com:** Alessandro Mascheroni (cb). **51 Dreamstime.com:** Travnikovstudio (cb). **52 Getty Images / iStock:** krblokhin (cr). **53 Alamy Stock Photo:** Image Farm Inc. / James Dawson (cla/wheelchair); Matthew Ashmore / Stockimo (cla). **Dreamstime.com:** Claudiodivizia (tl). **54 Alamy Stock Photo:** Moodboard Stock Photography (cr). **Getty Images / iStock:** E+ / martin-dm (crb). **DK Images:** Andy Crawford (br). **55 Dreamstime.com:** Vinicius Tupinamba (cl). **Getty Images / iStock:** E+ / xavierarnau (tl). **56-57 Shutterstock.com:** Nerthuz (b). **56 Dreamstime.com:** A1977 (c); Rostislav Glinsky (tc); Danflcreativo (tc/Museum); Leonid Andronov (tr); Konstantinos Papaioannou (ca); Saiko3p (ca/Cathedral). **Getty Images / iStock:** Fani Kurti (c). **58 Dreamstime.com:** David Brooks (crb). **Getty Images / iStock:** E+ / zeljkosantrac (crb/Family). **59 Dreamstime.com:** Denys Kovtun (tl). **Getty Images / iStock:** 0802290022 (clb). **60 Dreamstime.com:** Freesurf69 (bl). **Getty Images / iStock:** surachetsh (cb). **Shutterstock.com:** Sarymsakov Andrey (cr). **61 Alamy Stock Photo:** Cultura Creative RF / IS007 (cla). **Dreamstime.com:** Piotr Adamowicz (bl). **Getty Images / iStock:** yipengge (tl). **Ingram Image Library:** (cl). **62-63 Dreamstime.com:** Jennifer Thompson (c). **64 Alamy Stock Photo:** imageBROKER / Daniel Meissner (crb). **65 Ingram Image Library:** (tl). **Alamy Stock Photo:** Arcaid Images / Richard Bryant (clb). **Dreamstime. com:** Apiwan Borrikonratchata (cla); Vitalyedush (cla/traffic). **Getty Images / iStock:** piovesempre (clb/ bedroom). **Shutterstock.com:** Sarymsakov Andrey (cl). **66 Alamy Stock Photo:** Arcaid Images / Richard Bryant (ca). **Dreamstime.com:** Jennifer Thompson (tl). **67 Ingram Image Library:** (bl). **68 Alamy Stock Photo:** doughoughton (cr). **Dreamstime.com:** Arne9001 (c); Sander Van Der Werf (bl). **Getty Images / iStock:** E+ / alvarez (crb); PK-Photos (cb). **Shutterstock.com:** Weho (cra). **69 Alamy Stock Photo:** Ian Dagnall (cla). **Dreamstime.com:** Marcel De Grijs (cl). **Getty Images / iStock:** krblokhin (cr); nastya_ph (tl). **72 Getty Images / iStock:** doomu (bl). **73 Alamy Stock Photo:** imageBROKER / Harald Theissen (cla). **Dreamstime.com:** Charlieaja (tl); Konstantin Iliev (clb). **Getty Images / iStock:** E+ / Drazen_ (cla/supermarket). **74 Getty Images:** Beyond Fotomedia / Alessandro Ventura (r). **75 Getty Images / iStock:** leolintang (clb). **76 Dreamstime.com:** Arne9001 (fbr); Marcel De Grijs (fcrb). **Getty Images / iStock:** E+ / alvarez (crb); PK-Photos (bc). **Shutterstock. com:** Weho (br). **78 Alamy Stock Photo:** Luca DiCecco (cr). **79 Getty Images / iStock:** E+ / shapecharge (tl); E+ / shapecharge (cla); E+ / shapecharge (cl); E+ / shapecharge (clb). **Shutterstock.com:** zhu difeng (bl). **80 Dreamstime.com:** Robert Kneschke (cra). **82 Alamy Stock Photo:** Momentum Creative / John Sykaluk (cr). **Ingram Image Library:** (cr). **Getty Images / iStock:** Bim (crb). **Shutterstock.com:** Gorodenkoff (cra). **83 Alamy Stock Photo:** wildphotos.com (cla). **84 Shutterstock.com:** Ground Picture (mc). **84-85 Shutterstock. com:** Pressmaster (c). **85 Getty Images / iStock:** PeopleImages (tc). **Shutterstock.com:** Drazen Zigic (c). **Ingram Image Library:** (crb). **86 Alamy Stock Photo:** Luca DiCecco (br). **89 Getty Images / iStock:** Damir Khabirov (tl). **DK Images:** David Jordan (cla); Stephen Oliver (cl). **Ingram Image Library:** (clb). **91 Dreamstime.com:** Sebnem Ragiboglu (tl). **92 Getty Images / iStock:** E+ / FatCamera (cra). **93 Dreamstime. com:** Roman Egorov (cb); Prostockstudio (tl). **94 Getty Images / iStock:** E+ / Morsa Images (cra); E+ / Tempura (br). **95 DK Images:** Stephen Oliver (tl). **Dreamstime.com:** Shawn Hempel (clb). **Getty Images / iStock:** seb_ra (cl). **97 Dreamstime.com:** Prostockstudio (b). **Getty Images:** Beyond Fotomedia / Alessandro Ventura (ca). **98 Dreamstime.com:** Rawf88 (bl). **98-99 Alamy Stock Photo:** Keith Levit (c). **99 Alamy Stock Photo:** Itsik Marom (tc). **Dreamstime.com:** Laupri (ca). **Getty Images / iStock:** E+ / CreativaStudio (c). **Shutterstock.com:** Gajus (tl). **100 Dreamstime.com:** Draftmode (cb). **Getty Images / iStock:** sihuo0860371 (cr). **102 Getty Images / iStock:** cjp (cr). **102-103 Getty Images / iStock:** DigiStu (b). **103 Dreamstime.com:** Welcomia (cla). **Getty Images / iStock:** Imagesines (tl). **Ingram Image Library:** (cr). **106 Dreamstime.com:** Draftmode (bc). **Getty Images / iStock:** sihuo0860371 (br). **107 Alamy Stock Photo:** Itsik Marom (cl). **Getty Images / iStock:** Imagesines (bc). **109 Getty Images / iStock:** mediaphotos (cla). **110 Getty Images / iStock:** Biserka Stojanovic (cr). **111 Dreamstime.com:** Welcomia (cl). **112 Getty Images / iStock:** E+ / freemixer (cr); nullplus (bl). **113 Getty Images / iStock:** RossHelen (tl). **Ingram Image Library:** (cl); **Shutterstock.com:** Evgeny Atamanenko (clb). **114 Dreamstime.com:** Amsis1 (br); Brett Critchley (crb). **Getty Images / iStock:** Ridofranz (cr). **115 Alamy Stock Photo:** Michelle Bailey (br). **Dreamstime.com:** Ulianna19970 (cla). **Getty Images / iStock:** Tatsiana Volkava (cl). **116 Dreamstime.com:** Laupri (ca); Welcomia (cra). **Getty Images / iStock:** mediaphotos (br). **118-119 Dreamstime.com:** Vladwitty (c). **119 Dreamstime.com:** Prostockstudio (cb). **120 Dreamstime.com:** Sergeyoch (bc/Ball); Wavebreakmedia Ltd (cr); Skypixel (cb); Volkop (bc). **121 Getty Images / iStock:** E+ / AscentXmedia (cla). **122-123 Alamy Stock Photo:** Tony Tallec (c). **123 Getty Images / iStock:** nastya_ph (cla). **124-125 DK Images:** Paul Bricknell tc(2); Geoff Dann tc(5); Max Gibbs tc(3); Frank Greenaway tc(4); Dave King tc(1); TracyMorgan tc(6). **124 Dreamstime.com:** Sergeyoch (crb); Wavebreakmedia Ltd (bc); Skypixel (cb/Basketball); Volkop (cb).

All other images © Dorling Kindersley